STRUCTURES, RESTRUCTURATION AND SOCIAL POWER

Structures, Restructuration and Social Power

MARK HAUGAARD
Department of Politics
University College of Dublin

Avebury

Aldershot · Brookfield USA · Hong Kong · Singapore · Sydney

Published by
Avebury
Ashgate Publishing Limited
Gower House
Croft Road
Aldershot
Hants GU11 3HR
England

Ashgate Publishing Company
Old Post Road
Brookfield
Vermont 05036
USA

A CIP catalogue record for this book is available from the British Library and the US Library of Congress.

ISBN 1 85628 312 7

Printed and Bound in Great Britain by
Athenaeum Press Ltd., Newcastle upon Tyne.

Contents

Introduction: The Framework of Analysis   1

Section One
Perspectives of Power

1. Conflictual Power   7
2. Consensual Power   26
3. Power and Structure   40

Section Two
Giddens, Structuration and Power

4. Giddens and Time-Space   65
5. Structures as Rules   75
6. Power, Structures and Resources   88
7. Giddens: A Critique   102

Section Three
Restructuration and Power

8. Interaction and Restructuration   121
9. Paradigms and Interaction   140
10. Restructuration and Consensual Power   153
11. Conflictual Power and Restructuration   187
12. Destructuration, Institutions and Powerlessness   204
13. Structural Constraint and Inequalities of Power   220

Appendix 1   238
Appendix 2   241
Notes   247
Bibliography   251

Introduction: The framework of analysis

This introductory chapter aims at providing a general orientation which will enable the reader to approach this work with a clearly defined idea of both its place in sociopolitical theory and the problems which it is intended to resolve. For the sake of clarity, I have kept the introduction as short and succinct as possible. It is divided into three parts: the first is a description of the background debate from which this work developed, the second is a short summary of the methodological division of the book into a number of distinct sections and the third concludes with a brief commentary on the nature and scope of this work.

Within mainstream social and political science there are two dominant theoretical positions which broadly define the analysis of power. They are the conflictual and consensual traditions. Between, and within, these traditions there has been much debate concerning the exact conceptual borders which define the area of phenomena covered by the concept of power. Much of this debate has been a direct result of a gradual analytical shift of attention towards the relationship between the constitution of inequalities of power and more structural or systemic elements. It is a change of focus which is particularly manifest in the attempt to distinguish power from structural constraint and control. Viewed overall, this slow change is the direct result of a theoretical move, by both power traditions,

1

into the terrain of the agent-structure debate. Within this context, Lukes' position represents the explicit recognition of the fact that, when developed to their logical conclusion, both conflictual and consensual traditions inevitably move into the theoretical arena of the agent-structure debate. In short, this means that the analysis of power becomes inherently linked to the resolution of the problem of theorizing the relationship between agency and structure. This implies two alternative approaches: the problem can be defined out of existence by opting for theoretical neatness through semantic rigour or the theoretical implications of this new position can be resolved through the development of an alternative framework which specifically tackles the relationship between agency and structure.

To date, the most sophisticated contemporary attempt at theoretically delineating the relationship between agency and structure is represented by Anthony Giddens' theory of structuration. It is a perspective which claims to resolve the perceived dichotomy between agency and structure through a conceptual move away from the dualism, which characterizes social and political debate, to a duality. It is a move which is facilitated by placing the concept of structuration at theoretical centre stage. However, in this work it is argued that Giddens' position contains inherent theoretical problems which manifest themselves in a number of ways. Among these are an inability to account for systemic change and, importantly in this context, a lack of adequate theoretical space for the analysis of the production of power. It is a theoretical inadequacy which can be tackled only through the reorientation of theoretical perspective brought about by the introduction of the concepts of restructuration and destructuration.

The development of restructuration theory is an attempt to analyse the relationship between power and structure through an explanatory theorization of the process by which agents produce power and recreate structure. This explanatory theorization is then used as a conceptual tool for analysing the relationship between conflictual and consensual power, and the related phenomena of structural constraint and control.

With this theoretical schema of debate in mind, I have divided the book into three parts. Section one deals with the mainstream conflictual and consensual theories of power, their development into the conceptual area of agency and structure and the overt recognition - but irresolution - of this position by Lukes, Jessop and Clegg. Section two is an analysis and critique of Giddens' attempt to resolve the agency-structure problem through the theory of structuration. The third section concerns the development of an alternative theoretical framework which goes beyond the position of Giddens. Central to this is an emphasis on, and discussion of, the concepts of restructuration and destructuration. Restructuration theory is then used to develop an explanatory analysis of the phenomena of conflictual and consensual power, and structural constraint and control.

As is manifest in the above, I have continuously limited the scope of this work to specific problems associated with social power and their analysis within the framework of some of the more fundamental problems of analytical social and political theory. The confined focus has also meant a continual monitoring of an almost irrepressible urge to show how restructuration theory can be applied to the resolution of a number of non-power based problems and subjects in politics and sociology. However, these self-imposed restraints have been necessary in order to provide a continual clear thread of argument and prevent the book from becoming conceptually disjointed through either the attempt to combine theoretical development with a general review of literature or numerous digressions.

Section One
PERSPECTIVES OF POWER

1   Conflictual power

In this chapter I will analyse some of the more important
phenomena associated with the conflictual 1-D, 2-D and 3-D power
debate. As a work of analytical political theory, I intend to
methodologically bracket the more normative or descriptive
elements of this debate as far as possible. In this manner, I wish to
extract analytical elements for two purposes: 1) as a measure of the
type of phenomena for which any adequate theory of power must
have conceptual space; 2) as a methodological tool for showing
where ambiguity exists between power and related phenomena
such as structural constraint and determinacy. While the chapter
will center on the work of Dahl, Bachrach, Baratz, Lukes and their
associates, it also contains a short introductory section dealing with
the background theoretical debate out of which Dahl's work grew.

It is part of the thesis of this chapter that there is a central core
concept of power which is implicitly inherent in any generally and
loosely defined conflictual view of power. Where thinkers such as
Dahl and Lukes differ is not with respect to their implicit concept of
power but with regard to the type of phenomena to which this
concept is most aptly applied. Consequently, the first part of this
chapter is a short section dealing with their shared 'conflictual'
concept of power. The second is a short, context setting description

of the elite theories to which Dahl's work was in part intended as an answer. The third is devoted to the pluralists. The fourth is concerned with the more 'radical' positions of 2-D and 3-D power. In the fifth, and concluding section, the overall conceptual drifts and problems inherent in these positions are drawn together.

Like Terence Ball, I would argue that both the pluralists and their 2-D and 3-D critics used an implicitly similar concept of power. In addition, I would further wish to claim that this point can be extended to include many of the elite theorists who were Dahl's early adversaries. Central to this definition of power is a causal conceptualization of power relations between actors (Ball 1988 p. 88). Individual actors act with respect to each other when acted upon. The form which such a causal relationship takes is illustrated by the following example from Dahl: "Suppose I stand on a corner and say to myself, ' I command all automobile drivers on this street to drive on the right side of the road'; suppose further that all the drivers actually do as I 'command' them to do; still, most people will regard me as mentally ill if I insist that I have enough power over automobile drivers to compel them to use the right side of the road. On the other hand, suppose a policeman is standing in the middle of an intersection at which most ordinary traffic moves ahead; he orders all traffic to turn right or left; the traffic moves as he orders it to do. Then it accords with what I conceive to be the bedrock idea of power to say that the policeman acting in this particular role evidently has the power to make automobile drivers turn right or left rather than go ahead." (Dahl 1957 p. 202). Hence, "For the assertion 'C has power over R' can be substituted the assertion 'C causes R's behaviour'." (Dahl 1968 p. 410). Inherent in this is the counterfactual claim that if C had not acted in the manner in which he/she did then R would not have reacted as manifest through his/her action. This can be summed up in Dahl's intuitive notion of power: "A has power over B to the extent that he can get B to do something that B would not otherwise do." (Dahl 1957 p. 202-3).

It is with respect to the particular focus or emphasis placed upon this definition that the divergence between Dahl and his more radical critics takes place. Both the pluralists and elite theorists are primarily interested in actor A: the persons who govern (Polsby 1960 p. 476,), or those that can command (Hunter 1953 p. 2), or the elite who make decisions that really matter (Mills 1958 p. 29). Rather than the behaviour of actor A, who has power, the radical power theorists are much more interested in B and the manner in which his/her behaviour is inherently shaped by his/her powerlessness relative to A (Gaventa 1980 p. 8).

The point of divergence between the pluralists and the elite theorists is at the level of the identification of actor A. Or more correctly, which attributes define A as a possessor of power relative to actor B. It is disagreement over this issue which forms the background to the emergence of the pluralist concept of power.

Rather than an explicit conflict over the defining characteristics of actor A, one of the motivating factors which drew Dahl, Polsby and Wolfinger into the power debate was desire to assess the 'democraticness' of American society vis-a-vis criticisms made by elite theorists. The latter group can be divided into two general theoretical orientations: 1) there was C. Wright Mills working from a 'leftish' reinterpretation of European classical elite theory and; 2) there were the 'reputational' community power theorists who were working from a less explicitly developed theoretical position [1]. Dahl's primary target was the former whereas Polsby and Wolfinger concentrated upon the latter.

The theoretical roots of Mills' elite thesis are in part derived from Weber and the classical elitists Mosca and Michels. From Weber, Mills absorbs the rejection of Marxist mono-causalist interpretations of history (see Gerth and Mills 1948 p. 47). There are three (and in previous centuries, five) primary sources of power in society. These sources are institutionally bureaucratically organized according to Weberian principles of increased rationalization (Gerth and Mills 1948 p. 49-50). From Mosca and Michels, he takes over the importance of unintended consequences in the constitution of capitalist society as dominated by elites. Like Michels, he believed that social power is power organized (Meisel 1962 p. 37 Michels 1915 p. 30-40). However, the latter ultimately has the unintended consequence of creating a reified worship of the organizational means of power (Michels 1915 p. 89, 366, 373, Mills 1956 p. 23) and an organizing class, with a highly developed class consciousness, dedicated to the pursuit of its own interests (Mosca 1939 p. 149, 277-8).

In Mills work, these influences are integrated with an implicitly mechanistic image of society (Giblan 1981 p. 2) which bears a remarkable similarity to Hobbes' concept of the Leviathan. The Leviathan - which for Hobbes is a self propelling clock-like artificial animal of which man is the artificer - in the hands of Mills, becomes transformed into modern giant organizational machines. These are major institutions of society which constitute the means of power within modern social organization (Mills 1956 p. 5). They carry within them an ever greater amount of resources which are the primary source of the expansion of power within society as a whole

(Mills 1956 p. 7; 1958 p. 31). The manner in which he visualized these institutional machines is possibly best exemplified by his description of the Pentagon: "This concrete and limestone maze contains the organized brain of the American means of violence....Three football fields would reach only the length of one of its five outer walls.... [It has] seventeen and a half miles of corridor, 40,000 phone switchboards, fifteen miles of pneumatic tubing, 2100 intercoms, connected with one another and with the world,.... it has four full-time workers...watching the master panel which synchronizes its 4000 clocks." (Mills 1956 p. 186-7).

While Mills classifies five major institutional orders (Eldrige 1983 p. 59), he claims that within advanced capitalism three have emerged as predominant. They are the economic, political and military orders (Mills 1956 p. 6). In pivotal positions, which constitute command posts within these organizational hierarchies, there is a small group who constitute the power elite (Mills 1956 p. 4). This elite forms a triangle of power which is unified by two factors: 1) interrelationship based upon "...an awareness of the interdependence of the major institutional orders."(Mills 1956 p. 8); 2) common class consciousness derived from common interests and a shared socialization process (Mills 1956 p. 11). This elite is comprised of the key decision makers who, in contemporary society, are making history - even if it is in circumstances which are not of their own choosing (Mills 1958 p. 30; see Bachrach 1962 p. 445).

Unlike Mills, the 'reputational' elite theorists did not premise the occurrence of elites on an organizational theory. It was much more based on a generalized notion that the existence of a stable social order is in some manner attributable to the existence of a permanent elite (Ricci 1976 p. 88; Abu-Laban 1965 p. 37; Wolfinger 1960 p. 644). Possibly, this is implicitly derived from the Hobbesian hypothesis that centralized power is the key to the orderedness of the social world. Hence, they take it as given that someone governs. It is their task to find out who, when and how (Abu-Laban 1965 p. 36).

Identifying those who have power is made complex by the fact that, given that there is a high circulation of those observed to make important decisions[2], it is implicitly the case that the monolithic elite responsible for social order and stability are not the ones who are immediately visible as decision-makers. The latter tend to be those who wield a highly limited governmental institutional power (Blakenship 1964 p. 208; Gitlin 1965 p. 39). Those who have real power tend to work 'behind the scenes'

(Bonjean 1963 p. 678). They exert power over others through subtle channels of influence based upon 'anticipated reaction'. When decisions are made by those observed to decide things, who do not have real power, they do so based not on criteria of personal or public interests, but upon their assessment of the anticipated reactions of those with great power resources at their disposal (Ehrlich 1961 p. 92). Consequently, the 'true' power elites need not have to take part in actual decision-making. This point is well exemplified by a transcript of an interview made in Bigtown by Pellegrin and Coats: "Only a man who is naive would accept invitations to participate in important community affairs without the blessing of Mr. A, the top executive in our company. For a man to ignore the usual procedures...he'd...have to be a complete ass."(Pellegrin and Coats 1956 p. 417). The company executive does not have to initiate decisions because everyone knows what his/her interests are: interests which are ultimately reducible to class stratification and are known locally (Abu-Laban 1963 p. 131-40; 1965 p. 36-39). Hence, the importance of a technique which can tap local knowledge (Miller and Dirksen 1965 p. 548).

In order to get to know what happened behind the scenes, based on local knowledge, they opted for what has become known as the reputational community power approach. This typically involved the following steps: 1) A list is made of those who are considered 'likely to know', based on position, what is 'going on' in the community. 2) These individuals are then asked to compile a list of those with power in the community. 3) The latter are then interviewed in order to obtain information on their level of 'cohesiveness' and who among them has most power. 5) Finally a certain number are selected as key leaders [3].

There were many criticisms made of this approach. One of the most persistent was that it constituted a valid analytic device for assessing who had a reputation for power but not who actually had it (e.g. Wolfinger 1962 p. 637-44). Another was that, as in Mills, it failed to distinguish between actual and potential power (Dahl 1958 p. 463-9; Polsby 1960 p. 474-84) [4]. In order to overcome these shortcomings the pluralists continually emphasized the importance of using research methodologies which do not act as self-fulfilling prophesies. While this insistence was partly intended to de-legitimize much of the work done by the Elite theorists, it also guided and shaped the work done by Dahl, Polsby and Wolfinger. It is to the latter I will now turn.

As already stated, when attempting to establish who has power empirically, the pluralists place great emphasis on the

11

methodological importance of avoiding tests based on criteria which will implicitly produce self-fulfilling prophesies. As such, when wishing to assess 'who governs?' the key orientating question should not be in the form 'Who runs this community?' because the latter presupposes that someone does run things by assuming the existence of a power elite. In order to avoid such a self-fulfilling prophesy the correct question should be: 'Does anyone at all run this community?' (Polsby 1980 p. 113).

Consistent with this fear of predetermining the outcomes of their work through preconceived ideas, Dahl, Polsby and Wolfinger insist on focusing primarily on manifestly observable, and hence verifiable, phenomena. Hence, in his critique of Mills, Dahl insists that "*I do not see how anyone can suppose that he has established the dominance of a specific group in a community or a nation without basing his analysis on the careful examination of a series of concrete decisions.*" (Dahl 1958 p. 466)[5]. This means that a political scientist should study "...who actually prevail in community decision making."(Polsby 1960 p. 476). Prevailing being defined in terms of succeeding "...in initiating a policy or vetoing a proposed policy." (Dahl 1961a p. 484).

Conflict between A and B, as revealed in concrete decision-making, is a manifestation of differences of preference between the two actors (Dahl 1958 p. 464). A system within which there is complete consensus is one in which there is no power conflict or there is enforced consensus (Dahl 1958 p. 464). However, Dahl claims that this level of enforced consensus exists only in a totalitarian regime. Hence, the possibility of enforced consensus can be methodologically bracketed when studying power distribution within a democratic system (Dahl 1958 p. 468). This does not apply to minor decisions where the inherent cost of engaging in power conflict will make participation not worthwhile (Polsby 1960 p. 480). However, in major issue areas differences in preferences will always manifest themselves in the breaking of consensus through conflict (Polsby 1980 p. 114-5). Hence, any attempt at enforcing consensus, through the exercise of power by A over B, can be studied "... *by an examination of a series of concrete cases where key decisions are made*: decisions on taxation and expenditures, subsidies, welfare programmes, military policy and so on." (Dahl 1958 p. 469). In other words, the pluralist researcher will tend to identify power with its exercises as manifest through visible conflict in decision-making. As such his/her concerns are to "...(a) select for study a number of 'key' as opposed to 'routine' political decisions, (b) identify the people who took an active part in the decision-making process, (c) obtain a full account of their actual behaviour... (d) determine and analyse the specific outcome of the conflict." (Bachrach and Baratz 1962 p. 948; see Polsby 1980 p. 4).

The act of choosing to study particular acts of decision-making is linked to the Pluralist hypothesis that the power of a given actor is not necessarily general. An individual may be powerful in one area but not in another (Dahl 1968 p. 408). "Therefore 'general power' rankings are misleading." (Wolfinger 1960 p. 638). For example, stemming from his position as university professor, Dahl has power over his students with respect to the issue of what they study. Due to their legal status, the Police Department has power over the parking habits of students at Yale University. Neither Dahl nor the Police Department have power in both areas (Dahl 1957 p. 206-7). In addition, if an actor wished to have power in both areas there appears to be no obvious way of achieving this goal. The power resources of university professor and policeman are inherently non-mutually-cumulative (see Bachrach and Baratz 1963 p. 635). This implies that the scope of an individual's power can be, and is often, issue specific (Polsby 1960 p. 477; for a quantified empirical study of this specific point see Agger 1956 p. 322-31). Hence, it is both meaningless and impossible to assess the power of a given actor without studying the exercise of power in specific different issue areas (Wolfinger 1960 p. 638; 1962 p. 845). For the purposes of their study of New Haven, Dahl and his team choose the issue areas of: 1) the making of party nominations, which determines who will hold public office; 2) the New Haven Redevelopment Programme, which was the largest per capita in the U.S; 3) public education, which was the most expensive item on the city's budget (Dahl 1961a p. 121-2; Polsby 1960 p. 477). After investigating the patterns of influence in these three issue areas, Dahl concluded - by way of verification of the hypothesis that power is usually issue specific - that, with only the exception of the mayor, no "...particular individual exerts a significant amount of direct influence in... more than one of the three issue areas studied." (Dahl 1961a p. 181). The latter serving as an empirical substantiation of the Pluralist conceptualization of the polyarchic workings of the American political system (Dahl 1961b p. 82).

Because power is inherently linked to its exercise, the Pluralists place great emphasis upon distinguishing potential from actual power (e.g. Polsby 1980 p. 109; Wolfinger 1960 p. 644). This means that great attention is continually paid to the difference between power, as manifest in conflict, and the type of phenomena which are necessary prerequisites for having power and/or are often associated with its possession (see Ricci 1976 p. 127).

The most important differentiation between actual and potential power is based upon the distinction of power from power resources. There are a number of reasons why power resources are not synonymous with actual power. The first is that, since there is usually a cost associated with converting potential into actual power, there must be a will in order to convert it (Clarke T.N. 1967a p. 281). A good example of this point is given by the Lynds in their examination of Middletown. The X family ran Middletown through their possession of massive wealth. However, they were not the only wealthy family in the town. There was the Y family who were clannish and absorbed with family affairs, hence demonstrating "...the ability of great wealth to live in Middletown with a large degree of isolation from the city's central interests..." (Lynd 1937 p. 91). In other words both X and Y family had wealth as a potential power resource but the former, unlike the latter, had the will to use it. In short, "Individuals with the same amounts of resources may exert different degrees of influence because they use their resources in different ways. One wealthy man may collect paintings; another politicians."(Dahl 1961a p. 270).

By themselves, intentions and resources are not sufficient for the realization of power. In addition the possessors of resources must have a requisite level of skill in order to organize resources appropriately. In this context, skill means a number of things, among them must be included: an ability to perceive which resources are appropriate for power of given scope, political ability and organizational acumen (Polsby 1960 p. 482-4; Wolfinger 1960 644; Dahl 1961b p. 81). The importance of skill, the diversity of power resources [6] and the necessity for motivation means that the comparative power of actors is inherently dependent upon a whole variety of contingent factors. Hence, in order to postulate that a group X has more power than a group Y it is, at the very least, necessary to assess whether or not group X and Y have similar resources, levels of motivation, organizational ability, and an identical interest in the same issue area (Dahl 1961a p. 272).

When attempting to assess the extent to which a society is governed by a ruling elite, the Pluralists would insist that all these contingently related factors must be taken into account. In effect, this implies that for there to be a ruling elite there must be a conscious effort by a group to overcome the necessities deriving from the contingently related prerequisites for having power. There must be what Meisel called the three C's: group consciousness, coherence and conspiracy or will to common action (see Meisel

1962 p. 361; Parry 1969 p. 32; Clegg 1989 p. 48). For example, in New Haven, with respect to any given issue - say redevelopment - it is undoubtedly true that "... if the Economic Notables were much more unified, influential, skillful, and dedicated to redevelopment than they are in New Haven, they could provide... dominant leadership..." (Dahl 1961a p.115). However, the point is that, while they may have had on aggregate a high level of potential power resources at their disposal, they lacked organizational unity of purpose on the issue. This implies that the power or "...actual *political effectiveness* of a group is a function of its potential for control and its potential for unity." (Dahl 1958 p. 465). In other words, there is a double contingency: at an actor level that potential power can be converted into actual power and at a social systemic level that the actor in question is capable of combining with another actor who is similarly able to realize his/her personal social power. The latter presupposes a unity of purpose so that they can form a well-defined group capable of acting together (Dahl 1958 p. 466). It is due to the necessity for the combination these variables that "... a group with a relatively low potential for control but with a high potential for unity may be more politically effective than a group with a high potential for control but a low potential for unity." (Dahl 1958 p. 465). Since "[t]here is no a priori reason for supposing that the rich will display more unity than the poor... the unequal apportionment of potential power does not inherently imply a parallel inequitable distribution of actual power." (Dahl 1961b p. 81).

The pluralists would argue that inherent in the nature of the American democratic process there are also additional factors, linked to anticipated reactions, which militate against the emergence of a unified elite. The first is based on the often mutually exclusive competing demands of the polity and the economy. Not only are political and economic power resources often non-mutually-cumulative but the interests deriving from them can be mutually exclusive. A leader may experience acute personal conflict between a desire to increase wealth and a wish to pursue political power (Dahl 1961a p. 139; p. 98). While the former is based on individual egotistic criteria, the latter is linked to an ability to anticipate the reactions of voters to specific future acts of political decision-making (Dahl 1961b p. 78). The importance of the ability to predict political reaction is illustrated by the success of Mayor Lee. In 1953 he became New Haven's most popular mayor (65% of the vote) and most powerful leader (measured by his ability at initiating decisions) by correctly predicting that urban

15

redevelopment would be the single most highly politically advantageous cause to use as a political power base (Dahl 1961a p. 121-40).

In the political sphere, anticipated reaction not only works positively as a power resource, which can be sought, but it also has an inherently constraining element. On an ideological level, it can define the limits of what is possible. The power of those who use their resources effectively in decision-making is ultimately dependent upon the non-conversion of potential power resources by others. A political elite is dependent on a majority who are content to remain unpolitical (Dahl 1961a p. 276-81). However, that unpoliticalness is conditional upon a certain level of consensus. At the outer limits, this consensus is defined by the non-transgression of what is considered legitimate with respect to either ideologically based legal or democratic criteria (Dahl 1961a p. 305-25).

Conceptually linked to the discussion of anticipated reaction, Dahl developed his distinction between having and exercising power. As exemplified in this context, the key decision-makers *exercise* power through decision-making whereas, the people have power through an ability to influence derived from anticipated reactions (Dahl 1968 p. 413)[7].

While it is without doubt true that anticipated reaction acts as a constraint upon those who have power and hence reinforces the workings of pluralist democracy, it is an unduly narrow conceptualization of the workings of this phenomenon. It only focuses upon the effect of anticipated reactions upon actor A, who has power, but fails completely to take account of the applicability of this concept in explaining the behaviour of actor B. This restricted focus is in part a manifestation of the pluralist methodological approach to the study of power whereby the distribution of power within a system can be examined purely through the analysis of who has power as manifest through decision-making. However, the inherently narrow focus which results from this approach is well complemented by the radical power theorist's[8] examination of actor B, the one acted upon.

Bachrach and Baratz fundamentally accepted Dahl's critique of the premises of elite theory. In particular they explicitly acknowledge its pertinence with respect to the following: 1) the inherent nonvalidity of the elite hypothesis that the existence of social order presupposes either the existence of a stratified power elite or 2) a stable power structure controlled by that elite 3) the fallaciousness of equating power with power resources or a reputation for power and 4) their failure to take account of such

16

phenomena as scope and intensity of power (Bachrach and Baratz 1962 p. 947-948).

The point where Bachrach and Baratz diverge from Dahl and his associates is derived from the criticism that the latter tend to confuse their criteria for the investigation of the distribution of power with the essence of the phenomenon of power itself. While it is without doubt correct - from the point of view of empirical investigation - that the examination of key decision makers and making leads to the collection of highly scientifically verifiable evidence, this does not imply that the exercise of power is thus confined or restricted in form and nature (Bachrach and Baratz 1962 p. 948). In particular it fails to take account of the fact that: 1) "... power may be, and often is, exercised by confining the scope of decision-making to relatively 'safe' issues" and 2) "...the model provides no *objective* criteria for distinguishing between 'important' and 'unimportant' issues arising in the political arena." (Bachrach and Baratz 1962 p. 948). With respect to the first point, "...power is also exercised when A devotes his energies to creating or reinforcing social and political values and institutional practices that limit the scope of the political process to public consideration of only those issues which are comparatively innocuous to A." (Bachrach and Baratz 1962 p. 948). In effect, this implies that A can exercise power over B by (hence the second point) defining what is to count as an important issue about which decisions should be made (Bachrach and Baratz 1962 p. 950). In effect, the latter means that a certain analogy could be made between the pluralist concentration on what, in essence are, reputedly important decisions and the reputational elite theorists examination of those reputed to have power (Bachrach and Baratz 1962 p. 949).

On a theoretical level their expansion of the concept of power was derived from an analysis of the structures of organization which are presupposed when decision-making is spoken of. In the words of Schattschneider (1960 p. 71): "All forms of political organization have a bias in favour of the exploitation of some kinds of conflict and the suppression of others because *organization is the mobilization of bias*. Some issues are organized into politics while others are organized out." (Bachrach and Baratz 1962 p. 949). Not only is power exercised, as within the pluralist framework, in the arena of decision-making but it is also exercised by preventing issues from reaching that arena. The procedure of limiting the process of overt decision-making to what, for A, comprises relatively safe issues is in essence nondecision-making with respect to issues or interests of importance to actor B. The latter constitutes

17

the other face of power (Bachrach and Baratz 1970 p.18) or its second dimension (Lukes 1974 p. 16).

Nondecision-making is the process through which the grievances or demands of B are kept *outside* the system (Bachrach and Baratz 1970 p. 49) Bachrach and Baratz and latter Crenson list a number of ways in which this is done[9]. The principal ones are as follows: 1) the most direct and visible is the terrorization of B into acquiescence (Bachrach and Baratz 1970 p. 44); 2) just as overt would be threats based upon potential deprivation (Bachrach and Baratz 1970 p. 44-5); 3) a more indirect form is the invoking of procedural norms and rules to make a demand illegitimate. Thus, the discussion of an issue can be branded socialist or immoral (Bachrach and Baratz 1970 p. 45); 4) more indirect yet, is the setting up an organizational procedure which has built into it institutional practices which are specifically geared to filtering out certain demands by B. "For example, the demands of rent-strikers can be blunted or dulled by insisting that tenant-landlord relations are a purely private matter." (Bachrach and Baratz 1970 p. 46); 5) the latter can be legitimized by an emphasis on the 'democraticness' of given institutional procedures. Hence, giving the illusion of a voice to those whose demands are organized out of the decision-making procedure (Bachrach and Baratz 1970 p. 45); 6) to these methods of nondecision-making must be added the importance of the role of anticipated reactions. In this context, " [t]he reference is to situations where B, confronted by A who has greater power resources, decides not to make a demand upon A for fear that the latter will invoke sanctions against him." (Bachrach and Baratz 1970 p. 46). The latter Bachrach and Baratz do not strictly speaking classify as a nondecision but prefer to say "...that A 'possessed' power in a nondecisional form and B reacted to it." (Bachrach and Baratz 1970 p. 46; 1962 p. 952). 7) Expanding upon the role of anticipated reactions in creating reinforcing acquiescence in B - and possibly drawing upon a point made by Erlich (1961 p. 926); D'Antonio and Erickson 1962b p. 370) in defence of the reputational approach - Crenson pointed out that in this case, B's behaviour is based upon his/her *subjective* perception of A. B is acquiescent based not upon an assessment of A's actual resources but upon A's reputation for power. In this case and "[t]o the extent that it has an identifiable effect on local politics, the reputation for power is itself a form of power." (Crenson 1971 p. 80). Hence, "[w]hen adherents of the pluralist alternative dismiss the mere reputation for power as a scientifically worthless datum, they may be dismissing an important part of political reality." (Crenson 1971 p. 80).

Aside from a new dimension to the exercise of power, Bachrach and Baratz introduced a number of conceptual clarifications, pertaining to power and related phenomena, which could be used as analytic tools when interpreting 1-D and 2-D power. With respect to the concept of power itself, they pointed out that it is inherently not acceptable to conceive of power as a property or thing possessed by actor A, even though "[i]t is customary to say that this or that person or group 'has power',..." (Bachrach and Baratz 1970 p. 19). The reason why such a concept of power is unacceptable is related to its inherent nature as a sociopolitical phenomenon. For them power is a purely *relational* concept which only exists or has meaning within the process of social interaction. Hence, A only has power with *respect to* actor B. A does not *have* power in personal isolation irrespective of the existence of B. Consequently, the possession of power resources and the ability to exercise power is inherently linked to the existence "...of conflicting values *in the mind of the recipient* in the power relationship." (Bachrach and Baratz 1970 p. 19).

Aside from adding to the analysis of the concept of power, Bachrach and Baratz also introduced distinctions between power, force, influence and authority. In so doing, they unfortunately add a certain level of confusion to their position. When speaking generally about the two faces of power they use the word 'power' as a concept to cover most forms of successful control of B by A. However, in their typological analysis of power and related phenomena they use the word power in a highly restricted sense. In dealing with this problem, Lukes relabelled the latter restricted form of power 'coercion'. I have not followed this lead because it would obscure some relevant points, with respect to the concept of conflictual power, which I develop in chapter 11. Instead of the word 'coercion' I have used 'power*' for the restricted term and the simple 'power' for the generic term. (For a further discussion of this point and an alternative more theoretically satisfactory rerendering of Bachrach's and Baratz's position see appendix 1).

Power* is defined as a relationship between A and B where B complies with A based upon reasoned calculation of the ability of A to impose sanctions upon him/her in the case of non-compliance. In this sense power* is based on both reason and communication. It is derived from the ability of B to understand what it is that A desires and his/her ability to assess the dis/advantages of compliance or noncompliance (Bachrach and Baratz 1970 p. 20-4). In such or similar conflict between A and B where power* ends force begins without any overlap between the two. If A threatens B with force

19

and B complies, A has successfully exercised power* over B. However, if B refuses to act in the manner desired by A and if A carries out his/her promised sanctions with respect to B, then the latter exercise of force does not indicate A's power* over B but rather A's powerlessness when attempting to control the action of B. "By the same token, if and when thermonuclear weapons are transformed from instruments of a policy deterrent into activated missiles of death, power[*] will have given way to force." (Bachrach and Baratz 1970 p. 27). Linking back to the distinction already made earlier between social and natural power, force also fails to qualify as an act of *social* power because it is inherently non-relational (Bachrach and Baratz 1970 p. 28) (see chapters 10 and 11 for development of this theme). While both power* and influence are similar in that they are both relationally based concepts, they are inherently different because "...the exercise of power* depends upon the potential sanctions, while the the exercise of influence does not." (Bachrach and Baratz 1970 p. 30-1). Explicitly rejecting the traditional definition of authority as formal or institutionalized power*, they claim the concepts to be antithetical (Bachrach and Baratz 1970 p. 32-3). In the case of authority, B complies with A through social interaction because he/she considers compliance reasonable based upon an assessment of A's position within a institutionalized structure or organization. Hence, B is not complying because he/she fears severe deprivations by A as in the exercise power* by A over B (Bachrach and Baratz 1970 p. 32-4). To illustrate this distinction Bachrach and Baratz use the following example: "Imagine,..., an armed military sentry who is approached by an unarmed man in uniform. The sentry levels his gun at the intruder and calls out, 'Halt or I'll shoot!' The order is promptly obeyed. Did the sentry therefore have power[*] and exercise it?" (Bachrach and Baratz 1970 p. 20) The answer is: yes if the intruder obeyed for fear of being shot but no if, as a fellow soldier, he was simply obeying orders irrespective of threatened sanctions. In the latter case compliance was based upon authority (Bachrach and Baratz 1970 p. 20).

Inherent in the above example is the view that the classification of the nature of A's affecting of B is inherently linked to B's subjective reasons for compliance. In the case of the guard and uniformed stranger the causal relationship between A's action and B's compliance appears, to an outside observer, to be one classifiable as power*. It may even be the case that A thinks that he is exercising power* over B. However, Bachrach and Baratz would wish to argue that in reality the causal relationship is one of authority derivable from an assessment of B's conscious intentionality. They represented this hypothesis in figurative form as follows:

Means by Which Compliance Reason Why Compliance
Is Sought Is Forthcoming

----
1. Power[*]------------   ------ 1. Power[*]
2. Influence-----------   -------2. Influence
3. Authority-----------   DECISION   -------3. Authority
4. Force---------------   -------4. Force

(Bachrach and Baratz 1970 p. 41).

As already emphasized, central to the 2-D view of power is an emphasis placed upon the actor B. Consistent with this, Bachrach and Baratz also make the intentions and motivations of actor B central to the core notion of power and the typology of power they develop with it. It is B's state of mind which is crucial in classifying whether or not A is controlling him/her by exercising power*, influence, force or authority. It is also B's ideological perceptions of the world which are being played upon when he/she is told that 2-D power is inherently democratic and consequently legitimate.

Central though B's subjectively defined intentionality is to Bachrach and Baratz's theoretical position, they refuse to acknowledge the possibility that power could be exercised over B through control of his/her intellect. In fact they deliberately copy Dahl in limiting their concept of 2-D power to visible decision-making. They explicitly claim that nondecision-making is a *decision*-making act whereby the grievances of others are kept outside the system (Bachrach and Baratz 1970 p. 44, 49). Consequently, nondecision-making should not be confused with not making decisions (Bradshaw 1976 p. 124). This limiting of 2-D power to decision-making intrinsically precludes control of B through control over his/her perceptions of the social world and his/her choices within it.

There are two principal reasons why Bachrach and Baratz limit their 2-D concept of power to active decision-making and overt grievances. The first is linked to their desire to show that 2-D power is empirically identifiable in exactly the same manner as Dahl's 1-D power. 2-D is just a more widely encompassing way of

21

assessing how power is exercised through decision-making. Being linked to decision-making, 2-D is just as 'scientific' as Dahl's work on New Haven (see Bachrach and Baratz 1970 p. 67-106). The second reason for the insistence on decision-making is more implicitly theoretical. Essentially what Bachrach and Baratz wish to add to Dahl's position is the issue of how the structures of organization organize certain issues out. For Bachrach and Baratz an organization is an intentional product created by conscious actors through active decision-making. In many respects, this means that they are conceptually working within the Hobbesian tradition where the orderedness of the social world is attributable to an organizational Leviathan created and maintained through intentional action. What this position inherently ignores is the fact that actor B is rendered powerless within a social system which has inherent in it many more power resources than those contained or defined by the deliberately created institutionalized decision-making bodies. Taking up a point made by Lukes, this is probably one of the main reasons why Bachrach and Baratz attempt to study race relations in Baltimore, through the examination of overt institutionalized decision-making procedures, is so relatively short and lacking in substance (Lukes 1974 p. 37).

Luke's third dimensional view of power is derived from a critique of those untheorized aspects of Bachrach's and Baratz's position. In particular Lukes focuses upon the artificial boundaries placed upon their concept of power originating from curtailing the more radical implications of their analysis of actor B and their emphasis on organizationally defined decision-making.

With respect to actor B, Lukes asks rhetorically "Indeed, is it not the supreme exercise of power to get another or others to have the desires you want them to have - that is, to secure compliance by controlling their thoughts and desires?" (Lukes 1974 p. 23). Enforced consensus is, in many respects, the most insidious and effective use of power because it prevents conflict from arising in the first place (Lukes 1974 p. 23). In other words, it is not a question of keeping conflict outside a given decision-making procedure but, more importantly, 3-D is created through the control of the production of interests which are the prerequisite for conflict.

When discussing the theoretical constraint placed upon Bachrach's and Baratz's 2-D power hypothesis, brought about by confining the concept of power within the conceptual parameters of organized decision-making, Lukes criticises them on two counts. The first is their failure to take into account the fact that organizations and systems are not produced by individual decision-makers but, more importantly, are *reproduced* through an aggregate of acts none of which are attributable to individual actors (Lukes 1974 p. 21-2). Secondly, they fail to accept the full implications of Schattschneider's hypothesis. Central to the concept of organizationally based nondecision-making "...is the phenomenon of 'systemic' or organizational effects, where the mobilization of bias results...,from the form of organization." (Lukes 1974 p. 22). Drawing these factors together "..the bias of a system is not sustained simply by a series of individually chosen acts, but also, most importantly, *by the socially structured and culturally patterned behaviour of groups*, and practices of institutions, which may indeed be manifested by individuals' inaction." (Lukes 1974 p. 21-2, emphasis not orig.). While it is without doubt true that collectivities and organizations are made up of individuals, this does not imply that "...the power they exercise...[can] be simply conceptualized in terms of individuals' decisions or behaviour. As Marx succinctly put it: `Men make history but they do not make it just as they please; they do not make it under circumstances chosen by themselves, but under circumstances directly encountered, given and transmitted from the past.'" (Lukes 1974 p. 22).

Lukes' 3-D view of power is in many respects "...a thoroughgoing critique of the behavioural focus of the first two views as too individualistic..." (Lukes 1974 p. 24). This involves an extension of the concepts of 1-D and 2-D of power by removing the barriers placed upon them by the insistence on focusing upon overt conflict as revealed in decision-making. Inherent in this 'radicalization' of power there is an almost natural progression with 2-D power as a half-way house between 1-D and 3-D power. In order to deal with this progression it is necessary to preface it with some observations on the definitional adjustments which Lukes makes to the concept of power.

On a general level Lukes contends that power is an 'essentially contested concept' (Lukes 1974 p. 26). By this he appears to be saying that any definition of power will inherently tend to reflect the normative, theoretical and analytic framework of whoever attempts to determine the exact nature of the phenomenon (Lukes 1974 p. 26-30). However, this is not intended to imply that some definitions are not better and/or more explanatorily encompassing than others (Lukes 1974 p. 30-1). Indeed, he argues that central to all theories of power must be the causal"...notion that A in some way affects B." (Lukes 1974 p. 26). As a social phenomenon, he claims that A's affecting of B must be "...in a non-trivial or significant manner." (Lukes 1974 p. 26).

In the 1-D and 2-D view of power 'significant affecting' can be measured with respect to the criterion of conflict in decision-making. In 3-D power this option is obviously closed. Having made the manipulation of B's interests the prerequisite of control without conflict, Lukes defines significant affecting in terms of interests. The revised concept of power now reads: "...A exercises power over B when A affects B in a manner contrary to B's interests." (Lukes 1974 p. 27). Wishing to subsume 1-D and 2-D views of power into his 3-D framework based on interests, he argues that: 1-D power is where actor A realizes his/her interests in observable decision-making conflict with B; 2-D power is where B's interests are kept covert - outside the arena of decision-making - through A's acts of nondecision-making; in 3-D power, power is exercised by keeping conflict latent through the suppression of B's real interests (Lukes 1974 p. 25).

With reference to Bachrach's and Baratz's typology of power, interests become a major defining criteria. Both force and coercion are forms of power because they are clearly contrary to B's interests. Authority and influence are power only when used to affect B in a manner contrary to B's interests. To these four typologies of power Lukes added a fifth: the manipulation of B's interests through influencing his/her consciousness - the instilling of 'false consciousness'. (Lukes 1974 p. 32-3).

I would argue that the emergence of the centrality of the idea of interest in conflictual power is part of the, already referred to, natural conceptual drift from 1-D to 3-D power. In 1-D power A is a decision-maker who exercises power. B is only considered relevant to the extent to which he/she can become a potential A. If B organizes him/herself he/she can become an actor A who exercises power. As a potential A, B has power and is consequently of interest to Dahl and his colleagues. In 2-D power A is taken out of his/her isolation as a lone decision-maker. A is part of an organization which militates against B. B's ability to voice his/her grievances in the decision-making arena becomes a key factor in analysing power. The increased importance placed upon B is further reflected in Bachrach and Baratz's typology of power. However, the rise of B does not eclipse the importance of A as a decision and nondecision-maker. In 3-D power the structural contextuality of social action places actor A in the shade. Institutions and collectivities can now exercise power (Lukes 1974 p. 39). Power within the system is assessed by the extent to which B is controlled through the shaping of his/her interests in social action (see Gaventa 1980 p. 13). In short, two things are happening at once: A, the individual actor, disappears with the emergence of the acquiescent B and simultaneously the autonomy of both is subsumed by the gradual emergence of the importance of structural and organizational factors. In this context, the tension brought about by Bachrach and Baratz's attempt to emphasize both organizational bias and the individual actor/decision-maker can be conceived of as in a limbo at the center of this tendential conceptual flow.

Aside from empirical difficulties such as identifying 'true' interests, the demise of A and the problematic autonomy of both A and B creates a number of theoretical difficulties. These difficulties are linked to the inability to delineate structural effects from those attributable to power. It is a move which fundamentally shifts the debate into a different terrain of sociopolitical theory and necessitates an adequate theorization of the relationship between power and structure.

Lukes has made actor A into a reproducer of social institutions who exercises power unconsciously (Lukes 1974 p. 39, 51). B is an actor whose consciousness is shaped, by his/her experiences, into a quiescent being who fails to realize his/her interests (Gaventa 1980 p. 20-5). The questions this perception of A and B begs are of the nature: what are the criteria which could be used to analytically distinguish between A's effect upon B as defined by power or by structural constraint? How can the shaping of B's consciousness through 3-D power be separated from B's socialization as a social actor? In other words, with the demise of the importance of A - the conscious decision-maker - and the emergence of B - the victim of the structural, cultural and organizational environment - the power debate has drifted into the waters where the relationship between agents, power, social structures, and structural constraint and control cannot be left untheorized. In the last chapters of *Power* (1974) Lukes acknowledges this point and in "Power and Structure" (1977) he makes an attempt at dealing with it. However, before discussing Lukes' handling of the problem I want to turn to Parsons' consensual view of power. I want to deal with Parsons' concept of power next because it also has inherent within it the hypothesis that power is not ultimately attributable individual actors but is a systemic effect. While Lukes sees power 'over others' as emerging from social structures, Parsons perceives power 'to do' as derived from the social system. In short, while working within different intellectual traditions, there is enough mutual convergence between them for the same analytic and theoretical problems to be of relevance to both.

2 Consensual power

In this chapter I will examine Parsons' concept of power as a paradigmatic example of a consensual theory of power. As such I will deliberately narrow the scope of my examination to specific aspects of his theory which contribute to the overall direction of this work. I will focus on five factors: 1) the zero-sum problem, 2) the concept of polity and economy, 3) the analogy between power and money, 4) the tie-up between power and trust, 5) the relationship between power and authority.

One of the first places where Parsons confronts the problem of power is in a review of C Wright Mills' book *The Power Elite* (see 1960 p. 199-225). Aside from from defending the pluralist position with respect to the distribution of power, Parsons was critical of Mills' implicitly zero-sum concept of power. As interpreted by Parson, the zero-sum concept of power places special emphasis on power *over* others, where "[t]he power A has in a system is, necessarily and by definition, at the expense of B." (Parsons 1960 p. 219). While Parsons accepted the idea that the ability of A to prevail over B - in conflict and at the expense of B - is an exercise of power, he argued that as an overall conceptualization of power it was unduly narrow. "What this conception does is to elevate a secondary and derived aspect of a total phenomenon into central place." (Parsons 1960 p. 220). Aside from several implied inadequacies, it falls short on two counts: 1) power is not only power over others but it is also enabling as power to (see Wrong 1979 p. 238-9), 2) if power exists as something to be distributed, implicitly it also has to be produced (see Nagel 1975 p. 159).

Power to and power over are not necessarily two mutually exclusive concepts or manifestations of inherently different and mutually incompatible theoretical systems. As emphasized by Hobbes, actors desire power over others so as to secure their ability to act. Parsons conceived of individuals as primarily social actors. Defined as such, they derive their ability to act as members of a society. Within this paradigm power exists as "... a generalized facility or resource in... society." (Parsons 1960 p. 220). Parsons' social actor is a product of the social system of which he/she is a part and it is the power within that system which enables him/her to become an actor in the sense of being able 'to do'. Of course, this does not to negate the possibility that power may be more or less evenly distributed, as emphasized by Mills (Parsons 1960 p.221). However, it does relegate the question of power distribution to a secondary level. It is something which can be examined meaningfully when the significance of power, as a property of social systems, is understood. Taking an analogy, studying the distribution of wealth of a given society will be an inherently superficial exercise if no attempt is made to understand the economic system upon which the given distribution is based. Studying the economy means analyzing the production of wealth. Similarly, Parsons argued that political theory should be concerned with the production of power.

Because power is a phenomenon of the social system as a whole, it is interpreted on a macro level. It is assessed on a systemic level where the needs of the social system are perceived as identical to the needs or desires of individual actors. It is a position which is premised upon Parsons' interpretation of the actor as a social product or (as more critically put by Garfinkel) a cultural 'dope'.

As a social creation, power is produced in order to realize systemic goals. These systemic goals are defined in terms of the minimal functional needs which are necessary for a system to survive as an entity. Parsons postulated that for a social system to survive it will be confronted with four functional problems: "1) adapting to the environment; 2) achieving collective goals; 3) maintaining, motivating and controlling tension within the system; and, 4) integrating the actions of members." (Mitchell 1967 p. 59). Parsons further thought that, as a surviving entity, the social system must by definition have organs or parts specifically designed to cope with each of these needs. These four dimensions

27

are functional exigencies (Parsons and Smelser 1956 p. 47). As a collectivity, the system can be analytically subdivided into a number of subcollectivities specifically oriented toward the particular functional requirements of the system as a whole (Parsons 1967a p. 300). Concentrating on the main functional needs: for adaptation there is the economy; for goal attainment the polity; for tension management there is pattern maintenance (or cultural subsystem); and for integration the integrative subsystem (Parsons 1966a p. 108; Parsons and Smelser 1956 p. 47-9, 53). While each of these subsystems has specific functions with respect to the system as a whole, they are also microcosms of the system in terms of functional requirements (Rocher 1975 p. 108). For example, like the economy, the polity must adapt itself to the environment, confront problems of goal attainment, tension management and integration (Mitchell 1967 p. 133).

For the purposes of analysing power, and more generally political aspects of the social system, the "... key orienting concept is the *polity*. It is defined as a primary functional subsystem of a society, strictly parallel in theoretical status to the *economy*, as that concept is broadly used in modern economic theory." (Parsons 1967b p. 71). With respect to the functional needs of the social system, "[t]he polity of a given society is composed of the ways in which the relevant components of the total system are organized with reference to one of its fundamental functions, namely effective collective action in the attainment of the goals of collectivities." (Parsons 1967a p. 300). In other words, Parsons is postulating that as an undivided whole, in order to survive, the social system has within it an analytically separable subcollectivity oriented toward the organizational prerequisites involved in attaining systemic goals. As subcollectivities they should not be identified with specific entities such as given government institutions or businesses (Parsons and Smelser 1956 p. 48; Bourricaud 1981 p. 140). Rather, the polity and the economy are abstract analytical entities serving distinct functional needs within the system (Parsons and Shils 1967 28-9, Rocher 1975 p. 87-8; Bourricaud 1981 p. 139). Each of these conceptually and analytically defined collectivities should be examined within the framework of separate theoretical disciplines: political and economic theory (Parsons 1967a p. 300; Parsons and Smelser 1956 p. 57).

In order to understand the functioning of the polity Parsons attempted an analysis which moves from the theoretically familiar to the as yet opaque and under-theorized. He developed his interpretation of the polity by analogy derived from the economy (see Barnes 1988 p. 14). This implies the assumption, as a premise, that the two spheres are analogically comparable. It means claiming that "...there is an essential parallelism in theoretical structure between the conceptual schemes appropriate for the analysis of the economic and political aspects of societies." (Parsons 1967a p. 299).

The parallel between the economy and the polity can be used in assessing major theoretical structures and criteria of analysis: "...there is an essential parallelism in theoretical structure between the conceptual schemes appropriate for the analysis of the economic and political aspects of societies." (Parsons 1967a p. 299). For example, the main criteria used for assessing success within the economy are derived from an assessment of production. The analogical derived criterion for the polity, which can be equated with production, is collective action (Parsons 1960 p. 181; 1967a p. 301). The general standard of evaluative judgment used in the economy to assess the worth of that which is produced is 'utility' of outputs. The parallel concept, pertaining to the polity, is 'effectiveness' (Parsons 1967a p. 301; 1967b p. 75). In order to realize the factors necessary for production in an advanced economy a necessary prerequisite is some form of circulating medium upon which the economy can be based. This circulating medium is money. The equivalent to money in the economy is represented by the concept of power in the polity (Parsons 1967a p. 301; 1960 p. 181).

The development of the parallel between power and money gave Parsons an analogical tool for transcending the narrow focus of the zero-sum concept of power. The central concern of economic theory is not so much the distribution of wealth but, more importantly, an attempt to account for its creation. In developing his ideas in analytical political theory, - as distinct from Mills' implicitly normative theory (Parsons 1960 p. 222-3) - Parsons attempted to account for the production and circulation of power within the polity (see Savage 1983 p. 150). Possibly the best way of understanding the production and circulation of power is by beginning with Parsons' use of hypothetical historical analysis of the development of money.

In an economically underdeveloped society objects change hands in a market place based on barter. Value is conceived of purely in terms of utility. Within such a society securing possession of an object is not a monetary transaction (Parsons 1967a p. 308). As society develops, money is created for the purposes of convenience. Contrasted with barter, money can be spent by its possessor on what, where, when and how he or she desires (Parsons 1967a p.

307). However, early money, where value is defined in terms of metal content, is an inherently unsophisticated form in the sense that it is still very close to being a commodity (Parsons 1967a p. 307). The economy is restricted in growth by the amount of metal put into circulation. As the economy expands more and more money is needed in circulation to sustain economic expansion. The need to produce more and more money eventually results in the printing of paper money backed by a relatively small quantity of metal. Over time this quantity of metal shrinks until it finally disappears. This final disappearance only goes to emphasize, or is an explicit recognition, of the fact that, except in the most underdeveloped economies, currency lacks any intrinsic worth and the worth actually imputed to it is purely symbolic or conventional. Even prior to this final stage, money has become intrinsically 'valueless' "...for the simple reason that the total quantity of metal is far too small to redeem more than a few [notes]." (Parsons 1967a p. 307).

The ultimate referent for the worth of money is not the worth of metal "...but the ordered reliability of an organized collective system of productive activities." (Parsons 1967a p. 275). The value of money is defined on the systemic level by reference to the economy. Worth is systemically created through confidence in the economy and its circulating medium, the monetary system. In transactions within the economy "...the acceptance of this 'valueless' money rests on a certain institutionalized confidence in the monetary system." (Parsons 1967a p. 307). Seen from the point of view of the social actor, participating in the recreation of the economy, "...such a system is a case of 'operation bootstrap'." (Parsons 1967a p. 275). That is to say, the monetary system is a self-perpetuating mechanism within which "[t]he rational ground for confidence in money is that others have confidence in money and that this confidence is generally shared..." (Parsons 1967a p. 275).

This hypothetical historical account of the development of money within the economy, can be extended analogically to interpret the role of power in the polity. Similar to the economically underdeveloped barter society would be a society within which the main means of securing the compliance of others is through force. Force is direct and unmediated and, consequently, does not necessitate an intermediary medium. In the same way that barter does not involve the use of money, so force is not mediated through power (Parsons 1967a p. 308).

With development of the polity power comes into being as a medium analogous to money. This early form of power has, as an ultimate deterrent, the threat of coercion in case of noncompliance. Force is a base to which compliance can ultimately be reduced. As such force, as an instrument of coercion, serves a function within the polity which is parallel to metal in the economy (Bourricaud 1981 p. 150). Just as metal is the ultimate base for primitive coinage, so force represents an ultimate deterrent to noncompliance (Parsons 1967a p. 313).

As the polity expands the need to ensure effectiveness becomes greater. In a manner analogous to the expansion of currency relative to metallic base, the ultimate deterrence of force becomes less and less significant relative to the expansion of power. As with the institution of paper money, eventually large amounts of symbolic power may be underpinned by a small quantity of coercive resources. (see Rocher 1974 p. 90). In essence, power becomes more and more intrinsically worthless as based on violence. The total amount of power in the system vastly outstrips the level of coercive resources available within the system in order to secure ultimate compliance (a point made by Hannah Arendt in assessing the relative weakness of many regimes with high levels of coercive sanctions at their disposal (see Arendt 1970 p. 55)). Both are "...a symbolic medium which circulates much like money..." (Parsons 1967b p. 79). Both have systemically defined value as circulating media based on confidence in the ability of a subcollectivity functionally to fulfil certain needs. Just as system based trust or confidence is purveyor of the value of money, so the value of systemic power, as a circulating medium, depends on confidence in the ability of the polity effectively to contribute to the attainment of collective goals (Parsons 1967 p. 276).

Not only do power and money both derive their intrinsic 'value' within social system through trust but both perform a parallel function based on confidence within the economy and polity respectively. In the economy the trust placed in money, as a case of operation 'boot-strap', is derived from confidence in the expectations of the behaviour of others. When a person parts with an object of intrinsic use value in exchange for paper money, he or she is doing so because they believe that others will similarly part with objects of use value in exchange for money (Parsons 1967a p. 276). Implicit in this trust is the idea of knowing how others will behave, their behaviour is not random but is controlled through the medium of money. As such, money is a medium of exchange operating as a medium of social control (Parsons 1967a p. 278). "The money held by a social unit is, we may say, the unit's capacity, through market channels under given rules of procedure, to command goods and services in exchange, which for its own reason it desires." (Parsons 1967a p. 276). In short, from the point of view of the individual social actor, money is a means of procuring the services of others through control over their action (Parsons 1967b p. 78).

When a social actor exercises power over another he or she does so with the purpose of gaining compliance. This compliance will be derived from the symbolic significance of the power exercised. This symbolic significance in turn arises from confidence in the polity as a producer of effectiveness with respect to the collective goals of the social system. Power then is the mechanism for mobilization of the actions of others in the interest of effective collective action (Parsons 1967a p. 280). As a medium based on trust, circulating for the purposes of securing collective goals, power is inherently based on legitimation. That legitimation imposes on actors an obligation to act in a particular manner. It is an obligation to behave in a particular manner which is considered binding as a form of social control. In case of nonfulfilment of such obligations force exists as an ultimate base. "Power then is [a] generalized capacity to secure the performance of binding obligations by units in a system of collective organization when obligations are legitimized with reference to their bearing on collective goals and where in case of recalcitrance there is a presumption of enforcement by negative situational sanctions - whatever the actual agency of that enforcement." (Parsons 1967a p. 308).

When actor A gives actor B a unit of paper money, in exchange for an object B wishes to sell, A knows how B will react. B is not going to say 'What do you mean giving me a bit of paper?'. B will either accept the paper or ask for more paper money. The money carries within it prescriptive meaning for both A and B: by giving B paper money A expects to control B's behaviour so that he/she will give A the object of use value. Similarly, when A exercises power over B, B acts in controlled manner through an understanding of the prescriptive content of the exercise of power. Therefore, "[w]e regard power as a generalized medium of social control....[which] has in common with money that it is essentially a mode of prescriptive communication. Its effectiveness is not mainly based on any particular base but rather on confidence.... There is, however, an ultimate symbolic basis of security of value in the medium: In the case of money, it is monetary metal; in that of power, physical force". (Parsons 1967a p. 296). As media of communication, they are means for ego and alter to prescribe the action of each other within a framework of complementary expectations (Parsons and Shils 1967 p. 16).

Money based on confidence is a necessary prerequisite for an advanced economy. Within such a system it is the prerequisite for the creation of new wealth (a point disputed by Cartwright and Warner 1976 p. 643). This wealth is derived from the economy as a productive subsystem. It is *not* created by simply printing more money. By analogy, the expansion of power within an advanced polity takes place through the creation and production of new power within the polity. In other words the production of power, which obviates any zero-sum concept of society, takes place through the complex workings of a polity. As explained, within such a polity trust in the circulating medium is a necessary prerequisite for the creation of more circulating medium but it is not the primary means through which total systemic levels of power are expanded (a point misunderstood by Cartwright and Warner 1976 p. 643). For the purposes of simplification, the complex workings of the power creation processes in the polity can best be explained through an analogy with the role of banking in the economy.

When a depositor places money in the bank, for the purposes of safe-keeping, that money is made available to the bank for lending or investment. This implies that the same units of currency do a double duty. They are being put to work by the bank in order to earn more money while simultaneously remaining the property of the depositor (Parsons 1967a p. 333). The feasibility of this 'miracle of loaves and fishes' is partly dependent on the predictability of the behaviour of the depositors. Their banking practices must be routine. If they were all to decide to withdraw their money at the same time there would be a run on the bank and the system would collapse (Parsons 1967a p. 334-5). Conversely, the depositor must also have confidence in the banking institution. He/she must feel sure that the bank will invest the money placed at its disposal properly. The creation of wealth through banking is based on mutual confidence in one another. The depositor trusts the bank not to squander his/her money and the bank has confidence that the depositors will demand their money in a routine fashion. It is this mutual trust which enables the bank to make itself notionally insolvent so as to produce wealth for the economy (see Bourricaud 1981 p. 151).

In the polity power is 'banked' in leadership. In effect members of a social system deposit power with their leaders by putting "...elected leadership in a position analogous to that of the banker." (Parsons 1967a p. 339). This power is revocable at election time in much the same manner that money can be withdrawn during banking hours (Parsons 1967a p. 339). The depositors place this power in the hands of their leadership because they trust them to use it in the pursuit of collective goals. Not using the power for collective goals would be the economic equivalent of a bank squandering its depositors money. Conversely, the leaders expect the depositors of power to give the support necessary in order to realize collective goals.

In the case of banking there are clearly defined rules setting out the manner in which the depositors' assets may be handled. In the polity leaders are also bound by rules. These rules are legitimized prescriptive system rules of behaviour. These rules Parsons defined as institutions: "Institutions are generalized patterns of norms which define *categories* of prescribed, permitted and prohibited behaviour in social relationships, for people in interaction with each other as members of their society and its various subsystems and groups." (Parsons 1960 p. 177). The binding of leadership through institutions performs very much the same function as contract does in the economic sphere. The institutionalization of leadership is the central element of authority, where authority is defined as "...the legitimated right to make certain categories of decisions and bind a collectivity to them." (Parsons 1967b p. 76). The words 'certain categories' should not be confused with the idea of specific decisions. The decisions made are not a constant but change with the desire for new collective goals and in response to changes in contingent exigencies posed to the system by the 'outside' environment. As such, the institutional binding or regulation of behaviour is "...always *conditional* in some sense. *If* you occupy a certain status in a social group or relationship, and *if* certain types of situation arise, you are expected to behave in certain ways..." (Parsons 1960 p. 177). Consequently, authority is "...an institutionalized complex of norms which do not involve the prescription, permission, or prohibition of particular acts, but which on a general level define the conditions under which, in the given social structure, and in the given statuses and situations within it, acts of others within the same collectivity may be prescribed, permitted, or prohibited." (Parsons 1960 p. 180). Extending the economy/polity analogy still further: "Authority is thus comparable to rights in property, on which the legitimate use of money is based." (Cartwright and Warner 1976 p. 642).

In the case of banking the miracle of 'loaves and fish' depends upon mutual obligation. In the polity, "...the pattern of authority defines or specifies complementary obligations and rights; in the case of the leader it is the *right to expect support* and the *right to regulate*, whereas in the case of the ordinary member it is the *right to expect leadership responsibility*". (Mitchell 1967 p. 112). In the case of the banker, responsibility was defined in terms of 'sound investment'. In the polity, responsibility, with respect to authoritative leadership, means the effective use of binding obligations in the pursuit of collective goals. In short, the leader in authority is under institutional obligation to use power responsibly. "[A]uthority can be conceived of as the institutional counterpart of power..." (Parsons 1967a p. 320). It is the institutionally defined right to use power, the circulating medium of the polity (Parsons 1967a p. 320).

The institutionally defined right of leadership is the ability to draw upon collective obligations in the pursuit of collective goals. If a given leader is particularly talented at drawing upon collective obligations so as to increase systemic effectiveness then more and more collective goals will be realized. From an increased realization of collective goals there will be systemic feedback: those that owe obligation to the leader will tend to trust him/her more. This increase in confidence on the part of the led will make them wish to extend higher levels of power credit to their leaders (Parsons 1967a p. 342). Hence, the net result of a change in the total level of confidence will result in increased levels of support for the leaders to draw upon (Giddens 1969 p. 260). In other words, a cycle has been established whereby "...the totality of commitments made by the collectivity as a whole can be enhanced." (Parsons 1967a p. 340), an increase in collective commitments being another way of saying an overall increase in power. In diagram form the parallel transcending of zero-sum conceptualizations of the social system through increased wealth and power can be represented as in figure 2.1 (see next page).

Power credit, like monetary credit, is based on confidence. If power credit has been extended too far - relative to effectiveness and consequent attainment of collective goals - then the attempt to invoke obligations will be met with less than full commitment (Parsons 1967a p. 242). This can, in a certain limited number of cases, be overcome through forcing actors to fulfil their obligations. However, as there are insufficient resources of coercion to enforce even a fraction of social obligations, large scale nonfulfilment of obligations will result directly in a lowering of effectiveness and consequently of the total amount of power in circulation. At this point a cycle of power deflation can set in: the lowering of power levels means lowering of collective goal attainment which in turn

Fig. 2.1

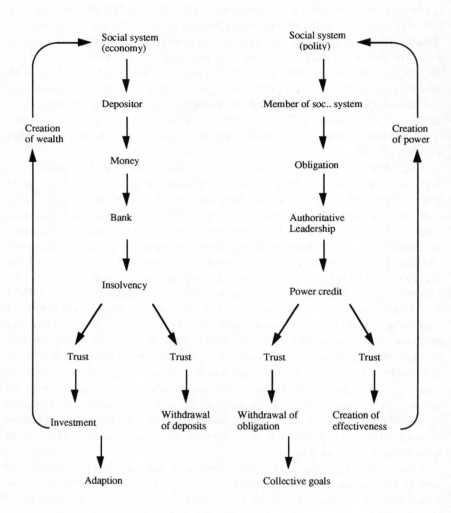

results in the general lack of confidence feeding back to a further decrease power credit (Parsons 1967a p. 343). Lack of power credit is the equivalent of depositors withdrawing their money from the bank. The leaders have less to invest, so effectiveness decreases and with it the total power in the system. In short, this implies that just as trust provides the key to an systemic increase of power so the absence of confidence creates power deflation. This implies a dual concept for the role of trust with respect to both money and power: 1) trust is the vital prerequisite for an advanced polity and economy, with power and money as symbolic circulating media, where value is created through conventions of mutual obligation based on self- perpetuating conventions of mutual trust (Parsons 1967a p. 342); 2) trust in the ability of others, to use responsibly the circulating media of both polity and economy, provides the means through which the zero-sum concept of power and wealth in the social system can be transcended by showing how total systemic levels of both media can be increased (Parsons 1967a p. 344).

Most criticisms of Parsons' concept of power focus on two points: 1) that power is portrayed as a purely consensual normative phenomenon which precludes illegitimate and conflictual manifestations of power (e.g. Giddens 1969 p. 263; Wrong 1977 p. 246; Clegg 1989 p. 132); 2) the inherent lack of validity of the analogy between power and money (see Cartwright et al 1976 p. 642-52; Barnes 1988 p. 19-20; Alexander 1984 p. 168). As both criticisms are well known I will not regurgitate them but instead comment on a couple of points associated with them.

It is undoubtedly true that Parsons leaves conflictual power untheorized. However, this does not necessarily mean that a consensus based concept of power necessarily precludes illegitimate and/or conflictual power. Contrary to what most commentators assume, there could be conceptual space for illegitimate and conflictual power within a framework where power is socially produced through consensus. Using a Parsonsian type analogical argument this can be illustrated with by example. Imagine an actor A who is ideologically committed to the overthrow of the capitalist system. The value of the currency within that system is determined by confidence in the overall system of production. The manner in which that confidence is assessed is through the willingness of social actors to consent to accept units of currency in exchange for products. When actor A accepts units of currency in exchange for his/her labour power he/she is actively contributing, through social practice, to an overall social consent that one unit of currency equals so much labour time. Through social practice he/she is giving consensual value to a given piece of paper. However, as a Marxist he/she may despise the capitalist relations of production and, consequently, consider the creation of capital through wage labour as inherently illegitimate. Therefore, through social practice he/she is giving his/her consent to a system which he/she considers illegitimate. In this case consensus and illegitimacy are combined through a mismatch between ideological commitment and social practice.

Speaking more generally, the social system only exists through its reproduction in social action. The social system is realized in the moment of action. To the extent to which that action is not coerced it must be voluntary. As such, any social system is, by and large, consensually based unless a conspiracy or determinant metaphysical forces are postulated to be at work. However, as revealed in social practice, consensus is not necessarily linked to, or a product of, an ideological commitment to the legitimacy of the system produced. This point is well illustrated by the behaviour of revolutionary revisionist states which, while committed to the overthrow of a particular system of international relations, actually actively contribute to its recreation through participation in it (Buzan 1983 179-86; Carr 1966 p. 105) (for a specific example see Waltz 1979 p. 127-8). On a general theoretical level, another example of a mismatch between practice and perceptions of legitimacy is described in the type of situation classified by Elster as one of counterfinality (Elster 1978 p. 106). The central point is that the social system may be produced through voluntary consensual action of individuals but the resultant system is an unintended consequence and, as such, could quite logically be perceived as illegitimate by its creators. When actor A decides to accept a pound note as valid legal tender he/she may be acting out of consent but this does not necessarily mean that he/she accepts as legitimate the unintended consequences of his/her action - the recreation of a market economy. Hence, it is conceptually possible to subscribe to the idea of a consensually produced power system and simultaneously account for illegitimate power. However, such a perspective must be able to accommodate different levels of consensus and legitimacy. The latter Parsons failed to do. Indeed his systemically based theory of normative action would have precluded it.

Aside from a theoretical lack in dealing with the issue of conflictual power, Parsons' theory calls for a certain paradigmatic leap of faith. On a general level it calls for an acceptance of his cybernetic orientation. On a more specific level, it calls for an act of unsubstantiated imagination to accept the idea of power as circulating medium analogous to money. I would argue that his idea of power, as an entity which explains certain phenomena but yet cannot be concretely shown to exist, leaves the political theorist with an unsatisfactory metaphysical concept of power.

While Parsons' theory of power suffers from having left large areas untheorized and is flawed by being premised on a functionalism which precludes any meaningful level of intellectual autonomy for the intentional social actor, Parsons does draw attention to some important aspects of consensual power which can be reinterpreted within an alternative framework. I will conclude by drawing attention to the potential insight it offers with respect to the relationship between power, violence and systemic stability, a point which so interested Hannah Arendt: "Where commands are no longer obeyed, the means of violence are of no use:... Everything depends on the power behind the violence. The sudden drastic breakdown of power that ushers in revolutions reveals in a flash how civil obedience -...- is but the outward manifestation of support and consent." (Arendt 1970 p. 49).

3   Power and structure

In the previous chapters I described the manner in which both conflict and consensus theories of power tend to converge on the hypothesis that power is inextricably linked to structural or systemic effects. Such a position inherently calls for the theorization the relationship between power and these structurally systemic elements. It necessitates the development of a framework which can deal with conceptually 'fuzzy edges' emerging between causal effects derived from power and those attributable to structure. In particular, it demands the theorization of the conceptual borders which analytically distinguish power from structural constraint. Ideally speaking, such a theorization should be meaningful both with respect to the idea of actors exercising power as agents and take account of the structurally/systemic social environment in which social action takes place. In short, this inherently implies rejecting as superficial any position which theorizes individual actors A exercising power over actors B, as if these actors were decontextualized and desocialized beings operating in a vacuum isolated from structural and systemic forces. Further, it means the elaboration of conceptual borders which render the concepts delineated inherently mutually meaningful and significant. For example, in this context, the theorization of the phenomenon of false consciousness as 3-D power is only a true enrichment of the political theorist's analytical vocabulary if such a gain is not accompanied by the loss of structural constraint as a meaningful conceptual tool for theoretical analysis. In short, not only should it be possible to theorize the ability of individual actors to prevail over each other in moments of interaction but, simultaneously, it should be possible to provide conceptual space for the structurally and systemically constituted environment in which such exercises of power take place.

A number of thinkers have attempted to deal with this problem. For the purposes of this chapter I have chosen to focus on three such attempts. Each is formulated within a different perspective. The first is by Lukes and is representative of an analysis combining agent centred and structuralist positions. The second is by Jessop and sketches the conceptual contours of a Marxist structuralist position. The third focuses on Clegg and is a more recent post-modernist formulation of the power/structure problem. With regard to the thematic organization of the chapter, the main body of the text will constitute an analysis of the three positions.

Lukes framed his analysis of the relationship between power and structure within the conceptual parameters of the Poulantzas/Milliband debate. He used the former as an exemplar of a structuralist Althusserian position (Lukes 1974 p. 63, 1977 p. 16) and the latter as a methodological individualist (1974 p. 54). Lukes starts from the premise that power and structural constraint are at opposite ends of a continuous spectrum. The problem is essentially to determine where the one begins and the other ends (Lukes 1977 p. 18). What distinguishes one end of the spectrum from the other is contingency. At one end a hypothetical actor A could have acted differently. At the other, A has no possibility of acting differently than he/she did. "[I]n other words, to identify a given process as an 'exercise of power', rather than structural domination, is to assume that it is *in the exerciser's or exercisees' power to act differently.*" (Lukes 1974 p. 55). " The point,...is that to the extent to which the explanation of a given outcome is structural, the claim being made is that to that extent the agents involved in bringing it about are powerless to act otherwise." (Lukes 1977 p. 9).

This conceptual link between power and contingency means that, in claiming a given act to be an exercise of power, an implicit counterfactual assertion is being made. The counterfactual claim is that the agent in question could have acted differently. To say that A has exercised power over B is also to maintain that A could have acted differently. "All those, whether observers or agents, who deny

41

structural explanations of outcomes, explaining them rather in terms of power, make counterfactual claims to the effect that some specified agent or agents could have acted (that is, had the ability and the opportunity to act) in a certain way." (Lukes 1974 p. 24).

With power and structural constraint at the opposite ends of a spectrum, measured with respect to contingency, it is inherently the case that any model of society characterized by structural determinacy would preclude power. Conversely, a voluntarist agent-centered social theory would deny the possibility of structural determinacy (Lukes 1974 p. 55; 1977 p. 7, 15-7; Jessop 1976 p. 10).

It is Lukes' thesis that the constant disputes which "...occur over whether (specifiable) options were within (specifiable) agents' power or beyond it,..." (Lukes 1977 p. 23) only make sense if society is characterized neither by the level of structural determinacy/constraint claimed by Althusser nor by the level of openness implied by agent-centred positions. In real life people are continuously arguing over counterfactual claims. For example, 'could Bukharin have resisted Stalin?' is a meaningful question (Lukes 1977 p. 24). It is a question concerning levels of contingency or determinacy. For Lukes, "...social life can... properly be understood as a dialectic of power and structure, a web of possibilities for agents, whose nature is both active and structured, to make choices or pursue strategies within given limits, which in consequence expand and contract over time." (Lukes 1977 p. 29)

The theoretical implications of this are that "[a]ny standpoint or methodology which reduces that dialectic to a one-sided consideration of agents without (internal and external) structural limits, or structures without agents, or which does not address the problem of their interrelation, will be unsatisfactory. No social theory merits serious attention that fails to retain an ever-present sense of the dialectic of power and structure." (Lukes 1977 p. 29). If an actor has no choice - through structurally imposed constraints - but to do what he/she does then he/she does not have power as an agent. "If one cannot choose, it is because one is without power or in some sense subject to structural determination." (Barbalet 1987 p. 4). As an agent, an actor has power which he/she can use to impose constraint upon another. In other words, "...the possession and exercise of power by some can be a structural fact of the situation of others - so what is structural with respect to the recipient(s) may not be so with respect to the exerciser(s)." (Lukes 1977 p. 9). In other words, subjection to power can be experienced as structural determination. In this sense, structural determination and power

42

can be both sides of the identical act (Barbalet 1987 p. 5). While both can refer to different sides of the same interaction, power and structure are still antithetical in the sense that, in many cases, "[t]o have power is...to be free from determination; to be subject to power is to be structurally determined." (Barbalet 1987 p. 6). In short, "The point,..., is that to the extent to which the explanation of a given outcome is structural, the claim being made is that to that extent the agents involved in bringing it about are *powerless* to act." (Lukes 1977 p. 9; emphasis not orig.).

In essence, what Lukes has done is to attempt differentiate power from structural constraint using the "...basic opposition between structure and agency..." (Lukes 1977 p. 8). Agency pertaining to power and structure to determinacy. Power "... is tied to agency in the 'freedom to act otherwise clause', and structural determinism is...concerned with agency only in the mechanical fashion i.e. where action is totally determined by structure." (Layder 1985 p. 137). In effect, Lukes has incorporated both sides of the debate between agent-centred theories and radical structuralist into his framework of power and structure (Lukes 1977 p. 15, 17). What he is saying is that both voluntarism and structuralism are commensurable (Lukes 1977 p. 18). Society is characterized by areas both of contingency and determinism and, hence, free agency and structural determination. Power is to be found at the contingent, agent-centred, end of the spectrum and structural constraint at the radical structuralist side.

The interplay between the contingent and the determinate takes place at the micro actor-based level. As observed by Jessop, inherent in this theorization of the relationship between agency and structure is the problematic of free will. If free will is interpreted as cognitively purposeful action, it must be fundamental to the definition of agency (Jessop 1976 p. 14). On the other hand, determinacy is conceived of in terms of the behaviour of individuals who are the mere carriers of social structures and, as such, are epistemologically programmed. This "...implies a fundamental antinomy between social causation (...) and reason..." (Jessop 1976 p. 16). Taken to its logical conclusion, to say that B could not have done otherwise could be construed as meaning that: a) he/she has diminished responsibility or, b) that he/she was morally not culpable for his/her actions (Barbalet 1987 p.7). As observed by Jessop, while this makes sense in the world of legal jargon it is a doubtful base upon which to construct a sociopolitical theory (see Jessop 1976 p. 15).

Even without asserting that the opposition between free will and

43

determinacy only makes sense in the world of legal jargon, I would agree with Bob Jessop that Lukes' position leaves large areas of social life untheorized. In many respects Lukes' position is a descriptive analysis which calls for theoretical development. As a general observation it is true that both radical structuralism and agent-centric theories do, each in a specific manner, constitute conceptual tools which describe facets of social life. It is both true to say that agency is meaningful and that actors realize this agency within a structurally constituted contextuality. While there is nothing inherently contradictory about the hypothesis that contingency and determinism both characterize social life, it is an observation which calls for the development of a theoretical perspective which has theoretical space for both these facets of social life. Without such a theorization, the sociopolitical theorist is left with the unsatisfactory situation of working with two sets of conceptual tools each pertaining to mutually excluding perceptions of the constitution of social order.

Wishing to avoid the pitfalls inherent in attempting to reconcile two theoretical perspectives, Bob Jessop attempted to resolve the power/structure problem by working within, and modifying, one theoretical tradition. He broke "...decisively with the concept of the individual posed within the humanist problematic of the subject." (Jessop 1976 p. 14). What he meant by this was a rejection of the problematic of agent-based theories. Instead Jessop asserted that Althusserian structuralism was not so inherently deterministic as to negate the possibility of developing a coherent theory of power: "It would seem that Lukes interprets the Althusserian project as the construction of a structural problematic of the subject in which all the properties of social formation are totally determined by a single principle of structuration.... this interpretation is incorrect." (Jessop 1976 p. 18). In short, Jessop attempted to differentiate power from structural determinism by rejecting the problematic of agency while simultaneously creating space for contingency within the Althusserian problematic.

While Jessop recognizes that *Reading Capital*, one of the principal texts of Althusserianism, does appear to imply a high level of structural rigidity and determination, he further argues that in the work of Poulantzas there is conceptual space for both the exercise of power and structural determinism. "Indeed, although Lukes claims that Poulantzas assimilates power to structural determination, it is in the latter's work that we find the most careful discussion of power and structural constraints in the whole school." (Jessop 1976 p. 19).

Nicos Poulantzas conceives of society as divided into two interrelated parts: that of social structure and that of social practices (Poulantzas 1973 p. 64) This distinction does not imply the '...relations of synchronic structure to diachronic function, as in a current erroneous trend..." (Poulantzas 1973 p. 67) where the synchronic is conceived of as static and the diachronic as dynamic.

Rather than the framework of synchrony/diachrony, "Social structure refers in an abstract fashion to the articulation of social space..." (Jessop 1976 p. 25) in which social practices take place. In turn these practices are the effect of social structure (Poulantzas 1973 p. 111). As a set of assembled structures, the social system only continues to exist, as an entity, through its ability to produce the conditions necessary for its own reproduction. Taking capitalism as an example: "The basic dynamic of capitalism is to expand reproduction of the capitalist relations of production through the capitalization of surplus value realized on the market. It is only when commodities are sold at a profit that the entrepreneur or corporation can renew capital investment and thus continue production. This leads to specific constraints if capital is to be reproduced and reinforces the operation of the law of value." (Jessop 1976 p. 26). The need for capitalism to survive through the reproduction of self means that capitalism "...cannot overcome the effects of the law of value without dissolving capitalism." (Jessop 1976 p. 26). Capitalism is so structured that "...capitalism simply produces its own reproduction." (Poulantzas 1978 p. 27) This necessity for reproduction constitutes "...first-order limits associated with the overall articulation of a social formation..." (Jessop 1976 p. 27) through social practice.

There is also a second level of structural constraint associated with the particular conjuncture in which action takes place (Jessop 1976 p. 27). At any point in time, social practices are doubly limited both as the effect of social structures and with respect to other practices which are themselves limited as the effects of structure (Poulantzas 1973 p. 95). This means a combined and compound constraint upon action. In short, constraint operates on two levels, with respect to: 1) the production and reproduction of a system of structures as a whole and 2) the actual contexts of other practices which are in turn structured on two levels. Within this dualistic framework "...power is conceptualized at the level of social relations," and constraint in terms of social structure (Jessop 1976 p. 25).

Within capitalism social relations are characterized by class struggle based on opposition: "Social relations consist of class

45

practices, in which classes are placed in *opposition*: social classes can be conceived only as class practices in opposition which *in their unity, constitute the field of class struggle*". (Poulantzas 1973 p. 86).

If social practice is the effect of social structure and, within the capitalist relations of production, practices are constituted as struggle, this implies that class struggle exists as the effect of structure. Class is not defined relative to specific structural features but as the global effect of structures in the field of social relations (Poulantzas 1973 p. 64). Class exists within a structured whole which constitutes the social system as geared toward a particular mode of production. As such, "*social class is a concept which shows the effects of the ensemble of structures, of the matrix of a mode of production or of a social formation on the agents which constitute its supports: this concept reveals the effects of the global structure in the field of social relations.*" (Poulantzas 1973 p. 67-8; see also 1973 p. 85-6).

In general, social practice is the effect of structure. Therefore, the struggle which appears in social relations is in itself, as a structural phenomenon, a manifestation of the contradictions inherent in the capitalist relations of production. Not only is class struggle a manifestation of the contradictions within the capitalist relations of production but, as socially defined entities, classes are the effect of structural contradiction (Poulantzas 1973 p. 86). Inversely, the absence of these contradictions would appear to imply the nonexistence of class as constituted through struggle.

The manifestation of class struggle in the realm of social practice implies a clash of horizons of interest (Poulantzas 1973 p. 111-2). Since these class interests are found at the level of social practices, they are also indirectly an effect of structure. However, in contrast with the Parsonsian framework, these interests are not located at the systemic level for integrative purposes. Instead they are rather a manifestation of overall contradiction. When combined, the idea of class conflict and class interest is the arena for social actors to participate as actors in a struggle for class domination. Domination by one class over the other is manifest through the ability of one class to realize its interests in conflict with another class. As a facet of domination, power is "*...the capacity of a social class to realize its specific objective interests*" (Poulantzas 1973 p. 104).

The link between power and interests is reminiscent of Lukes' third dimension of power. Within the Poulantzasian framework, as pertaining to social practices, it is explicit that "*...power is conceptualized at the level of social relations.*" (Jessop 1976 p. 25).

46

Structural determinacy/constraint is a specific phenomenon confined to the realm of social structures. As the realm of social action, class struggle provides the arena for the exercise of power to take place. As the manifestation of structural contradictions, this arena is determined by structural factors which are systemically defined. However, this systemic perception of determination does not negate that social action is perceived by actors in terms of interests. It is the latter which provides the incentive for them to engage in struggle. In short, class struggle is the social space, within the parameters of systemically confining social structures, where meaningful exercises of power can take place. As this struggle is a fight over interests, success or failure of social actors in power conflict can be measured by their ability to realize interests.

There can be little doubt that Jessop was correct in drawing attention to the conceptual space provided for power within Poulantzas' framework. Taking the premises of Marxist structuralism as given, it is a position which does provide the broad conceptual contours of an internally consistent theorization of the relationship between structure and power. However, it is a theorization which works only if the relationship between structure and praxis is taken as given. In other words, there are problems with the analysis of the *creation* of structure and *production* of power. This manifests itself on two levels.

The first concerns the problem of developing a feedback mechanism from the arena of action to the level of the systemic. Not only is it necessary to have theoretical space for both but it is a truism that the systemic cannot exist, as an entity, without the realm of praxis. Hence, there must be a feedback from the latter to the former. This is not a chicken and egg situation where the systemic or the realm of action can be arbitrarily selected to explain the other as an epiphenomenon. They are both mutually constituting and as such neither can be analytically separated as causal. As such, they do not constitute separate realms as postulated by Poulantzas. Social practice is not a separate epiphenominal realm of the structural. The difficulty inherent in this position is compounded by Poulantzas' observation "...that social classes are never theoretically conceived by Marx as the genetic origin of structures..." (Poulantzas 1973 p. 62). In other words, a feedback process from action to structure appears theoretically precluded from his framework of political thought.

The second problem with the Jessop/Poulantzas position is an extension of the first. It centres around the role of individual actors in the creation of social structures. Poulantzas deliberately rejected the problematic of agency (Jessop 1976 p. 29). Instead, he focused on them as "...the supports or bearers of an ensemble of structures..." (Poulantzas 1973 p. 62). As such, individual actors engage in social practices as members of a given class. Within this framework it is social classes, not agents, who hold power. Power is an attribute of classes (Poulantzas 1973 p. 115). This implies that "...the different ideologies which locate power as an 'inter-personal' phenomenon..." are inherently mistaken (Poulantzas 1973 p. 106 fn. 12). Taken to its logical conclusion, this negates the possibility of explaining how the ability of A to prevail over B contributes to recreation of the systemic in the field of power conflict. In others words, not only are structure and systemic action schismatically separated but, even more radically, individual actors are theoretically divorced from the realm within which social action takes place.

While the Jessop/Poulantzas framework is a theoretical perspective which recognizes the necessity to accommodate both structure and power in the realm of social practice. I would argue that the inability to provide adequate feed-back mechanisms from practice derives from an over systemic interpretation of the relationship between power and structure. It is of course true that structure only becomes meaningful as part of a systemic whole. However, this does not inherently imply that the theorization of relationship between structure and actor is one way. In other words, it is not valid to argue that, because it is the system which gives structure meaning, the recreation of structure can only be interpreted with respect to systemically defined needs. This falls foul of the type of problem which is also found in a Parsonsian systemic functionalist perception of social order. When the true significance of agency can only be interpreted from the level of the systemic down, and not from of the level of actor up, actors become 'dopes' in a world where agency has lost all meaning.

Taking an overview of the relationship between Lukes and Jessop, it could be argued that Lukes' position represents a descriptive analysis derived from two mutually exclusive frameworks of social order. While accepting the central problematic of the relationship between power and structure as a problem worth analysis, Jessop argued that inherent paradigmatic incompatibility of structuralism and agent-centredness implied the need to theorize within one or other framework. He opted for the structuralist alternative and provided conceptual space within it for certain levels of agency and power, albeit, an agency which had lost most of its meaningful content. There is of course also a third option. It is to opt for a new and alternative framework of sociopolitical theory. If it is a sufficiently radical framework, then the problems found in the previous frameworks are not so much resolved as become subject to dissolution (see Clegg 1989 p. 202). In other words, if a change of framework is complete enough then the sociopolitical theorist will be faced with an inherently different set of problems. It is this third alternative solution for which Clegg opts.

Clegg frames his analysis of power against the hypothesis that, within the history of political thought, the analysis of power can be characterized as taking place within two traditions. The first he attributes to a development of ideas derived from Hobbes and culminating in Lukes. The second is a tradition extending from Machiavelli to Foucault. The Hobbesian perspective is described as modernist and the Machiavellian as post-modernist. Central to this division of political thought is an argument to the effect that the theoretical problems associated with Lukes' concept of 3-D are symptomatic of a general crisis within the paradigm of modernism (Clegg 1989 p. 99). Consequently, Clegg suggests that the adoption of a post-modernist perspective constitutes the next logical step in the analysis of social power. In particular, he states that the relationship between power and structure cannot be analytically advanced through the sharpening of old modernist conceptual tools. Hence, Clegg takes it upon himself to develop a new theoretical analysis of power within a paradigm of post-modernism (Clegg 1989 p. 186).

In sociopolitical theory terms, one of the fundamental elements, which characterizes the division between modernism and post-modernism, is the contrast between theoretical frameworks which are premised on the idea of social order as an architectonic product (modernism) (Clegg 1989 p. 7) and frameworks where social order is conceived of as inherently much less rigid (post-modernism) (Clegg 1989 p. 150). The architectonic product is the creation of a sovereign power. On the other hand, the less rigid social order is the effect of a continual flux which is analytically similar to language. The Hobbesian sovereign view of social order is a manifestation of the enlightenment project where it was considered possible to translate the laws of mechanical physics into the creation of a mechanically based organization of society. The two most archetypal and influential portrayals of this perception of society are to be found in Hobbes' description of society as a clock (Hobbes 1839 p. 5) and the copper plate frontispiece engraved image of the state as an artificial organism contained in the various reprints of the first edition of *Leviathan* (Clegg 1989 p. 27, 42).

The internal workings of the Leviathan were driven by seventeenth century laws of mechanical physics. The whole machinery of state was driven by the measurable movements of objects colliding and bouncing against each other (Clegg 1989 p. 4, p 22). These objects of volition are social actors, later called A and B, who cause things to happen in the agent-centred modernist vision of political theory (Clegg 1989 p. 42-3). It is a perspective which finds its most overt promulgation in the behaviourism of Dahl's analysis of power (Clegg 1989 p. 50-9).

The Machiavellian perception is derived from the concept of the Prince as a strategist of power. He does not create a power structure as Hobbes' sovereign does. Instead, he stays in power through the manipulation and understanding of fields of force which are the product of power flowing through society (Clegg 1989 p. 4-5). As the product of acute observation by 'the would be advisor' to Lorenzo de Medici, this analysis of power is *descriptive* in nature and offers a rich ethnography of power (Clegg 1989 p. 32). "Where Hobbes and his successors may be said to have endlessly legislated on what power is, Machiavelli and his successors may be said to interpret what power does". (Clegg 1989 p. 5). In place of agent A colliding with B, there are descriptions of strategy conceived of within a framework where power is taken as given (Clegg 1989 p. 32). In more recent times, this descriptive tradition becomes developed in Michel Foucault's histories. Here individual actors become part of, and players in, a system of power. Actors are not so much agents as actors who are integrated into society through regimes of discipline. These disciplinary practices are "... the micro-techniques of power which inscribe and normalize not only individuals but also collective organized bodies." (Clegg 1989 p. 191). This disciplining is inherently bound up with surveillance, where "...surveillance is not simply about...direct control. It may range from cultural practices of moral endorsement, enablement and suasion to more formalised technical knowledge." (Clegg 1989 p. 191). These are the rules which subjects have to learn and play by in everyday life from the school to the factory (Clegg 1989 p. 175). These disciplinary practices are continually ordered according to principles of increased rationality, thus creating an indissoluble link between power and knowledge (Clegg 1989 p. 192). These are routines which increase the calculability of individuals, the purpose being to increase normalization (Clegg 1989 p. 174) With regard to the objects of power, "[d]isciplinary power works exactly through the construction of routine." (Clegg 1989 p. 167). "Such practices are not simply constraining: they do punish and forbid but more especially they also endorse and enable obedient wills and constitute organizationally approved forms of creativity and productivity through a process both transitive (via authoritative externalities such as rules, superiors, etc.) and intransitive (via the acquisition of organizationally proper conduct by the member)." (Clegg 1989 p. 192).

The centrality of rules in the creation of disciplined practices is, in part, a development of themes found in his earlier work - in particular *Power, Rule and Domination* (Clegg 1975). In this book there is a central emphasis upon the idea of a link between rule-following and the ordered flow of power. They are concepts of rule-following which are influenced by Wittegenstein's language philosophy and concepts of Weberian rational domination (Clegg 1989 p. 209). In *Frameworks of Power*, social power is an ordered medium which derives its channels of flow from rules which constitute the 'rules of the game'. Not only do these rules define the nature of social relations and the momentary episodic exercise of power but they are also considered integral in making some players more powerful than others. To take an analogy with the game of chess: "'Obviously, in an ongoing game, a piece like the queen would start in a more privileged position than a pawn, simply because the extant rules, which are now open to interpretation [in the act of play], enable her to begin the sequence with more potential moves to make.'" (Clegg 1975 p. 49 quoted in 1989 p. 210). According to the rules of chess the queen is inherently more powerful than the pawn, she is not simply more powerful when she is moved. Relating this to Dahl's example of the traffic police: "Policemen can be said to have the power to direct traffic not only while they actually do it but also when no vehicle is in sight. If some traffic were to come along then the policeman would have the power to hold up his hand and make it stop. He can be said to have the power without exercising it." (Clegg 1989 p. 83). Borrowing terminology from Wrong (1979 p. 6), he termed the momentary exercise of power - which so concerned Dahl and the modernists more generally - *episodic* power and the power which actors possessed as *dispositional* power (Clegg 1989 p. 83). As can be seen in the traffic police example, in terms of analysing distributions of power within a community, it tells you substantially more about the distribution of power in a community to know that the police *have* this dispositional power than that he/she directed a particular car left or right in a specific moment of an episodic exercise of power. Episodic power is only a manifestation of the power which the police officer has according to certain rules. "Episodic agency power, the focus of Dahl's concerns, may be seen from this perspective as something which is based on effective utilization of resource control or possession." (Clegg 1989 p. 84). As such, "[e]pisodic power is seen to derive from the capacities of agents grounded in resource control." (Clegg 1989 p. 217).

An aspect of Clegg's shift of perspective from modernism to postmodernism was also a change of language derived from the differences in world view which separate modernism from post-modernism. Out the door went "...the metaphorical billiard balls,...flywheels, gears, levers and pulleys.... [and in came]....an imagery more redolent of the post-modern electronic age, an imagery which is crystallised as a circuit diagram: circuits of power." (Clegg 1989 p. 186). Both episodic power and dispositional power are described as part of a circuit of power. It is these circuits which mobilize "...relations of meaning and membership (...) and techniques of production and discipline..." (Clegg 1989 p. 219). These circuits are the channels of established patterns which characterize the organization of a social grouping (Clegg 1989 p. 222). These circuits exist at three levels: agency, social integration and system integration.

The focus of power within the agency level circuit is episodic power. This is "...the most apparent, evident and economical circuit of power." (Clegg 1989 p. 215). As observed with respect to the example of the traffic police and the queen in chess, this exercise of power is a manifestation of already existing sets of rules and practices. These are the rules and disciplinary practices which make agents what they are as actors with dispositional power. Dispositional power pertains to the circuit which defines the rules and practices through which all traffic must pass (Clegg 1989 p. 215). Dispositional power defines the abilities of agents, under specific conditions, to do what they do by making them what they are (Clegg 1989 p. 122). As such, this is the circuit of social integration which fixes the meaning of membership through the maintenance of the 'rules of the game' (Clegg 1989 p. 224).

In the circuit of social integration fixity of meaning and consistency of rules implies a fixed set of reference points establishing stability. Clegg refers to these junctures, through which all traffic must pass, as obligatory passage points. The fixity inherent in the idea of obligatory passage points is created through the reification of power. When reified, power appears as a thing-like entity which can confine the parameters through which power flows (Clegg 1989 p. 207).

In a game of chess the queen is guaranteed her power according to the rules whereby a game of chess is constituted as a game of chess. However, in real life, actors will tend to challenge the rules of the game. In other words, however permanent obligatory passage points may appear, they will always be open to challenge (Clegg 1989 p. 210, 215). Continuing the chess analogy for the purposes of explanation, in the real world the pawn or the bishop may challenge the obligatory passage points whereby he/she is defined as less powerful than the queen. Such challenges are the main sources of social change (Clegg 1989 p. 215).

In the moment of social change customary circuits of power vie for dominance with alternative organizational circuitry of power. The victory of one circuit over another Clegg calls organizational outflanking (Clegg 1989 p. 220-1). Alternatively, viewed from the angle of stability, organizational outflanking is also the process whereby the powerless are kept powerless through lack of access to an alternative circuitry of power which would define the pawns as queens (see Clegg 1989 p. 221-3). In other words, organizational outflanking refers to the process whereby the less powerful fail to organize an organizational challenge to existing organizationally constituted power circuits; circuits which define existing distributions of dispositional power (Clegg 1989 p. 289). When such a challenge is mounted, it is often a function of "...changes in the process of innovation which always pose potential transformations for the extant structuring of empowerment and disempowerment, dependent upon extant techniques of production and discipline." (Clegg 1989 p. 215). These new techniques are not only sources of innovation but also, almost invariably, bearers of new forms of domination (Clegg 1989 p. 215). Victory through organizational outflanking results in transformations "...leading to a new 'constitution' of the power configuration." (Clegg 1989 p. 220). In short, the concept of organizational outflanking is both a tool for the continued maintenance of the existing power circuits - social control - and similarly it is also a method of instigating social change (Clegg 1989 p. 225).

The maintenance of continuity or the creation of change points to yet a third circuit of power. This is the circuit of power whereby the obligatory passage points of the dispositional power circuit are kept intact or are undermined. This is the circuit of system integration whereby conditions of empowerment and disempowerment are maintained through the stabilization of obligatory passage points in the circuit of social integration. "Social and system integration can thus be conceptualized as the pathways through which fields of force are fixed and stabilized on 'obligatory passage points' in the circuits of power." (Clegg 1989 p. 224). Inversely, and by the same process, it is also the circuit whereby existing distributions of power are altered. In other words, "[i]t should be apparent that these circuits may be termed 'integrative' but they should also be viewed as double edged: they may be disintegrative as well as integrative, particularly where exogenous sources of change are involved." (Clegg 1989 p. 224). Analysed as such, the circuit of social integration is the circuit where structures of dominance are maintained or overthrown. Consequently, it is both true to say that existing structures of dominance are central to the continued existence of organizational inequality and they are also the tools of organizational overthrow. "[E]xisting structures of dominance are thus in principle always open to subsidence, disruption and innovation, since new techniques may open up new conduits and passages which undermine the presently entrenched structures." (Clegg 1989 p. 224). (for Clegg's figurative representation of the relationship between the three circuits of power see 1989 p. 214).

Taking an over-view of Clegg's position, at the analytical core, the success of his project inherently hinges upon his ability to transcend the modernist problematic of the relationship between power and structure through a retheorization of power within postmodernism. Clegg does not offer a theorization of the relationship between agency and structure. Instead, he offers an alternative framework where such a theorization is unnecessary for an adequate conceptualization of power. Clegg attempts to remove the agent/structure problem as a target for debate, by offering postmodernism as a framework which does not contain this 'target' (see Clegg 1989 p. 130). Commenting upon this, I would fully accept such a solution is theoretically possible. However, I would argue that Clegg must show that such a change of framework has actually taken place. It is not sufficient to introduce a new linguistic terminology to political theory. It must be clearly demonstrated that the new vocabulary, or imagery, is part of an inherently different theorization of social power. Otherwise, the apparent dissolution of agent/structure problem could be a linguistically created illusion produced by a swapping of labels. Possibly, this point can best be explained through an imaginary example.

Imagine that there exists a framework of political theory which is usually referred to as Poligology. Within this perspective three phenomena X, Y and Z are considered of central importance. While the distinction between Z and the other two is clear, due to extensive social research, there is a theoretical crisis because the difference between X and Y has become conceptually problematic. In order to deal with this problem some political theorists have attempted to create various conceptual tools for dispelling the analytical blurring emergent between X and Y. Imagine further that most of these attempts have been theoretically problematic for various reasons. Then along comes a political scientist who claims to resolve, or dissolve, the problematic pertaining to X and Y. He/she does this by developing an alternative framework called Post-poligology. Within this new framework A, B and C emerge as conceptual categories of analysis. However, for this position to be a true advancement upon the old, it is not sufficient simply to assert that because it uses the language of A, B and C the problematic pertaining to X and Y has been resolved. The political scientist in question must show that the new framework has conceptual space for the type of phenomena analysed in the old and, more importantly in this case, that A, B and C are, in some significant manner, different from X, Y and Z. With respect to the latter, he/she must demonstrate that A, B and C are capable of doing the same work as X, Y and Z without being fundamentally analytically synonymous to them. If A, B, and C are analytically too similar to X, Y and Z, then the supposed alternative framework simply consists of a swapping of labels which resolves nothing. In other words, the problem of X and Y has simply been replaced with that of A and B.

Relating this to the debate at issue, if Clegg wishes to theoretically supersede the problem posed by the relationship between power and structure, he must show that the language of circuits of power involves a meaningful replacement of modernism by postmodernism. Inherent in this must be a clear demonstration that he is not giving us old problems dressed up in new linguistic clothes. This, I would claim, is precisely what Clegg fails to do. To substantiate this assertion, I will focus on three key areas of analysis within modernist power/structure debate. With respect to these problems, I will show that they actually exist under a different name within Clegg's 'new' 'post-modernist' framework. In terms of the imaginary example, I will examine whether or not X and Y would appear to have been turned into A and B.

Central to Clegg's dissolution of the relationship between agency and structure is the conceptualization of agency, at the circuit level, as manifest in the form of causal episodic power. This power does not exist in insolation but "..may move through circuits in which rules, relations and resources that are constitutive of power are translated, fixed and reproduced/transformed." (Clegg 1989 p. 211).

Consequently, episodic power "... involves not only securing outcomes, which is achieved in the episodic circuit of power, but also securing or reproducing the 'substantively rational' conditions within which the strategies espoused in the circuit of episodic power make contextually good sense." (Clegg 1989 p. 212). These conditions are rules, relations and resources which convey meaning in the circuit of social and system integration (see Clegg 1989 p. 211-2). At the level of social integration, dispositional "[p]ower will always be inscribed within contextual 'rules of the game' which both enable and constrain action." (Clegg 1989 p. 200). When analysed closely, this concept of dispositional power is virtually identical with the modernist concept of structure. Within Giddens' structuration perspective, structure can be conceived as a recursively constituted set of rules and resources which are both constraining and enabling (see Giddens 1984 p. 25, also chapter 5 of this work). In other words, it would appear that there is remarkable similarity between Clegg's second circuit of power and what is referred to as structure within the modernist framework. This point is well illustrated by Clegg's description of the creation of new circuits of dispositional power within the early Christian church:

"One of the first designers of a recognisably modern monastic form was the Egyptian Pachonious, who died in 346. Some of the rules he set up concerned the construction of a monastery. A big wall should isolate the monks from the outside world.... The novices had to stay for some time in a boarding house for strangers. They had to receive preparation for the entrance examination. After passing it, they were all to be dressed formally in a new gown. They received new names. All of these ceremonies symbolized that a new monk was taking on a new identity. Other rules dealt with religious ceremonies and communal meals. Pachonious' principles solved the problem of how to lead an ascetic life. *The structure of an ascetic life* was no longer a personal problem. The solution was to be found in obeying the rules of the monastic order and obedience to these rules became the ascetic ideal." (Clegg 1989 p. 169 emphasis not orig.).

Within a 'modernist' framework, Pachonious' creation of a new structure of ascetic life, according to specific impersonal rules, would constitute a creation of novel structural practises. While there is nothing inherently the matter with calling this a form of power, if Clegg wishes to argue that this dissolves the agent/structure problem, he must specifically demonstrate that he is not involved in an act of pure label swapping. In other words, in order to defend superiority of postmodernism, it is incumbent upon him to show that the agent/structure problem has actually disappeared and that it cannot simply be relabelled as the episodic/dispositional power problem.

The lack of an analytical distinction between the second circuit of power and structure appears not only on the theoretical and descriptive level but also manifests itself in the analysis of specific forms of dispositional power. Clegg argues that Foucault's concept disciplinary power makes him an important post-modernist theorizer of dispositional power. As Schram observes, for Clegg "[t]he macropolitics of sovereignty is dissolved into the micropolitics of disciplinary practices." (S.F. Schram 1991 p. 263). Hence, Foucault's description of disciplinary practices is a fundamental specific post-modernist conceptualization of dispositional power. However, despite having the post-modernist vocabulary of Foucauldian thought at his disposal, the strong structural component inherent in his concept of disciplinary practices is immediately apparent. In the introduction to chapter 8, where Clegg develops the concept of power circuits, he argues: "In this chapter the notion of disciplinary power will be conceptualized as a distinct 'circuit of of power' in which disciplinary technique, in the broadest sense of what Foucault suggests, *structures the relations of power...*" (Clegg 1989 p. 206, emphasis not orig.). In the vocabulary of modernism, the description of disciplinary practices as structuring the relations of power is a statement to the effect that the exercise of power, as a social act, is structurally constituted. The idea of calling the structural component of such an exercise of power disciplinary power is only an act of label swapping which adds nothing to the richness of the vocabulary of political theory. In fact, it could be argued that it constitutes an unnecessary linguistic conceptual confusion. It obscures the central analytical point whereby it is possible to theorize the relationship between an actor's ability to exercise power and the inherent structuredness of his/her action with respect to certain disciplinary practices. Disciplinary practices give form, continuity and predictability to actor's actions. Among these actions are acts which are specifically directed towards the exercise of power. However, the specific disciplinary structuredness of an actor's exercise of power is not in itself an exercise of power.

Clegg's inability to show the difference between the modernist concept of power/structure and the post-modernist perception of episodic power/disciplinary power is brought home, with particular force, in Clegg's theorization of Foucault's analysis of the transition from physical torture to disciplinary power. On this Clegg writes: "This shift from physical torture to a highly regulatory apparatus of power, *which seeks to structure the total institutional environment of the offender*, is but one of a number of forms of what Foucault termed disciplinary power. Disciplinary power works exactly through the construction of a routine." (Clegg 1989 p. 167, emphasis not orig.). Here, the use of the terminology of structure, combined with the idea that disciplinary power as rooted the construction of a routine (on structure as routine, see Giddens 1984 p. xxiii), makes Clegg's post-modernist concept of disciplinary power virtually indistinguishable from the modernist theorization of structure.

Central to any 'modernist' structural interpretation of social reproduction is the phenomenon of structural constraint. Constraint is the phenomenon which gives the concept of structured action meaning by establishing a fixed predictability to social action. Using the language of Lukes, constraint constitutes the 'could not have done otherwise' component of structured social action. Without this phenomenon actors would be completely free to order their action as they wished. Consequently, structures would never be reproduced. Like the modernists, Clegg is also in need of a conceptual device which ensures that structures, or dispositional power as he calls it, are reproduced. For this purpose the establishment of obligatory passage points as "...the construction of a conduit through which all traffic must pass." (Clegg 1989 p. 205) performs the theoretical task of structural constraint. In short, obligatory passage points constitute points of fixity of meaning which manifest themselves as constraint. Again, if Clegg wishes to claim that his perspective yields the relationship between power and structural constraint unproblematic, Clegg must spell out what the inherent difference is between the modernist concept of structural constraint and the post-modernist concept of obligatory passage points.

Inherent in any conceptualization of structure and constraint there is always the formulation of a theory of 'deep' systemic structures. These are the structures which give an assembled set of structures its characteristic systemic form. For a political theorist with a conflictual perception of the creation and maintenance of social order, these are the structures of domination which characterize a specific system. Without these structures of domination conflict would reduce the social system to a state of relative formlessness. In his perception of the constitution of social order, Clegg is a conflict theorist. Consequently, Clegg has a theoretical need to incorporate structures of domination into his overall framework. Without such structures Clegg would be unable to explain the maintenance of relative systemic inequality of power. Again I would wish to argue that by calling the modernist concept of structures of domination a third circuit of power he has done nothing more than apply a new, not very helpful, label to an old concept. At the very least, he has not provided us with any analytical criterion by which to distinguish the post-modernist third circuit of power from the conventional modernist analysis of structures of domination. This point is made particularly obvious in the language he uses to describe organizational outflanking. On this he writes: "Existing structures of dominancy are thus in principle always open to subsistence, disruption and innovation, since new techniques may open up new conduits and passages which undermine the presently entrenched structures." (Clegg 1989 p. 224). I would like to ask Stewart Clegg, what is the theoretical advantage of calling the structures of dominance a circuit of power? The only advantage that is immediately obvious is that it obscures the fact that, within Clegg's framework, the relationship between power and structure is as theoretically unresolved as it is in the 'modernism' of Lukes. In short, Clegg's postmodernism is not sufficiently different from modernism to be able to transcend or dissolve the central problematic of the relationship between agency and structure.

In many respects I would argue that calling structure, structural constraint and structures of domination all forms of power (dispositional power, obligatory passage points and facilitative power respectively) is a manifestation of a crisis in the power/structure debate. When Clegg's electrifying language is analysed more closely, he (not Lukes) represents the ultimate culmination of a crisis within the theoretical tradition from which he wishes to distance himself. While the concept of 3-D implies a development of power into the analytical sphere of structural phenomena, Lukes does provide us with a set of scalar concepts by which to distinguish power from structure. The scalar opposition between contingency and determinacy is an explicit recognition of the need to provide conceptual tools which can be used to distinguish power from structure. The problem with Lukes' position is that he does not provide a framework which has theoretical space for the conceptual tools provided. He does not theorize the process by which agency and structure characterize fundamental facets of social life. In contrast, Clegg extended the concept of social power to cover all facets of social life which have any influence whatsoever upon relative distributions of power and powerlessness. In effect, what Clegg has done is to perceive that the structuredness of interaction has a direct impact upon distributions of power. He continually emphasizes this by referring to the failure of the modernists to take account of the fact that their metaphorical billiard balls are bouncing against each other on a billiard table which is skewed due to structural power (see Clegg 1989 p. 209). Similarly, he argues that they fail to take account of strategic agency (Clegg 1989 p. 209). What Clegg has missed in all of this is that the development of the theorization of power into the arena of the agent/structure debate is a manifestation of an acute awareness of the extent to which the billiard table is structurally skewed. It is an awareness which is coupled with a sophisticated understanding of the importance of distinguishing between the various phenomena which contribute to the constitution of relative inequalities of power and power itself.

Clegg's inability to distinguish between social power and the structural factors which contribute to relative inequalities of power also manifests itself in an extension of power and agency to cover physically causal phenomena as well. Clegg does this through the proud claim that he has abandoned the problematic of agency as specifically pertaining to humans. Instead he argues that agency can be attributed to, amongst others, machines, buildings and animals. He argues that some of these agencies can have profound historical consequence. As an example of machine agency, he cites the instance of the "...undoubted agency exercised by the complex, highly coupled, computer decision-making systems introduced by the Securities Industry Automatic Corporation to Wall Street Trading. Some analysts regard these as a major contributory factor in the 19 October 1989 stock market crash..." (Clegg 1989 p. 200). With regard to animal agency, Clegg cites the part played by the rat as agent of historical change in the Medieval period. In terms of the massive social displacements between country and city which took place within feudal society "...the humble rat was one of the principle agents of these transformations, as it was the 'Black Death', the bubonic plague virus carried by infected rats, which altered the balance of feudal power on the land between lord and peasant by weakening the taxable capacities of the lords and strengthening those of the towns." (Clegg 1989 p. 244).

It is without doubt correct that, as a carrier of bubonic plague, the rat had a tremendous effect upon relations of empowerment and disempowerment during the mid fourteenth century. Indeed, it is not far fetched to suggest rats did more to shape the history of that century than any specific human agent. However, while the total causal effect wrought by the rat may be greater than that of the main instigators of the Hundred Years War (Edward III and Philip VI), in political theory terms, the nature of this effect is analytically fundamentally different in a number of crucial respects. Using Clegg against himself, "Power involves not only securing outcomes, which is achieved in the episodic circuit of power, but also securing or reproducing the 'substantively rational' conditions within which the strategies espoused in the circuit of episodic power make good sense." (Clegg 1989 p. 212). In other words, in exercising power through agency, social actors reproduce the social contextuality within which their agency made sense. In analytical terms, this means the agency of human actors, in the moment of making sense, reconstitutes the facets of social organization which give that social action meaning. In the language of 'modernism', in the moment of agency an actor unintentionally reproduces the structures of a social system which give meaning to his/her action. In the language of 'postmodernism', the episodic agency of actors inherently reproduce the rules and disciplinary practices of the dispositional power circuit. For the political theorist, the ability of actors to realize agency through structural reproduction (or recreating the rules and disciplinary practices pertaining a particular configuration of dispositional power) is analytically fundamentally different from any effects derived from non-socially based causal sources. While a historian may wish to argue that the rat had profound consequences upon the history of the fourteenth century, this consequence was not realized through the ability of an actor to draw upon and reproduce characteristic features of his/her society. To compare Edward III and the rat, it is true that the rat may have had a greater effect than Edward III on relations of empowerment and disempowerment in France. However, when Edward III began the Hundred Years War by declaring war upon France, Edward III was acting as an actor realizing his/her agency through the reproduction of the structural configurations pertaining to the definition of Kingship in the fourteenth century. Edward III was exercising power over others through his ability to realize agency by drawing upon (to use Clegg's language) the specific rules and disciplinary practices which were integral to the constitution of English society as a specific assembled set of interpersonal relations and obligations. In contrast, the rat displaced populations irrespective of any social relations whatsoever. The rat had an unintentional causal effect which was

61

not based upon the ability to draw upon any of the social rules and resources which characterize agency as a social phenomenon. The rat could have realized exactly the same magnitude of causal effect upon a group of people living in a Hobbesian state of nature.

In conclusion, I have shown that the work of Lukes, Jessop and Clegg have all been unable to provide a sufficiently sophisticated theoretical framework to explain the relationship between power and structure. Lukes provided a good descriptive analysis of the relationship based upon a scalar opposition between contingency and determinism. However, he did not provide the necessary theoretical depth to go any further. Jessop did attempt to give an explanatory theorization of the relationship between power and structure but it was within a framework which provided no conceptual space for meaningful agency. Clegg provides an alternative framework which primarily consists in a label swapping exercise. It leaves the original power/structure problematic intact under a new name. In the next section of this work I will look at Giddens' attempt to analyse the relationship between power and structure through an explanatory theorization of the recreation of structure. Here it will be argued that the theory of structuration is flawed because it is too agent centred and fails to provide a consistent account of the production of power. The third and main section of this work represents a resolution of the relationship between power and structure through an explanatory theorization of the re/creation of structure and the production of power.

Section Two
GIDDENS, STRUCTURATION
AND POWER

4 Giddens and time–space

This section is intended as an exploration of the ability of structuration theory to provide an adequate theorization of the creation of structure and the production of power. When analysing these processes of creation and production, account will also be taken of the ability of the structuration perspective to provide conceptual space for the basic analytical distinctions associated with both power and structure. The latter will include such phenomena as structural change, structural constraint, A prevailing over B and power resources. It must be observed that I am primarily interested in the theory of structuration and have chosen to focus on Anthony Giddens as the most important and best promulgator of the structuration framework. Consequently, I am not interested in the intellectual process whereby Giddens developed the theory of structuration nor do I intend to give an exposition of the body of secondary literature surrounding Giddens' work. As observed by I. Cohen in his introduction to *Structuration Theory*, since Anthony Giddens is the founder of structuration theory, it should be obvious that any work on structuration must be based on his writings (I. Cohen 1989 p. 5) However, "[g]iven the range and diversity of Giddens' themes it should be evident why a choice must be made between dealing with the nature and influence of his work at large, or dealing with structuration theory at length and in detail." (I. Cohen 1989 p. 5). Like I. Cohen, I have chosen to deal with the theory of structuration as a framework for resolving certain problems in sociopolitical theory. Consequently, there has been a certain methodological bracketing both of an account of Giddens 'the thinker' and of his critics. In terms style and references, this means that I make use of the full range of Giddens' writings between 1976 and 1990 without explaining which facets of structuration theory Giddens developed at what time. Similarly, I make use of secondary literature, to the extent to which it aids exposition, without giving an account of the overall nature of the secondary works referred to.

With respect to my interpretation of Giddens' ideas, it should also be observed that this is not a summary of his work or of all facets of structuration theory more generally. I am simply concentrating on what I consider core concepts for the purposes of understanding the relationship between power and social structure.

One of the main problems faced by any one wishing to explore structuration theory is that Giddens 'inhabits' the theoretical universe which he has created. Because his theoretical perspective almost constitutes a complete paradigmatic perception of social order, he presents his theories as a conceptual whole (see Bernstein 1989 p. 24 for a similar point). For example, in page three of the introduction to *Central Problems in Social Theory* the reader is told: "According to the theory of structuration an understanding of social systems as situated in time-space can be effected by reading structure as non-temporal and non-spatial, as a virtual order of differences produced and reproduced in social interaction as its medium and outcome." The choice of words in this sentence is both highly deliberate and succinct. However, because it makes sense only when viewed from within an already constituted conceptual system, it is extremely difficult to know how to 'unpack' the meaning of such a sentence when coming from outside Giddens' framework.

In interpreting Giddens, I intend to separate different strands within his system in order to break into his hermeneutic circle. In disconnecting mutually dependent ideas some temporary distortions are bound to occur. I apologize for these in advance. However, I hope that they are excusable if what has been taken apart, when put back together, constitutes a new whole which is identical to the original.

In exploring some of Giddens' ideas I use some fairly simple illustrative examples by way of explanation. I do this in order to avoid misunderstandings. For example, in the *Constitution of*

Society "Giddens suggests that the sense of 'rule' most relevant to the analysis of social life is that expressed by a formula such as $a_n = n^2 + n - 1$. " (Thompson 1989 p. 64). In interpreting this John B. Thompson wonders if Giddens means "... most implausibly, that semantic rules and moral rules should be seen as quasi-mathematical formulae, as if 'butterfly = moth 2 + colour - cloth'?" (Thompson 1989 p. 64). In interpreting Giddens' intended meaning of rule following I use an example which Wittgenstein also used when discussing the concept of rule following - a child attempting to write a series of numbers.

Giddens' structuration theory was an attempt to deal with the theoretical schism in sociopolitical theory posed by the hermeneutic tradition on the one hand and the structuralist and functionalist traditions on the other. Together they represent an essentially schizoid vision of society. In the former, society is viewed only from the perspective of the *cogito*. In the latter, the social actor is an effect of structures (structuralism) or, more derogatorily, a cultural 'dope ' (functionalism). "If interpretative sociologies are founded, as it were, upon the imperialism of the subject, functionalism and structuralism propose the imperialism of the object. One of my principal ambitions in the formulation of structuration theory is to put an end to each of these empire-building endeavours." (Giddens 1984 p. 2).

Heidegger believed that one of the fundamental problems of Western thought has been caused by an obsession with the epistemological. "This preoccupation has manifested itself both in those accounts which have begun from the subject and those which have begun from the object. Thus the Cartesian *cogito* did not enquire into the *am* of 'I am', presupposed as a background to the congnising subject." (Giddens 1981 p. 31).

The problematic of the traditional subject-object duality is premised on an attempt "...to compose a common ground 'between' entities that is not originally given, [whereas] Heidegger argues that the common ground is already 'there'..." (Fell 1979 p. 42-3) in the concept of Being. The desire to build such a bridge is what leads to many of the absurdities of western philosophy. In fact, "[f]or Heidegger, it is not the failure to produce [a solution to Descartes problem...that is the 'scandal of philosophy', as Kant thought: the scandal is rather that such proofs are still demanded." (Olafson 1987 p. 8).

Even those philosophers who "...have concerned themselves with the nature of 'objects' or 'things' have remained on the relatively shallow level of the 'ontic' rather than penetrating to the level of the 'ontological'." (Giddens 1981 p. 31). The ontic constitutes the being of particular beings whereas the ontological is the being of Being. In other words, the ontological constitutes the essence of being. The ontic is that which "...characterizes beings, not their Being." (King 1964 p. 64).

All things presuppose both the ontic and the ontological. It is not possible for a being to be in a particular manner and yet not to Be (Fell 1979 p. 45). The word which Heidegger uses to designate being in both its ontic and ontological form was *Dasein. Dasein* has been variously translated but approximately means `being-there' (see Heidegger 1973 (translated by Macquarrie and Robinson) p.H. 7-8 esp. Fn. 1; King 1964 p. 68 and Fell 1979 p. 40). The term *Dasein* is meant to convey the 'between' which is traditionally perceived to exist between subject and object. "... *Dasein is the Being* of this 'between'....where [t]he between is the *convenientia* of two things which are present-at-hand." (Heidegger 1973 p.H. 132). It is important to stress that the use of the word 'between' is in some respects misleading. *Dasein* does not imply "... the 'schema', in accordance with which the joining together is to be accomplished,... What is decisive for ontology is to prevent the splitting of the phenomenon..." (Heidegger 1973 p.H. 132). The state of *Dasein* as a unitary phenomenon can be conveyed through "[t]he compound expression 'Being-in-the-world.'" (Heidegger 1973 p.H. 53). In this context 'in-the-world' means both the abstract ontological concept and the ontic world of things as they are experienced (King 1964 p. 74).

In our contact with the world, in our everyday lives, things are always meaning given (King 1964 p. 7). Things are constituted by our 'being-in-the-world' as objects which exist for the 'sake' of our own existence (King 1964 p. 84). For example, when I see a table set for dinner, I do not see bits of metal and baked porcelain strewn on a hunk of timber. I see forks, plates and a table. I know what they mean, can interpret them, because I know them in terms of their use or their existence as defined for the 'sake of' man. In its being-in-the-world Dasein is discovered in "..*entities which are encountered in the world with involvement (readiness-to-hand) as their kind of Being*..." (Heidegger 1973 p.H. 87). This is "...the horizon within which such things as the world and worldhood are to be sought." (Heidegger 1973 p.H. 87). These meanings constitute the correct horizon against which to interpret *Dasein's* ontic being (Heidegger 1973 p.H. 87-8). However, Heidegger's "...*aim* is to work out the question of Being in general." (Heidegger 1973 p.H. 437). In order to do this "one must seek a *way* of casting light on the fundamental question of ontology..." (Heidegger 1973 p.H. 437). This implies finding a universal horizon against which to interpret *Dasein*:

"'Time' has long functioned as an ontological - or rather ontical - criterion for naively discriminating various realms of entities. A distinction has to be made between temporal 'entities' (natural and historical happenings) and non-temporal entities (spatial and numerical relationships).... It is also held that there is a 'cleavage' between 'temporal' entities and supra-temporal eternal entities,.... The fact remains that time, in the sense of 'being in time', functions as a criterion for distinguishing realms of Being.... 'Time' has acquired this 'self-evident' ontological function ' of its own accord', so to speak; indeed it has done so within the horizon of the way it is ordinarily understood." (Heidegger 1973 p.H. 18).

"If Being is to be conceived in terms of time, and if, indeed, its various modes and derivations are to become intelligible in their respective modifications and derivations by taking time into consideration, then Being itself (and not merely entities [ontic essence], let us say, as entities 'in time') is thus made visible in its temporal character." (Heidegger 1973 p. 18). In short, *time* is "...*the horizon for understanding of Being, and in terms of temporality, as the Being of Dasein, which understands Being.*" (Heidegger 1973 p. 18).

The concept of time, used in understanding the Being of beings, is not of the everyday sort. The latter is a contingently defined concept which is defined differently by different epochs. Our particular understanding of time is influenced by both Aristotle and Kant (Heidegger 1973 p.H. 26). For Aristotle time is a series of 'nows' or a linear progression of points in space (Aristotle 1947 § 219b). In the present day, these points are represented by historical 'clock time'. Kant added to this concept of time the idea that time is not found 'in' things themselves but is a *synthetic a priori* intuitive concept necessary for a person to make sense of the world (Kant 1963 74-6). Time and space - which are conceptually linked to each other through the concept of intuition - are inherently subjective, existing in the mind of the *cogito*. They enable the *cogito* to impose order upon the world.

For Heidegger, time is neither synonymous with a series of 'nows', nor subjectively intuited by the *cogito*. Time is not something which surrounds entities but is located in the very essence of Being. "Being exists in the coming-to-be of presence,

69

which replaces both the idea of the 'present', and the 'points in space'." (Giddens 1981 p. 31). "Time, Heidegger argues, should not be regarded as 'three dimensional' (past, present and future) but as 'four dimensional', the fourth dimension is the presencing which brings them together and holds them apart." (Giddens 1981 p. 31). It is here, in the concept of presencing, that the original unity inherent in the ontological Being of *Dasein* is to be found.

According to Giddens, the dualism found in sociopolitical theory is linked to that found in philosophy. In both there is a separation of the individual from the outside world. In the hermeneutic traditions the subject bears more than a passing resemblance to the *cogito*. The object is the creation of the cognicizing subject. In structuralism, society is an 'out-there' object acting upon a passive 'de-centred' subject. In effect, the subject is a creation of the object.

Influenced by Heidegger, Giddens tries to overcome the dualism of social thought by a move to ontological criteria (Giddens 1984 p. 2). Relative to structuralism and functionalism, this implies a return to the subject (Giddens 1982a p. 2). However, it does not mean a move to the Cartesian *cogito* (Giddens 1982a p. 8). For Giddens subjects are first and foremost agents. To be an agent means 'to make a difference' in the world through action (Giddens 1984 p. 9-11, 1979 p. 55). This action is not a mere reflex response to the object (society) but is intentional activity which is epistemologically grounded in reflexivity. (Giddens 1984 p. 2-3).

In order to understand action ontologically it is important to realize that action does not take place 'in' time and space, surrounded by time and space but is actually constituted 'through' time and space. (Giddens 1981 p. 34, also Heidegger 1973 p.H. 428). Because time "... is the horizon of all being, it follows that the 'human finds its meaning in temporality'" (Giddens 1987 p. 141). However, as Heidegger of post *Being and Time* came to implicitly acknowledge, a being cannot be only in time and not be in space. An object is always in both. Space is not reducible to time. Therefore, Giddens suggests that one should add space to Heidegger's concept of time. Because objects are always in both, and they are conceptually linked, Giddens often places a hyphen between the words to form the concept time-space (see Giddens 1987 p. 146). Bringing these threads together, Giddens views his ontological interpretation of society against the horizon of time-space. "An ontology of time-space as constitutive of social practices is basic to the concept of structuration,... " (Giddens 1984 p. 3). In practice, what does Giddens mean by this time-space ontological view? Possibly the best way of describing what Giddens means is through a 'thought experiment'. I imagine that I am an outer-space alien viewing a certain minute section of the globe over time (this experiment is based on Giddens' use of Hagerstrand's time geography in chapter 3 1984). I might observe a girl, Jane, getting up in the morning at a given time, eating breakfast in the kitchen and going to school. In school Jane will have very different behavioural patterns depending on whether she is in the class-room interacting with her teacher or in the school yard playing with her friends. After a period Jane will go home. There she will eat dinner in the dining-room. Then she will go into the sitting-room, phone a friend, watch T.V. and read a book. This scenario will be repeated the next day unless that happens to be Saturday. On that day Jane's time-space 'paths' will be altered. Continuing these observations over a longer period, Jane's time-space 'paths' will merge into a continuous 'weaving dance' through time and space, punctuated by a change in pattern into units of five and two days.

After a period there will be a total change in pattern. Jane will move into a different house. Instead of going to school, she will go to work. Then new time-space 'paths' will be set up around the place of work, the new home and a favourite cafe/pub. This will continue until retirement, when new patterns will emerge.

Continuing the experiment over generations, there will be a continual repetition of individual time-space 'paths'. However, the overall pattern will also be observed to change overall, very slowly, until it has a very different form.

What is manifest from analysing the experiment is that, in Parsonsian terms, there is order not chaos. Viewing things in this manner "[t]he problem of order is the issue of time-space distantiation." (Giddens 1987 p. 153). There is an obvious patterning of social action over time-space. Taking an ontological perspective means that "[t]he basic domain of study of the social sciences, according to the theory of structuration, is neither the experience of an individual actor, nor the existence of any form of societal totality, but social practices ordered across time-space." (Giddens 1984 p. 2). This order is a manifestation of ordering or organization by social actors. It is absurd to speak of a random order. There is ".. not just organization 'in' time-space, but organization 'of' time-space,... (Giddens 1987 p. 153).

In the thought experiment, the order created by Jane was produced by the continuous reproduction of action over time and space. Hence, Giddens conceives of the social system as the ordered totality which comprises of "...the situated activities of human agents, reproduced across time and space." (Giddens 1984 p. 25). A social system is a pattern of action which stretches across greater or lesser spans of time and space producing order by 'bracketing' time-space (Giddens 1987 p. 153). In the instance of action, time-space are brought together. It is these instants which, when viewed together, give action its systemic from. In each instant that time-space are bound together social structures are recreated. Structure refers "...to the structuring properties allowing the 'binding' of time-space in a social system, the properties which make it possible for discernibly similar social practices to exist across varying spans of time and space and which lend them 'systemic form'." (Giddens 1984 p. 17).

Taking Jane as an example, the routinization of her day constitutes part of an ordered totality. Her routine of getting up in the morning, playing games with her mates in the yard, watching T.V. in the sitting-room, means a contribution to the reproduction of the social system of which she is a part. She is contributing to the continual reproduction of social structures over time and space. It is because of her action, and many like her, that it is observed to be routine to sleep in the bedroom of a house and not in the kitchen. As such she 'binds' time-space through the routinization of her action. She recreates structures and in this manner contributes to the continual reproduction of the social system. In this sense, routinization "... is a fundamental concept of structuration theory..." (Giddens 1984 p. xxiii).

"The routine (whatever is done habitually) is a basic element of 'day-to-day' social activity....The term day-to-day encapsulates exactly the routinized character which social life has as it stretches across time-space. The repetitiveness of activities which are undertaken in a like manner day after day is the material grounding of what I call the recursive nature of social life." (Giddens 1984 p. xxiii).

Conceived of as the binding of time-space into systemic form, structures are the principles upon which the continuous reproduction of the social system takes place. As observed in the thought experiment, the social system exists in time-space. However, structures only have a 'virtual' existence in the act of binding time-space (Giddens 1982a p. 9). "Structures exist in time-space only as moments recursively involved in the production and reproduction of a social system." (Giddens 1981 p. 26).

Due to the fact that structures do not exist in time-space, it is conceptually impossible to take a time-space 'slice' of a system and emerge with a mechanical, Mecano like, set of structures which are static in time and space (Giddens 1982 p. 33). Instead structures are a set of transformative relations. This means that "...social systems, as reproduced social practices, do not have 'structures' but rather exhibit 'structural properties' and that structures exist as time-space presences, only in such practices..." (Giddens 1984 p. 17). However, "...this does not prevent us from conceiving of structural properties as hierarchically organized in terms of time-space extension of the practices they organize. The most deeply embedded structural properties, implicated in the reproduction of societal totalities, I call *structural principles*. Those practices which have the greatest time-space extension within such totalities can be referred to as *institutions*." (Giddens 1984 p. 17).

When the term time-space is used as a criterion for understanding the essence of system and structure, it has to be remembered that the concept of time-space used is not measurable Aristotelian and Kantian time-space. Referring to the thought experiment, there are at least six ways in which time-space is experienced by Jane who contributes to the recreation of the social system: 1) there is Jane's life, her being onto death or *durée* of her life span. This assumes the from of an irreversible linear progression from her school days to her death; 2) the *durée* of her life is made up of day-to-day routine activities or the *durée* of day-to-day life (Giddens 1987 p. 145); 3) the durée of day-to-day life in turn constitutes part of the *longue durée* of the society of which Jane is a part (Giddens 1987 p. 145; 1981 p. 35-6); 4) in school Jane interacted with the teacher who was physically present. Giddens refers to this as 'co-presence'; 5) the state of 'co-presence' does not happen in a vacuum. It is partly structured with respect to the physical environment in which a given social action takes place. When Jane was in a pub this forms the 'locale' of her action; 6) in these 'locales' behaviour is managed differently. Jane played in the yard but not in the classroom. In terms of time, the different behavioural patterns found in differing 'locales' mark 'episodes' in the day.

The introduction of time-space as inherent in structuration practices has a number of important theoretical implications. With respect the structuralist and functionalist traditions it means breaking with synchrony/diachrony divisions which figure prominently in both schools of thought. Neither the social system nor social structures exist outside of time-space in an 'out there' synchronic, static, form which make it possible for an observer to take timeless snapshots of society (Giddens 1979 p. 198). With respect to the subject object/dualism, structures do not exist as an 'outside' object which acts upon a passive subject. Structures only exist in the moment of action. The implications of this will form part of the central theme of the next chapter.

By way of closing this chapter, I should also mention that the integration of time-space into sociopolitical theory has a number of important implications for disciplinary boundaries with other subjects such as history and geography (Giddens 1987 p. 144). If time and space are inherent to theories of structure and system then "[h]istorians... cannot be properly be regarded as specialists along a dimension of time, anymore than geographers can be regarded as specialists along a dimension of space; such disciplinary divisions, as ordinarily conceived, are concrete expressions of the repression of time and space in social theory." (Giddens 1984 p. 355).

5 Structures as rules

In the previous chapter I showed how action gained systemic form when viewed against the horizon of time-space. Structures are the principles which 'bind' time-space and hence make social order possible. I explained this with the use a thought experiment which was a bit like viewing a T.V. with the sound turned off. It was visible that there was order but not how this systemic form could be reproduced across time-space. If structures exist only in the moment of action, in the instant of structuration, how are they carried from moment of action to moment of action?

In rejecting structuralist determinacy and Parsonsian functionalism, Giddens attributes cognitive awareness to agents. They are neither the 'effect' of social structures nor are they cultural 'dopes'. For Giddens action is a consciously intentional 'doing' which has the unintentional effect of reproducing structure. It is not illogical to suppose that if action is an intentional conscious act and structure exists only in action, then there is an inherent link between consciousness and the recreation of structure. It is Giddens' hypothesis that structures exist outside the moment of action as memory traces which are drawn upon in action in order to structure action. In order to make sense of this position I will divide this chapter into two parts: the first will deal with his theory of consciousness and the second will concern the form which structures take in the mind of the social actor.

In discussing the concept of consciousness, Giddens replaces the Freudian division of the individual into 'id', 'ego' and `super-ego' with discursive consciousness (d.c.), practical consciousness (p.c.) and the unconscious (u.c.) (Giddens 1984 p. 45). "Discursive consciousness means being able to put things into words." (Giddens 1984 p. 45). "Practical consciousness consists of all the things which actors know tacitly about how to 'go on' in the contexts of social life without being able to give them discursive expression." (Giddens 1984 p. xxiii). The unconscious is the source of various drives and motives which have to be controlled in order to maintain the security system of the adult personality (Giddens 1984 p. 49). With respect to the control of u.c. "...the motivational components of the infant and adult personality derive from a generalized orientation to the avoidance of anxiety and the preservation of self-esteem against the 'flooding through' of shame and guilt." (Giddens 1984 p. 57).

While d.c., p.c. and u.c. are analytically separate there is a continuous flow between d.c. and p.c.. However, there is a bar between d.c., p.c. and u.c.. This bar is based on repression which is necessary in order to maintain ontological security (Giddens 1984 p. 7). In this respect d.c. and p.c. are the key to the *control* of the motives and desires originating in u.c.. Without this control ontological security can not be maintained. Part of the way in which such control is preserved is through maintenance of trust in social action. This includes both trust with respect to self, in terms of bodily control, and others, in social interaction.

To a great extent, bodily trust involves the maintenance of 'front' and 'back' regions. This is well exemplified by the loss of ontological security manifest by concentration camp victims in having to defecate in public (Giddens 1984 p. 64). This bodily division is extended to the regionalization of surrounding 'locales'. The concentration camp victims suffered not only humiliation by having their 'back' bodily regions exposed but also by the inappropriateness of the locale in which the act of defecation took place (Giddens 1984 p. 63).

Ontological security with respect to others is first encountered by an infant in its relationship with mother: "As Erickson comments, 'The infant's first social achievement... is his willingness to let the mother out of sight without undue anxiety or rage, because she has become an inner certainty as well as an outer predictability.'" (Giddens 1984 p. 53). In this context, trust equals confidence based on the routine experience that mother always returns (Giddens 1984 p. 53).

76

The binding of time-space by the baby, and the maintenance of front and back regions, are both typical and archetypal of the sort of binding of time-space which goes into the constitution of the social system. "All social life occurs in, and is constituted by, intersections of presence and absence in the 'fading away' of time and the 'shading off' of space. The physical properties of the body and the *milieux* in which it moves inevitably give social life a serial character, and limit the modes of access to absent others across time-space." (Giddens 1984 p. 132). It is the time-space contextuality of structuration practices which links the binding of time-space to Saussure's notion of difference as defining. "According to the theory of structuration an understanding of social systems as situated in time-space can be effected by regarding social structures as non-temporal and non-spatial, as *a virtual order of differences* produced and reproduced in social interaction as its medium and outcome." (Giddens 1979 p. 2). If we take Saussure's famous Geneva to Paris train example: "What gives the train its identity, de Saussure argued, is the ways in which it is different from other trains: its time of departure, route etc." (Giddens 1979 p. 12). When Jane was in co-presence with her teacher in the classroom her behaviour was entirely different from that when watching T.V. in her kitchen. What characterizes the nature of her social action as inherently different in the two incidents is the contextuality of her action in time-space. The uniqueness of each encounter is constituted by what differentiates it from other encounters.

The creation of social structure, defined through the notion of difference in the contextuality of action, is dependent upon the ability of actors to monitor their conduct. Therefore, "...reflexive monitoring of conduct is a chronic feature of everyday action and involves the conduct not just of individual but that of others. That is to say, actors not only monitor continuously the flow of their activities and expect others to do the same for their own; they also routinely monitor aspects, social and physical, of the contexts in which they move." (Giddens 1984 p. 5). It is within this context that Goffman's work, on the ability of actors to maintain security and trust through the management of social action, assumes particular interest for Giddens (see Giddens 1984 p. 86).

The continuous monitoring of conduct manifests itself as knowledgeability of the social world. This knowledge is 'stored' in the memory of the social actor and recalled through d.c. and p.c. (there is a bar inhibiting u.c. recall). In most ordinary action, the most used form is p.c. (Giddens 1984 p. 49). Therefore, the bulk of social knowledge "...is not directly accessible to the [d.c.] consciousness of actors. Most knowledge is practical in character: it is inherent in the capability to 'go on' within the routines of social life." (Giddens 1984 p. 4).

The fact that social "...knowledgeability is founded less upon discursive consciousness than practical consciousness" (Giddens 1984 p. 26) should not obscure a number of points: 1) "...that human agents always know what they are doing on the level of discursive consciousness under some description." (Giddens 1984 p. 26). Without that knowledge action could not be described as acting intentionally - actors can usually explain why they decided. to engage in social action; 2) when faced with unusual circumstances (breaching experiments or different cultural norms) there can be a rapid transfer of knowledge from p.c. to d.c.; 3) p.c. knowledge is not inherently trivial or shallow. "The knowledge of social conventions, of oneself and other human beings, presumed in being able to 'go on' in the diversity of contexts of social life is detailed and dazzling. All competent members of society are vastly skilled in the practical accomplishments of social activities and are expert 'sociologists'." (Giddens 1984 p. 26). It is worth stressing that what Giddens means by this claim is that social actors are expert sociologist at the level of p.c.. At the level of p.c. social actors know as much as sociologists do at the level of d.c.. In fact, it can be argued, that most actors know more about the rules of social life than an expert such as Goffman is capable of promulgating at the level of d.c.. However, like is not being compared with like: the p.c. of actors is being measured against the d.c. of sociologists. Failure to understand this has led critics, such as Barbalet (1987 p. 11) and Clegg (1989 p. 143), into mistakenly thinking that Giddens is claiming that social actors have a profound discursive knowledge of social order and of the inner workings of the society in which they live.

It is this store of p.c. and d.c. knowledge which enables Giddens to place the cognitive intentional actor at center stage. The division or dualist vision of the relationship between actor and structure is overcome by postulating that structures are 'carried' outside the moment of action in the knowledge which actors possess. Outside the moment of action "[s]tructure has no existence independent of the knowledge that agents have about what they do in their day-to-day lives." (Giddens 1984 p. 26).

The knowledge in which social structures are 'carried' is the same knowledge which is necessary to maintain ontological security. Through routinization, this knowledge creates ontological security for individual actors and simultaneously gives their action a structured form. Not only does the routinization constitute the essence of social structures, replicated across time-space, but "[r]outinization is vital to the psychological mechanisms whereby a sense of trust is sustained in the daily activities of social life. Carried primarily in practical consciousness, routine drives a wedge between the potentially explosive content of the unconscious and the reflexive monitoring of action which agents display. Why did Garfinkel's 'experiments with trust' stimulate such a very strong reaction on the part of those involved ? Because, I think, the apparently minor conventions of social life are of essential significance in curbing the sources of unconscious tension that would otherwise preoccupy us most of our waking lives [and do in some cases of psychological disturbance]." (Giddens 1984 xxii-iii).

Bringing these threads together, the essence of the recursive nature of most action is directed toward tension management. This management is largely carried out by p.c. which, through action, binds time-space in routinization. This means that routinization is both the key to the maintenance of ontological security and the recreation of social structures. "The concept of *routinization*, as grounded in practical consciousness, is vital to the theory of structuration. Routine is integral both to the constitution of the personality of the agent as he or she moves along the paths of daily activities and to the institutions of society, which are such only through their continued reproduction." (Giddens 1984 p. 60).

The continued reproduction of structure takes place through action. Social structures have no existence in time-space except in the instance of social action. In short, structures are only realized in praxis (Cohen 1987 p. 298). Praxis is the instantiation of structure in the Heideggerian concept of the present as the past flowing into the future (Giddens 1979 p. 70). Praxis is the link between action and structure which both presuppose each other and yet have appeared as antinomies (Giddens 1979 p. 49, 53).

It is at the level of the centrality of praxis, in the constitution of social life, that there is a convergence between Giddens and Marx and Wittgenstein. With respect to the former, the link with historical materialism can be "...stated in the quotation 'human beings make history', that social life is formed and reformed in praxis - in the practical activities carried out in the enactment of every-day life. This is exactly the kind of view I have tried to argue for in setting out the basic tenets of structuration theory." (Giddens 1984 p. 242).

Referring to Wittgenstein, Giddens states that "... the significance of Wittgenstein's writing... consists in the association of language with definite social practices." (Giddens 1979 p. 4). The recursive reproduction of designated practices is what lies at the core of Wittgenstein's concept of rule following (Giddens 1979 p. 41). In this sense, "... rules are procedures of action, aspects of praxis" (Giddens 1979 p. 41). In other words, when stored in memory, structures take the form of a rule. Explaining this statement leads me on to the second part of this chapter.

A rule is the form in which structures are stored in memory. Following a rule implies knowledge of that rule. This knowledge, retrieved through p.c., is learned through reflexivity and is manifest in action. Reflexivity is the way in which rules are both learned and preserved. However, this statement does not tell one the kind of rules which are stored in memory. What kind of rules are being invoked when Jane goes about her day-to-day action? "Consider the following possible instances of what rules are:

1) 'The rule defining checkmate is...'
2) 'A formula: $a_n = n^2 + n-1$;'
3) 'As a rule R gets up at 6.00 every day;'
4) 'It is a rule that all workers must clock in at 8.00 a.m.;'
(Giddens 1984 p. 19).

Number three describes quite effectively how Jane behaves. However, it fails to explain how she knows to behave in that manner. It is an observation of the type we used in the 'thought experiment'. Rather than two different forms of rule, rules one and four express the constitutive and regulative content of most rule-governed behaviour. " To explain the rule governing checkmate in chess is to say something about what goes into the very making of chess as a game. The rule that workers must clock in at a certain hour, on the other hand, does not help define what work is; it specifies how work is to be carried on." (Giddens 1984 p. 20). While these two aspects of rule-governed behaviour have often been seen as a dualism expressing two distinct types of rules, Giddens prefers to see them as a part of a duality. "(1) is certainly part of what chess is, but for those playing chess it has sanctioning or regulative properties; it refers to aspects of play that must be observed." (Giddens 1984 p. 20). Four also has constitutive aspects. Aside from forcing Jane into work every day, it is also constitutive of capitalist relations of production. One and four tell us how Jane may experience rules as constitutive of meaning and legitimating certain social practices. Neither tell us what form of memory traces enable her to behave the way she recursively does.

Following Wittgenstein, Giddens believes that number two constitutes an example of the essence of rule following. What is meant by this strange claim can be best interpreted by referring to the example which Wittgenstein used in *Philosophical Investigations*. A person A writes down a series of numbers and person B watches him. " A has written down the numbers 1, 5, 11, 19, 29; at this point B says he knows how to go on. What has happened here? " (Wittgenstein 1968 p. 59 § 151). Among the possibilities are the following: 1) " After A had written the number 19, B tried the formula $a = n^2 + n - 1$; and the next number confirmed his hypothesis." (Wittgenstein 1968 p. 59 § 151). This constitutes a d.c. knowledge of the rule used by A. Not only does B know how to 'go on' indefinitely but he/she can express why, verbally. 2) "Or again B does not think of formulae. He watches A writing his numbers down with a certain feeling of tension, and all sorts of vague thoughts go through his head. Finally he asks himself: ' What is the series of differences?' He finds the series 4, 6, 8, 10, and says: Now I can go on." (Wittgenstein 1968 p. 60 § 151). The ability too formulate this series of differences is again an attribute of d.c.. 3) " Or he [B] watches and says 'Yes, I know *that* series' - and continues it, just as he would have done if A had written down the series 1, 3, 5, 7, 9,.. - [4)] Or he says nothing at all and simply continues the series. Perhaps he had what may be called the sensation 'that's easy!'" (Wittgenstein 1963 § 151). In cases three and four B knows the rule but is incapable of providing a discursive formulation of it. This p.c. knowledge of the rule enables B to 'go on'. B knows the rule because he/she can continue the series. If B said: 'Ah yes, the rule is $a_n = n^2 + n - 1$.' and then continued the series with the numbers 197 and 10005, we would say B didn't know the rule. He/she could utter the formula but he/she couldn't continue the series. He/she didn't understand, couldn't apply, the rule. Hence the ability to 'go on' constitutes the correct criterion for knowing a rule, not the ability to say it. Similarly, thinking a rule is not the same as 'going on'. Knowledge of a rule is manifest in praxis.

To take another example, if we were to assess whether two Spaniards, Maria or Louis, spoke better English, what criteria would we use? Let us imagine that Louis knew by heart all the most important rules of the English language. However, when spoken to in English Louis was completely incapable of replying. In this case we would say Louis couldn't speak English. Conversely, imagine Maria didn't know a single rule of grammar. When put on the spot she even claimed that in English adjectives always followed the noun. However, in conversation she spoke grammatically correct English. In interpreting this phenomenon, we would say that Maria had no d.c. penetration of the rules of the English language but that didn't alter the fact that she could speak it. At a level of p.c. she knew the rules so that she could 'go on'. She used the rules to structure a sentence and in that act allowing a discernibly similar word order to be reproduced time and time again. If one were to sum up the underlying principle of that reproduction discursively it might be a + b + c where a = subject b = verb and c = object. With a d.c. or p.c. knowledge of that rule Maria could say: 'I hit the dog'. Or, 'Louis lifted the glass'. Or,...........In short, whenever faced with a, b, and c she would know how to place them in the correct order according to the rule a + b + c.

As a word of caution, it should be observed that in analysing real life situations it is often difficult to neatly categorise any action purely as p.c. or d.c.. As analytical categories d.c. and p.c. constitute scalar concepts. In their abstract theoretical formulation they exist at opposite ends of a continuum where most observed social action can be placed somewhere between these extremes. At the p.c. end is action ordered with respect to rules which are completely taken for granted. At the d.c. opposite side of the spectrum one can imagine an actor sitting quietly formulating a strategy of social action. With regard to two such poles most observed action contains elements of both. Returning to the previous example, if Maria were actually put to the test, in all probability, she could tell one something about English grammar and, similarly, Louis would be able to speak to some English.

Translating this into the social context, structures are rules and resources which refer "...in social analysis, to the structuring properties allowing the binding of time-space...,the properties which make it possible for discernibly similar social practices to exist across varying spans of time and space..." (Giddens 1984 p. 17). This recursively organized set of rules or structures "... [are] out of time and space, save in [their] instantiations and co-ordination as memory traces,..." (Giddens 1984 p. 25). When seen as rules constituting part of an overall systemic form they are "...marked by an 'absence of the subject'." (Giddens 1984 p. 25). When we think of the rule a + b + c we do not necessarily think of Maria or the millions of people who recursively reproduce it. However, the existence of structures is dependent upon the memory traces of social actors which constitute their knowledgeability as social actors (Giddens 1982a p. 9). "Structure is not 'external' to individuals: as memory traces, and as instantiated in social practices, it is in a sense more 'internal' than exterior to their activities in a Durkheimian sense. " (Giddens 1984 p. 25). In the sense that structures enable social actors to 'go on', they are inherently enabling (structural constraint will be dealt with later).

Conceptually, returning to the 'horizon' of time-space referred to in the previous chapter, several things can be seen to be happening at once. On a micro level, we can see the agent again and again using social structures as rules and resources to repeat the same 'binding' of time-space over time and space. Viewed from a greater distance this repeated binding of time-space has an order which gives these patterns a systemic form. These " [s]ocial systems, as reproduced social practices, do not have 'structures' but rather exhibit 'structural properties'...structure exists, as time-space presence, only in its instantiations in such practices and as memory traces orienting the conduct of knowledgeable human agents." (Giddens 1984 p. 17). Social systems have structural properties, that are the result of the situated activities of human subjects which exist syntagmatically in the flow of time (Giddens 1979 p. 66). Structure "... refers to the 'structural property'; or more exactly, 'structuring property'...providing the 'binding' of time and space in social systems....these properties can be understood as rules and resources, recursively implicated in the reproduction of social systems. Structures exist paradigmatically, as an absent set of differences, temporally 'present' only in their instantiation, in the constituting moment of the social system." (Giddens 1979 p. 64). As such, structures "...are *characterized by the 'absence' of the subject.*" (Giddens 1979 p. 66). "Structure thus refers...to the structuring properties allowing the 'binding' of time-space in social systems...which lend them, systemic from." (Giddens 1984 p. 17).

This is the very core of Giddens' attempt to overcome the dualism between action and structure found in the hermeneutic and structuralist traditions. He replaces it with a *duality*. In structuration, the production of structure exists only as a product of agency. Agency implies action which is based on structures as rules and resources. The effect of using structures as rules, in action, is their recursive reproduction over time and space through the 'binding' of time-space. "The constitution of agents and structures are not two independently given sets of phenomena, a dualism, but represents a duality. According to the notion of the duality of structure, the structural properties of social systems are both the medium and outcome of the practices they recursively organize." (Giddens 1984 p. 25).

The decentring 'of the subject' implicit in the systemic existence of social structures does not imply that the social actor becomes a 'cultural dope' or the effect of social structures as in functionalism or structuralism. The existence of structures as rules and resources presupposes knowledgeability grounded in p.c. and d.c..

If structures are the product of intentional activity, does this imply that the social system is an intentional product? The answer is no, because there is a "...disjunction between individual acts, undertaken separately and their composite consequence" (Giddens 1984 p. 314). In other words, the result of a series of intentional acts is not necessarily an intentional product. Taking the analogy of language: "...one of the consequences of my speaking or writing English in a correct way is to contribute to the reproduction of the English language as a whole. My speaking English correctly is intentional; the contribution I make to the reproduction of the language is not." (Giddens 1984 p. 8). In Wittgenstein's terms, when I follow a linguistic rule I am doing something intentional in the act of speaking. However, simultaneously I am unintentionally contributing to the continued existence / recreation of a rule. In action "...*the consequences of actions chronically escape their initiators intentions in the process of objectification.*" (Giddens 1979 p. 44). Therefore, while the use of social structures as rules and resources form part of intentional action, the reproduction of social structures/system is not an intended act (Giddens 1979 p. 42-4). In this manner, while both structures and systems are the product of intentional action they are not intentionally created. Structures are neither an intentional product nor are they an 'other' acting upon a passive unintentional agent, the subject. The social system as an 'other' can be studied with respect to a 'de-centered subject' without implying either the separation of subject and object or the derogation of the subject as a cognitively and epistemologically aware intentionally acting agent. The social system is reconstituted as the unintentional effect of intentional action. Hence, the system is reproduced without the teleological implications of functionalism (Bernstein 1989 p. 22-3). This difference Giddens represented graphically (see next page).

While actors act intentionally, with respect to d.c. and p.c., the recreation of society does, in a way, 'happen behind their backs'. However, this is without the consequence of making them automatons programmed by society to create society (Bernstein 1989 p.24-4). It is the feedback of unintended effects which constitutes the essence the homeostatic causal loops necessary for integration within society. In a context of co-presence it is referred

Structuration Theory:

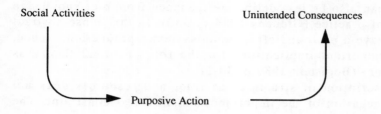

Social Activities   Unintended Consequences

Purposive Action

Functionalism:

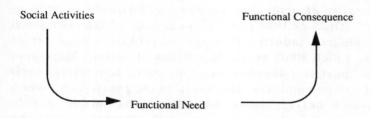

Social Activities   Functional Consequence

Functional Need

(Giddens 1984 p.294)

to as social integration. In the case of the individual and the greater systemic whole Giddens speaks of system integration (Giddens 1984 p. 28).

The explanation of the reproduction of social structures as an unintentional effect has to be qualified in one respect. Knowledge of the processes of social reproduction is sometimes discursively penetrated by social actors to some degree (e.g. sociopolitical theory). This knowledge may then be used in an "...attempt to monitor, and thereby control, highly generalized conditions of system reproduction..."(Giddens 1984 p. 27). This implies that in addition to homeostatic causal loops there also exists reflexive self-regulation in system reproduction (Giddens 1984 p. 28). Added to this there can also be less deliberate feedback from d.c. knowledge to structural practice (Giddens 1984 p. 350). In this sense abstract ideas can have a profound effect upon system reproduction. Hence, there are important implications for the role of social theory as critical theory (Bernstein 1989 p. 30-1).

The description of structures as rules and resources does not imply the negation of the importance of structural constraint. The very preexistence, with respect to action, of structures presupposes constraint. To elucidate this claim I will use the analogy of language. The rules of English enable me to communicate with others. However, these rules also determine the parameters of my expression and, consequently, the manner in which I express myself. The unintentional consequence of my speaking feeds into the systemic existence of the rules of English. The latter in turn constitutes a preexisting form delineating the parameters of future action.

Returning to social structures, the prior systemic existence of structures places "...*limits upon the range of options open to an actor, or plurality of actors, in a given circumstance or type of circumstance.*" (Giddens 1984 p. 177). For example, "The contractual relations of modern industry face the individual with a set of circumstances which limit available options of action. Marx says that workers 'must sell themselves' - or, more accurately, their labour power - to an employer. The 'must' in the phrase expresses a constraint which derives from the institutional order [highly embedded structures] of modern capitalist enterprises that the worker faces." (Giddens 1984 p. 177) This 'must' is not like a force of nature (Giddens 1984 p. 15) which drives non-cognitive actors along, as in some forms of structuralism. Structural constraint can only be described as absolute with respect to the subjective desires of the actor in question. The actor is not driven along by an outside force. People make history, but not in the conditions of their own making and it is the latter which is the source of structural constraint.

It is through the concept of structures as 'carried' in p.c. and d.c. that Giddens is able to bring together the concept of structures existing in the moment of action and simultaneously ordering action. Even though structures only exist at the moment of action, as rules and resources they can also order action by existing in potential form as knowledge of rules and resources. Hence, I would disagree with Derek Layder's criticism that, in conceptualizing structures as existing in the moment of action, Giddens fails to take account of the prior existence of structures as manifest in their systemic existence and in the phenomenon of structural constraint (Layder 1985 p. 144; 1987 p. 33). The point is that prior to their recreation in time-space, social structures are 'carried' - exist in potential form - as rules and resources in p.c. and d.c.. In p.c. and d.c. they are carried/exist as knowledge of the social system. Hence, it is at the level of p.c. and d.c. that structures are inherently both enabling (rules and resources) and, prior to action, exist as a form of constraint limiting the possibilities of future action.

6 Power, structures and resources

The previous chapter centred on the relationship between action and structure. I showed how the traditional dualism between the two was overcome by a duality. This involved placing the concept of agency at the center of social theory. However, as developed so far, within this theoretical perspective there is an inherent tendency to view agency within an almost ethnomethodological framework. Structuration practices are perceived as an out-growth of ontological insecurity and carried out between actors as if interaction were the mutual labour of peers (see Giddens 1976 p. 113). Basically, I concentrated on the relationship between agency and structure in the abstract and thereby methodologically bracketed other analytically inherent aspects of both structure and agency.

Inherent in the concept of agency is the ability 'to do'. Agents don't simply seek ontological security but they also make a difference in the world by intervening in it through action. The concept of agency implies "... capability of doing things in the first place (which is why agency implies power: cf. the Oxford English Dictionary definition of an agent as 'one who exerts power or produces an effect'). Agency concerns events of which an individual is the perpetrator....Whatever happened would not have happened if that individual had not intervened." (Giddens 1984 p. 9).

For an agent to be able to act structures must have a content which facilitates action. Structures cannot simply be viewed as an empty 'binding' of time-space. In essence, it could be argued that the 'binding of time-space' constitutes the ontological essence of social structures. However, structures are experienced ontically in their being-in-the-world. In their ontic form structures exist 'for the sake of man'. It is this 'for the sake of' existence which agents use so as to be able 'to do'. On an ontic level structures exist in three forms; as structures of signification, domination and legitimation (Giddens 1984 p. 24). On this level the essence of structure can be portrayed as follows:

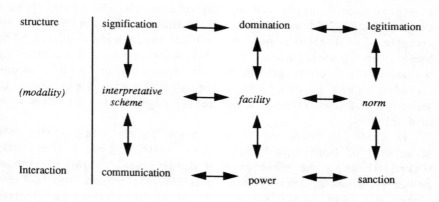

(Giddens 1984 p.29)

In the diagram structure stands for the ontic form of a given structure. Modality refers to the manner in which these structures are drawn upon in action. Interaction indicates the nature of social action between actors. (Giddens 1984 p. 28, 1976 p. 122). When actors interact they draw upon structures which they experience/use in a given modal form. In this act they intentionally shape the nature of a given interaction and in turn unintentionally reconstitute given social structures.

While it is analytically possible to distinguish three different structural dimensions to the social system, it is important to stress that they don't exist independently of each other. To illustrate this point I shall begin with the structures of signification. " The communication of meaning in interaction involves the use of interpretative schemes by which sense is made by participants of

89

what each says and does." (Giddens 1976 p. 122). This implies the existence of a 'cognitive order' which actors draw upon and reconstitute in that act. This knowledge of the world is not static but culturally bound and consequently ideologically linked. In this respect, what passes for social reality is inherently linked to structures of domination (Giddens 1976 p. 113).

The inherent interrelationship between different structures' 'being in the world' can also be observed to exist - on the level of interpretative scheme, facility and norm - as follows: "The stocks of knowledge which actors draw upon in the production and reproduction of interaction are the same as those where by they are able to make accounts, offer reasons, etc." (Giddens 1984 p. 29). "To be 'accountable' for one's activities is both to explicate the reasons for them and to supply the normative grounds whereby they may be justified'" (Giddens 1984 p. 30). In that act they reconstitute the structures of legitimation from which these norms derive. The imposition of social norms calls for some process of sanctioning whereby certain contingent normative claims can be 'made to count' (Giddens 1984 p. 30) Therefore, the continued existence of structures of legitimation is inherently dependent upon structures of domination.

In systemic form, as distinct from purely analytically, the structures of both signification and legitimation are inherently linked (through the structures of domination) to the particular power relations of that system. It is for this reason that Giddens makes it a fundamental supposition of his theoretical perspective that "...the articulation of time-space relations in social systems has to be examined in conjunction with the generation of power." (Giddens 1981 p. 3).

In power based social relations actors draw upon structures of domination which are reconstituted through social action. Structures of domination exist in time-space in the moment of action. The unintentional effect of this action is to structure the structures of domination. The intentional result desired by the actors in question is the realization of power. Hence, in structural form, " [d]omination refers to structured asymmetries of resources drawn upon and reconstituted in...power relations." (Giddens 1981 p. 51). This can be expressed as follows (see over):

Structures of domination

↓ ↑ (Unintentional)

Action ⟶

↓ (Intentional)

Power

   Implicit in this representation of the relationship between intentional action and unintentional effects is the need to clarify two points: Giddens' concept of power and structures of domination.

   Giddens has two concepts of power in mind. The first is very general and linked to the definition of agency. It is simply"...the *transformative capacity* of human action,..." (Giddens 1976 p. 110). This implies having dominion over both nature and other humans. As a subset of this general concept is a more restricted use of the word referring specifically only to dominion over people. This is a relational concept which is the property of social action and is linked to structures of domination (Giddens 1976 p. 111). "Power, in this relational sense, concerns the capability of actors to secure outcomes where the realization of these outcomes depends upon the agency of others." (Giddens 1979 p. 93). It is this subcategory of the general concept of power which feeds back into the structures of domination and is consequently of interest to sociopolitical theorists. This purely transformational concept of power is not linked to interest as in Lukes (Giddens 1979 p. 90). A given actor may have power to, and actually, do something which is inherently against his/her interests. Further, an actor A may have power over B without there being conflict between A and B. Only if there are differing interests implied in the power relationship between two actors will conflict arise. Hence, it is important to emphasize that power should not be defined in terms of conflict. (Giddens 1976 p. 112). While power is frequently associated with the twin concepts of conflict and interests this relationship is inherently contingent (Giddens 1984 p. 257).

   Aside from explicitly divorcing power from interests and conflict, Giddens added to his concept of power the hypothesis that "[u]nlike the communication of meaning, power does not come into being only when being 'exercised', even if ultimately there is no other criterion whereby one can demonstrate what power actors possess. This is important, because we can talk of power being 'stored up' for future occasions of use." (Giddens 1976 p. 111-2).

Like power, domination is not an inherently noxious phenomenon associated only with 'suppression'. In terms of having 'dominion over', domination expresses three aspects of power relations: 1) it is the ability of individual 'decision-makers' to realize their objectives, as in Dahl; 2) it is part of "... the structured properties of social systems." (Giddens 1981 p. 50); 3) it is the ability 'to do', as in Parsons. Social structures are not simply the binding of empty time-space. Ontically they are implicated in the ordering of resources which are drawn upon in order to act - make a difference as an agent or have power. Resources are structural elements of social systems which are "...drawn upon by actors in the instantiation of interaction." (Giddens 1981 p. 50) Hence, social actors realize power in interaction. "*Domination* refers to structured asymmetries of resources drawn upon and reconstituted in...power relations." (Giddens 1981 p. 50). Referring back to the distinction between general power and social power, "[i]t is in this sense that men have power 'over' others: this is power as domination".(Giddens 1976 p. 111).

When actors are agents through the act of doing things, they draw upon resources which, through structuration, are reconstituted as structures of domination. " Resources are drawn upon by actors in the production of interaction, but are constituted as structures of domination." (Giddens 1982a p. 38-9). Resources are inherently distinct from power: they "...are the media through which power is exercised, and structures of domination reproduced..." (Giddens 1979 p. 91). Structures of domination are reconstituted ontically through the drawing upon of resources through which power can be realized. "Resources are the media whereby power is employed in the routine course of social action; but they are at the same time structural elements of social systems, reconstituted in social interaction." (Giddens 1982a p. 39).

Being an agent implies having power, being able 'to do'. In social action, agents mobilize resources in order to realize power with respect to each other. Hence, "...power in social systems can thus be treated as involving relations of *autonomy and dependence in* social interaction." (Giddens 1982a p. 39). In this manner power relations are chronically recreated in interaction between agents. Part of the definition of being an agent is to have power. This implies that power relations in interaction can never be zero-sum. Both actors have power. If one of them didn't he/she would have ceased to be an agent. Therefore, with respect to social practices, when defining power in terms of relations of autonomy and dependence, it is of central importance to keep in mind that "...even the most autonomous agent is in some degree dependent, and the most dependent actor or party in a relationship retains some autonomy." (Giddens 1979 p. 93).

If all agents have some power this implies they all have some resources. Agent A has neither all power nor all resources with respect to agent B. Hence, structures of domination refer to asymmetries of resources (Giddens 1979 p. 93).

The combination of the claim that interaction is characterized by domination and the idea that every actor always has power may seem superficially strange. The image of a prisoner immediately comes to mind as an example of an actor with no power. Against this point Giddens would argue that even prisoners do have certain resources at their disposal which still make them agents (see Giddens 1981 p. 63). There is always the option of a 'dirty protest' or hunger-strike. If a prisoner were, in response, physically cleaned and forced to eat (possibly under sedation) then he/she would admittedly be powerless. However, he/she would also cease to an agent. The domination exercised over him/her would be over his/her physical body. In this sense the power involved would cease to be social. It would be domination over nature. Power over a person's physical body is not analytically separate from power over a stone. The latter is power only in the wider sense of the word.

Before turning to the examination of resources, I want to show how the introduction of the concepts of power and domination call for a reconceptualization of social structures and system reproduction.

Previously I described how structures exist as rules and resources. Within that context they appeared as rules purely in a Wittgensteinian form and only as resources with respect to the maintenance of ontological security. Through the notions of power and domination they now gain a different form. We have already seen that as rules they differ from rules in chess in being dependent for their existence upon continual reproduction within a framework of power and domination (Giddens 1979 p. 67). The constitutive and regulative aspects of rule-governed behaviour, expressed through structures, signification and legitimation, are dependent for their maintenance upon the mobilization of the structures of domination. This implies that the structures of signification and legitimation are 'stretched' over time-space through both conflict and consensus. Conflict appears through sanctions in the mobilization of the structures of domination. Consensus is a manifestation of a mutual recognition of interpretative schemes and norms. Structures are no longer just memory traces drawn upon as rules through p.c. and d.c. but continually reproduced within the framework of contending fields of conflict and consensus.

Structures in their ontic form embody structures of domination which give agents power. People do not just act for the fun of it or to steady their psyche. They do so in order to get things done, which means drawing upon structures of domination and resources. "Resources are the media whereby transformative capacity is employed as power in the routine courses of social interaction...." (Giddens 1979 p. 92). However many resources an agent may have at his/her disposal, in the act of exercising power he/she is dependent upon the action of another agent to realize a desired end. This implies not only dependence but also the need for reciprocal action (Giddens 1979 p. 76). This gives an entirely different slant to the concepts of social and system integration. Seeing that social and system integration take place within the framework of autonomy and dependence, "'Integration' can be defined...as regularized ties, interchanges or reciprocity *of practices* between either actors or collectivities." (Giddens 1979 p. 76). Reciprocity of practices is in turn "... to be understood as involving regularized relations of relative autonomy and dependence between the parties concerned." (Giddens 1979 p. 76). Integration takes place within the context of structures of signification and legitimation which are contested through the structures of domination. Therefore, "...*integration is not synonymous with 'cohesion', certainly not with consensus*." (Giddens 1979 p. 76) as in the Parsonsian framework.

Social and system integration have to be grasped in terms of the duality of structure. Structure presupposes system integration and system integration presupposes social integration. *Langue* presupposes *parole* and *parole* presupposes *langue*. Social integration is reciprocity, and autonomy and dependence, between actors on a face to face level. System integration is reciprocity between groups or collectivities based on relations of autonomy and dependence (Giddens 1979 p. 77). Social integration is concerned with the level of systemness manifest in co-presence(Giddens 1984 p. 28). System integration refers to systemness in connection with those who are physically absent in time-space(Giddens 1984 p. 28).

Both social and system integration are dependent upon the mutual interelatedness of structures. The structures of signification, legitimation and domination are maintained through structuration practices by the mobilization of resources in order 'to do'. When I previously discussed resources I methodologically bracketed an explanation of how resources exist with respect to structures.

Ordinarily when we speak of resources there is an inherent tendency to see them as 'out there' with respect to the parameters of the social world. However, for Giddens they are inseparable from structures as rules (Barbalet 1987 p. 10) which also exist ontologically as the binding of time-space. Resources are inherently bound up with the ontic existence of social structures. 'Out there' resources are the vehicles for social structures within the social system. This is in much the same manner in which specific symbols (words, signs) are used as carriers in a system of signification. As already emphasized, all structural forms are mutually sustaining. Therefore, 'out there' resources become social resources through structures as rules which exist as formulas with constitutive and normative content. The ownership of an acre of land is dependent both upon the structures of signification - whereby we understand the meaning of private property - and the structures of legitimation - by which we accept the inherent 'validity' of the institution of private property. If we reject such institutions and show this through trespassing then structures of domination will be applied(Giddens 1979 p. 104).

This distinction between 'out there' resources and social resources is in some respects directly related to the differentiation made between power in the abstract and social power; the latter being domination over nature, and the former over others. Social resources are those which are implicated in the reproduction of social relations whereas more general resources are those with an 'out there' existence. As previously developed, the reproduction of structures was purely the reproduction of a Wittgensteinian type rule through praxis. Through social power and social resources the reproduction of rules has been given 'flesh'. "Resources,...provide the *material levers* of empirical contents, including those involved in the operation of codes and norms." (Giddens 1979 p. 104). Power over a prisoner's body was not social power in that it was not based on interaction and structuration practices. Similarly, material resources such as raw materials, land, etc. "... become resources, in the manner in which I apply the term here [qua social resources], only when incorporated within the process of structuration." (Giddens 1984 p. 33). In order to explain this point I think a valid analogy can be drawn with a chair. At the moment I am sitting on a chair. The material resource out of which this chair is constructed is timber. This wood, as distinct from a tree in virgin jungle, exists as a material resource through being a chair. It exists 'for the sake of' me in its 'chairness'. As such, when I sit my chair 'carries' social structures. It is constituted as part of the social system by my act of sitting upon it. On the other hand, the tree in the virgin jungle does not, as yet, exist for the 'sake of' facilitating any social actor.

Giddens conceptually separates "...two major types of resource which constitute structures of domination, and which are drawn upon and reproduced as power relations in interaction." (Giddens 1979 p. 100). The two forms of resources are allocative and authoritative. By authoritative he refers "...to capabilities which generate command over *persons*..." and allocative "...to capacities which generate command over *objects* or other material phenomena." (Giddens 1979 p.100)

He represents his classification in the following form:

Allocative Resources	Authoritative Resources
1) Material features of the environment (raw materials, material power sources)	1) Organization of social time-space (temporal-spatial constitution of paths and regions)
2) Means of material production/ reproduction (instruments of production, technology)	2) Production/reproduction of the body (organization and relation of human beings in mutual association)
3) Produced goods (artifacts created by the interaction of 1 and 2)	3) Organization of life chances (constitution of chances of development and self-expression)

(Giddens 1984 p. 258)

It is important to emphasize that allocative resources are not 'out there' resources in the 'raw' so to speak. They are material things which are 'socially bound up' in society through the structures of domination. As such, they are an inherent part of the ontic existence of social structures. The ontic existence of structures can, of course, only be conceptually separated from the ontological. My chair may exist in the abstract as a set of material properties. However, in the Giddensian framework, its 'chairness' is defined through its historicity, that is the time 'in' it and hence is bound up with its contingently defined nature of being. While allocative resources are concerned with social structures as they are carried by resources, authoritative resources are more bound up with the management of time-space and hence implicitly relate more to the ontological, or time-space, aspects of social structures. They involve the management of time-space 'paths' of social agents.

Neither allocative nor authoritative resources are fixed resources. "They form the media of the expandable character of power in different types of societies." (Giddens 1984 p. 258) The inherent expandableness of these resources is the source of the expansion of power in the social system. Hence, as resources can be created or already existent ones expanded, power cannot be conceived of as zero-sum (Giddens 1981 p. 52). Because resources are the carriers of structures and the latter are the properties of social systems, "...authoritative resources, like allocative resources, are not possessed by individual social actors but are features of the social totality. Like other structural characteristics of social systems they are recreated as resources in and through the act of structuration which they facilitate. They make possible the intentional content of action, with the unintentional effect of being reconstituted as resources. Taken together the allocative and authoritative resources... are constitutive of the societal totality as a structural system of domination." (Giddens 1981 p. 52). Power is a property of social systems which is generated in and through the structures of domination (Giddens 1984 p. 258). Hence, power is related to both structural and systemic aspects of social life while being experienced as both power 'to' and power 'over'.

In analysing the expansion of power within social systems, Giddens accords neither primacy to allocative resources, as in Marxism, nor primacy to authoritative resources, as in Foucauldian or Nietszcheian perspectives (see Thiele 1990 p. 907-26). Expansion of power takes place through an interplay between the two. To illustrate this point I will adapt and simplify an example of Giddens' analysis of some of the major factors involved in the advent of the industrial revolution.

Prior to the industrial revolution the main means of production in England was small scale domestic or home-based workshop production. This form of production "...as E. P. Thompson has pointed out, had little of the regularity achieved within the factory or large centralized work-place." (Giddens 1981 p. 136). The change brought about by the industrial revolution involved two major changes in the routine time-space paths of everyday life (Giddens 1981 p. 153). One is the separation of workplace and home; the other is the division of the day into 'working time' and 'one's own' time (Giddens 1981 p. 137). Labour-power is transformed into wages and commodified through its sale "...for definite periods of time." (Marx 1979 Vol.1 p. 683). In the workplace the worker not only works through the machine but also as a machine in the sense that a new level of time-space precision is required of the body in order suit the demands of mechanization (see Marx 1975 p. 291). The process of industrialization on a large scale required not only the steam engine but, equally importantly, the commodification and precise organization of the time-space 'paths' of labour in a manner compatible with new capitalist/industrial modes/relations of production. Hence, the pertinence of Mumford's remark to the effect that "...it is the clock rather than the steam-engine that should be regarded as the epitome of capitalist industrialism." (Giddens 1981 p. 133).

Both allocative and authoritative resources are mutually dependent in social reproduction through their production through action. The conditions of production of action are at the same time the conditions of reproduction of the structures of domination. The ability to act, the use of power, reproduces both the structures of domination and their ontic existence through resources (Giddens 1981 p. 92-3). This can be represented in the following form:

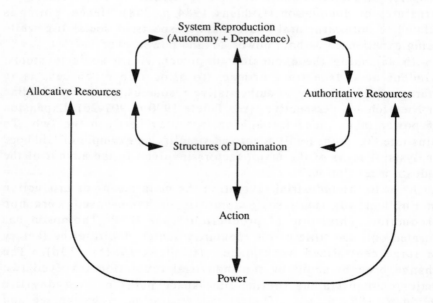

The intentional actor draws upon structures of domination as resources in order to act. In so doing he/she unintentionally contributes to their reproduction. These structures are inherently expandable as is consistent with a non zero-sum concept of power. This implies that not only does action reconstitute structures of domination but, in the longue duree, this action may contribute to their expansion. This expansion is in turn dependent upon an overall increase in social resources.

In the thought experiment, society was described as a series of interweaving time-space paths. Society existed both 'in' time-space and 'through ' time-space. In this sense the system can be described as 'bracketing' time-space (Giddens 1981 p. 91). Structures bind time-space in action. In the act of structuration actors also draw upon resources as the media by which power can be exercised and expanded in the social system. Therefore, expansion of resources is inherently linked to the time-space expansion of the systemic totality. In other words, expansion of resources implies the expansion of time-space distantiation of asocial system. The development of societies with a high presence availability (e.g. hunter-gatherer) to ones with a high time-space distantiation (e.g. capitalism) is facilitated through the incorporation of more and more resources 'in' the system.

The embodiment of resources 'in' the system points "...to the importance of *storage capacity* to time-space distantiation and the generation of power." (Giddens 1981 p. 94). The term 'storage capacity' is meant to convey the notion of resources as being 'placed into' or 'drawn into ' or 'forming part of' the structures of domination as they are 'stretched' across time-space through greater time-space control (Giddens 1981 p. 94, Held and Thompson 1989 p. 8).

There are two forms of storage "...corresponding to the two types of resources that enter into the structures of domination." (Giddens 1981 p. 94). I will describe the nature of the storage of allocative resources first and then authoritative second. As already explained, the storage of material resources is not synonymous with the physical containment of goods but rather a form of time-space control (Giddens 1981 p. 94). The expansion of allocative resources, as stored in the time-space 'bracketed' by the social system, can best be explicated through example. "Hunters and gatherers have little means of storing food and other material requisites and utilize the given store house of nature in providing for their needs the year round." (Giddens 1984 p. 259). They are also societies with a high level of presence availability. After a certain period of time these societies became agrarian. "In agrarian communities... the storehouse which the natural world provides is augmented in various ways that facilitate the 'stretching' of social relations across time-space." (Giddens 1984 p. 259). Jumping several millennia in world time: "In modern capitalism purchase and sale of manufactured foods is as fundamental to social existence as the exchange of the whole gamut of other commodities: it is not an exaggeration to say that the expansion of capitalism to form a new world economy would not have been possible without the development of a range of techniques for the preservation and storage of perishable goods, particularly food." (Giddens 1984 p. 259-60). Technical innovation is wasted if it cannot be channelled to produce goods which are storable or immediately consumable. A non-storable/consumable resource would cease to be a social resource and hence contribute to the overall social time-space distantiation.

The expansion of allocative resources should never be assumed to have primacy for social development as it does in materialist concepts of history. It is important to stress that such expansion could not have occurred without the parallel development of authoritative resources. With respect to the latter, "'Storage' is a medium of 'binding' time-space involving, on the level of action, the knowledgeable management of a projected future and recall of an elapsed past." (Giddens 1984 p. 261). In other words, when dealing with authoritative resources we are in essence concerned with the control of structuration practices as the binding of time-space. It is control over the manner in which social relations occur across time-space. Outside their instantiation in time-space, through structuration practices, structures exist as memory traces. These memory traces constitute the knowledge/ information necessary in order to 'goon'. Hence, "Storage of authoritative resources involves above all the retention of control of information or knowledge." (Giddens 1981 p. 94). In other words, authoritative resources involve the storage of information which feeds back to shape future structuration practices. "In non-literate societies knowledge is stored through its incorporation in traditional practices, including myth telling: the only storage container in such circumstances is the human memory." (Giddens 1981 p. 94-5). With the advent of writing, computers and other means of information storage time-space distantiation is radically increased (Giddens 1981 p. 95). These media of information storage of course also presuppose a group capable of retrieving or decoding this knowledge (Giddens 1984 p. 261). In short, with respect to authoritative resources,

100

Giddens appears to be postulating an almost Foucauldian connection between power and knowledge. Drawing these threads together, Giddens' concept of the storage of allocative and authoritative resources can be represented as follows:

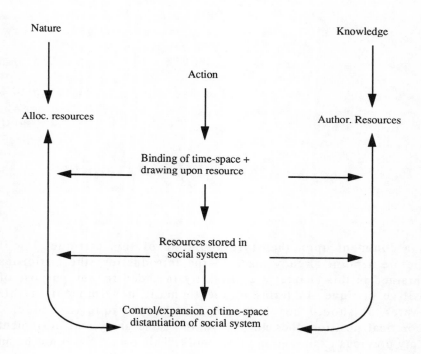

In conclusion, resources provide the key to the expansion of the social system as viewed against the horizon of time-space. Inaction they provide the means to realize power. Conceptually speaking, resources are dialectically interrelated with structures. They provide the ontic 'meat' of structures that 'bind' the time-space which the social system 'brackets'. In away, I have come back to where I started with Jane's weaving dance of time -space paths. Except now, the social structures which bind time-space exist as rules - retrieved through p.c. and d.c. - that also facilitate intentional action through resources and power. On an unintentional level, Jane's action not only has the potential for reproducing social structures but it can also constitute a contribution to the expansion of the total amount of power within a system.

7 Giddens: A critique

As a comment upon the style and tone of this critique, I will reiterate a point already made in the introduction: the criticisms contained in this chapter are primarily intended for the purpose of positive critique. In terms of the thematic development of this chapter, it should be observed that this critique of Giddens' theoretical position does not follow the same analytical movement as my previous examination of his work. This chapter will not be an inductively explained conceptual map of some of his core ideas but will instead focus on a couple of problematic issues within his position. Consequently, for example, I intend to gloss over Giddens' analysis of structures/system viewed against the horizon of time-space. In terms of critique, I intend to focus on two broadly defined issue areas: firstly, the adequacy of the structuration perspective as a conceptual tool for the analysis of the process whereby the reproduction of social structures takes place and, secondly, the theoretical contradictions inherent in Giddens' concept of power. Each of these broad subject areas will be further subdivided. Each will begin with an introductory analysis of the general theoretical terrain. This will gradually unfold into a critique of the position outlined. In the critique of structuration theory it will be argued that, while the perspective is highly satisfactory on the level of internal consistency, it suffers from an inherent lack in terms of the claims made for it with regard to the reproduction of structure. On the topic of power, it will be maintained that Giddens' analysis is flawed by conceptual contradiction. Each of these critiques will be followed by a discussion of the manner in which these inadequacies (re. structuration) and inconsistencies (re. power) manifest themselves in the analysis of social change.

Experienced as rules, structures exist primarily in the same form as a mathematical formula which can be expressed discursively as $a_n = n^2 + n - 1$. This formula allows the actor to 'go on'. When faced with a series of numbers 1, 5, 11, 19,... he/she knows the next number in the series to be 29. This knowledge may be either d.c. or p.c.. In drawing upon this rule, in order to guide action, the rule is reconstituted. In this sense, structures can be better compared with the 'rules' of a children's game rather than the those of a game of chess. This is a more valid analogy because the rules of a children's game only exist on the level of p.c. unless contested by one of the participants in the play: 'John is being unfair because...'. Similarly, in every-day life the rules of social participation usually exist on the level of p.c..

Rules are drawn upon in order to 'go on' and in that act are unintentionally reconstituted internally as memory traces and externally as the binding of time-space. The description of the reconstitution of rules/structures through such structuration practices makes *routinization* a linch pin concept for structuration theory (Giddens 1984 p. xxiii). In order to make this point, I am going to include a relatively long quotation form *The Constitution of Society*: "The routine (whatever is done habitually) is a basic element of day-to-day social activity....The term 'day-to-day' encapsulates exactly the routinized character which social life has as it stretches across time-space. The repetitiveness of activities which are undertaken in a like manner day after day is the material grounding of what I call the recursive nature of social life. (By its recursive nature I mean that the structured properties of social activity - via the duality of structure - are constantly recreated out of the very resources which constitute them.) Routinization is vital to the psychological mechanisms whereby a sense of trust or ontological security is sustained in the daily activities of social life. Carried primarily in practical consciousness, routine drives a wedge between the potentially explosive content of the unconscious and the reflexive monitoring of action which the agent displays." (Giddens 1984 p. xxiii). In short, routine is fundamental for both the creation of social structures and the maintenance of ontological security.

Most action, indeed "Any action that is repeated frequently becomes cast into a pattern,..." (Berger and Luckmann 1967 p. 70). "Even the solitary individual on the proverbial desert island habitualizes his activity. When he wakes up in the morning and resumes his attempts to construct a canoe of matchsticks, he may mumble to himself, 'There I go again', as he starts on step one of an operating procedure consisting of, say ten steps." (Berger and Luckmann 1967 p. 71). Repeating the thought experiment, used for observing Jane, on the solitary individual there is repetition and recursiveness. Viewed against the horizon of time-space there is order not chaos. The solitary individual moves through time-space 'paths' and, as a consequence, in action binds time-space. Through the act of binding time-space he/she is unintentionally reproducing structures. These structures exist as memory traces outside the moment of their presencing so that he/she can 'go on'. In the morning he/she can draw upon rules which allow him/her to repeat the same time-space paths as yesterday. His/her material resources will only be resources to the extent that they are implicated in the micro-system which he/she has created. Sticks with specific physical characteristics (e.g. pliability or absence of knots) will constitute part of the media of his/her structuration practices and in that act enlarge the overall power of the system set up. Once the canoe is constructed there may a large leap in the amount of time-space 'bracketed' by the system.

In nearly all respects the description of the individual on the desert island exhibits the same characteristics of time-space 'bracketing' as Jane. The only factor which is inherently different is the absence of others. In other words, the *recreation* of Giddens' concept of structures, as rules and resources which bind time-space in action, is not *theoretically* dependent upon the existence of others. Returning to the example of Jane, it might be part of her day-to-day routine never to walk on the lines in the pavement because she believes that such an act gives her good luck. Not walking on the lines exists in her memory as a rule concerning good luck which enables her to 'go on' when confronted with lines in the pavement. In the act of avoiding the lines she binds time-space, orders her time-space paths, and in that act recreates structures in time-space.

What I am using these examples to convey is that there appears to be a conceptual gap between the concept of structures in the abstract and as a property of *social systems*. Structure "...refers, in social analysis, to the 'binding' of time-space in social systems, the properties which make it possible for discernibly similar practices

104

to exist across varying spans of time and space and which lend them 'systemic form." (Giddens 1984 p. 17). "Social systems are composed of patterns of relationships between actors or collectivities reproduced across time and space." (Giddens 1981 p. 26) What is not clear is how structures, as Giddens describes the production of them, through structuration practices, inherently pertain to a systemic form which is also reproduced by others. As memory traces, or rules determining routine, they appear to be purely an effect of the behaviour of individual actors. While they may often be structured with respect to others, possibly taking account of others, the existence of social structures does not depend on the existence of others. Rather, structures are formed through the activities of *individual actors*. While this certainly places the intentional social actor back at centre stage, as Giddens desired, it also involves him in a series of interrelated theoretical difficulties.

There is not necessarily, depending on definitions, an inherent difficulty in accepting the idea that the person on the desert island, or Jane in avoiding lines, is creating structures - recreating rules and 'binding' time-space. Where there is a problem, for the social theorist, is if there does not exist any criterion whereby it is possible to differentiate the *creation* of these 'private' (in the sense of non-socially systemic) structures from those which constitute characteristics of a social system. As can be seen on a linguistic level, such a theoretical position falls theoretically foul of an aspect of Wittgenstein's analysis of the 'private language' fallacy. To take an example from Wittgenstein, the existence of a word for a given pain presupposes the existence of a "...a grammar of the word 'pain'..." (Wittgenstein 1968 § 257). Similarly, the existence of a *social* structure presupposes a grammar of that structure within the social system. Also, by the same criterion, ostensive definitions are not of sufficient explanatory content to theorize the creation of meaning. An actor might recursively fix the meaning of an object by pointing and saying that's an x. While this may be part of the process of creating rules it is not in itself sufficient to create the linguistically constituted word x (see Fogelin 1976 p. 103). For the word x to become a 'real' word it must become part of a language where its meaning is constituted through the way in which it is used - in combination with different words - in a manner which inherently distinguishes it from other words through difference. In fact, framed within the language of de Saussure's linguistic analysis, this point is appreciated by Giddens when he describes structures as "...*a virtual order of differences* produced and reproduced in social interaction as its medium and outcome." (Giddens 1979 p. 3).

On a systemic level, structures must have meaning with respect to the notion of difference with respect to other systemically defined social structures. However, while explicitly recognizing this point with regard to the nature of structures, *the process whereby structures are reproduced through structuration does not provide theoretical space for this essential structural characteristic.* In other words, although Giddens recognizes the systemic ingredient pertaining to the essence of structures, the concept of structuration does not inherently embody it. If social structures are a guide for social practice and produced through such practice, it inherently follows that structuration theory must show how they, as distinct from any other forms of rule imaginable, *must* in some manner be a unique product which pertains to a socially systemic reality. One of the obvious first steps for getting around this difficulty would be to make the basic building block out of which social structures are constituted an inherently different element than that which goes into the creation of 'private' structures. It is necessary to have a theory of the social system which makes its continuous reproduction, through action, a theoretically distinct phenomenon from the order created by a solitary individual on his/her own or in the non-social and/or 'private' 'bracketing' (for a discussion of the use of the terms non-social and 'private' see next chapter) of time-space. Without wishing to state the obvious, not all order produced through repeated action is necessarily social order. This applies even to recursive practices which *are* social as defined by the intentionality of the actor involved: *it is not sufficient to intend to create a new word x through recursive action in order to actually create it.*

The over-emphasis upon recursive structuration practices leads to inherent difficulties in providing an adequately theorized conceptual space for system change. Within his perspective Giddens theorized three main sources or types of system change: 1) time-space edges, 2) actor based structuration practices and 3) the enlargement of power resources. As a conceptual tool, the notion of time-space edges - even if slightly esoteric sounding - is highly satisfactory as an analytic device for the description of intersystemic change brought about by contact between different time-space patternings of social order. Consequently, I will methodologically 'bracket' any further discussion of this point in the context of a critique of Giddens' position. Actor-based social change through novel structuration practices will be the subject of what follows. Change brought about by expansion/contraction in power resources will be dealt with later in this chapter in the context of power.

On the micro actor level, in structuration theory, system stability presupposes a totally self-contained system which 'feeds' on itself. It is true that most structures already exist socially in one form or another and, hence, are learned. However, it is also equally true that people also 'make history' or, more appropriately in this context, new structures. Consequently, there exists a continual potential for social change. In a sociopolitical theory which is *not* completely structurally predetermined and where there is free will, *"[t]here is no guarantee that agents will reproduce regularities of conduct as they have previously done."* (I.Cohen 1989 p. 45). If actors are not simply the passive 'bearers' of structure, and structures do not have an 'out-there' existence outside of their recreation in the moment of social action, there must exist the continual potential for an actor to create new structures. Consequently, "...the seeds of social change are present in every moment of the constitution of social systems across time and space." (Giddens 1984 p. 27). This source of contingency constitutes the conceptual mechanism both for the theorization of imperfections regarding the exact reproduction of social routines and, simultaneously, "...provides the praxiological basis for social transformation." (I. Cohen 1989 p. 45). In other words, the praxiological basis for system reproduction provides a methodological tool whereby social change can be theorized through making the reproducers of structure more than structurally determined objects (radical structuralism) or, alternatively, cultural 'dopes' (functionalism). As such, the praxiological basis of continuity and change becomes inherently linked to the theorization of the relationship between determinacy and freedom of action.

On a systemic level, the source of continuity is the inherent systemic inertia whereby the system constitutes the contextuality of action which facilitates the reproduction of consistent social action. For social actors this contextuality manifests itself as structural constraint (see Giddens 1984 p. 176). It is a constraint which guarantees a certain consistency in structuration practices. This consistency is made possible through actors' knowledge of rules. This knowledge of a rule is experienced as both constraining and enabling for actors: actor A's knowledge of a given rule enables him/her to structure in a given manner and simultaneously constrains him/her from ordering his/her actions according to an inherently different rule. This points to the causal relationship between structural constraint and social change. In a social reality characterized by total structural constraint social change would be inherently impossible. Alternatively, in a situation where constraint were totally absent, action would be completely contingent and result in the disintegration of praxis into unremitting chaos (see I. Cohen 1989 p. 221).

Central to Giddens' position is the hypothesis that structures do not have an 'out there' time-space existence except in the moment of structuration. Consequently, for the reproducers of structure, constraint is not derived from being faced with a solid 'steel cage' where they are trapped. Actors are the knowledgeable 'carriers' of certain rules which enable them to reproduce identical structures over varying spans of time and space. Hence, the origins of constraint are the rules whereby structures are 'carried' by actors outside the moment of action. Through the concept of the duality of structure, they are rules which enable actors to act while, in a simultaneous and complementary fashion, also restrain them from ordering their action in an inherently different (and possibly chaotic) manner. Hence, while inherently enabling, the knowledge of the formula $a_n = n^2 + n - 1$ is a source of structural constraint.

Experienced as constraint, an actor's knowledge of $a_n = n^2 + n - 1$ is a barrier to social change or, stated differently, a source of systemic stability. On a praxiological level, the possibility that a given actor could conceivably substitute the formula $a_n = n^4 - 22 + n^6$ is the continually present contingent source for potential social change which is blocked through the knowledge of $a_n = n^2 + n - 1$. Consequently, the continually present potential for change is the possibility that a given actor may decide, for whatever contingent reasons (non-causally theorizable), to 'invent' a new rule by which to structure his/her behaviour.

The contrast between the continual use of the formula $a_n = n^2 + n - 1$ and the possibility of an actor creating a new formula $a_n = n^4 - 22 + n^6$ allows Giddens to theorize the relationship between stability and change in the context of a structural relationship between rules as a facility and as a source of constraint. As such, it is a perspective which has much to commend it. However, it does not contain sufficient theoretical mechanisms for the theorization of structural constraint: the only source of constraint preserving systemic stability is an actor's knowledge of rules pertaining to a specific contextuality of action. Consequently, once an actor has overcome internal personal p.c. and d.c. constraints, it would appear that he/she is free to initiate social change by creating new structures through the use of the formula $a_n = n^4 - 22 + n^6$. While this may be the case on a desert island, this is certainly not the case if $a_n = n^4 - 22 + n^6$ is going to become part of a social system and, hence, contribute to social change.

The actor on a desert island experiences two important forms of constraint to his/her action: the first derives from a lack of resources, the second form his/her limited knowledge of rules. Analytically speaking, the latter is the sole source of the structural constraint which prevents him/her indulging in innovative structuration practices. This knowledge, which has been manifest and reinforced (preventing ontological insecurity) through recursiveness, is the sole epistemological barrier to structural change. Consequently, an actors' p.c. and d.c. knowledge of rules constitutes the only barrier to novel or contingent structuration practices. Without such knowledge of rules, structures could no longer be reproduced as the unintentional effect of action. This form of constraint is the mechanism whereby structures - which only exist in time-space at the moment of action - can be reproduced across varying spans of time and space.

The social actor wishing interaction with other is also subject to the above sources of constraint: access to a limited set of resources and a specific p.c. and d.c. knowledge of rule-governed behaviour. However, *unlike* the person on the desert island, the social actor also experiences an additional source of constraint. The source of this constraint is derived from having to interact with 'other'. This 'other' is an actor with a given quantity of resources and, more importantly in this context, with a specific p.c. and d.c. knowledge of rule-governed behaviour. Hence, actor A is not only subject to constraint from the nature of his/her knowledge of rules. In social interaction, A experiences structural constraint derived from B's p.c. and d.c. knowledge of social reproduction. In other words, for structural change to take place, it is not sufficient that A should get the idea for the rule $a_n = n^4 - 22 + n^6$. Even if formula $a_n = n^4 - 22 + n^6$ has been conceived of with actors B and C in mind, this does not inherently imply that other actors B and C will *understand and accept* the formula $a_n = n^4 - 22 + n^6$ as systemically valid. In short, with respect to actor A, there are three areas which regulate the creation of praxiological structural change: 1) constraint derived from A's p.c. and d.c. knowledge of rules, 2) constraint based upon B's p.c. and d.c. knowledge of rules and 3) constraint derived from B's willingness to accept the new rule as valid - even if he/she understands the new rule, he/she may consider it inappropriate. While Giddens does theorize the first form of constraint, no conceptual space is provided for the latter two. In short, while Giddens wishes to emphasise that the theory of social reproduction through structuration "...does not imply emphasising stability at the expense of radical discontinuities in system organization" (Giddens 1981 p. 27) the theory of structuration lacks certain necessary theoretical mechanisms for analysing such change. The mechanism whereby some innovative structuration can either be rejected or made part of a social system is left unsatisfactorily theorized. There does not exist a method of 'converting' individual unlearned structures, used for the first time, into learnable social structures. Indeed, when faced with the rule $a_n = n^2 + n - 1$, Giddens has failed to provide the necessary theoretical mechanisms to analyse the process by which this rule was, at some point in time, made part of the social system whereas $a_n = n^4 - 22 + n^6$ was rejected. Leaving aside the motivational issue of why an actor might decide to invent the rule/structure $a_n = n^2 + n - 1$, the theorization of actors creating and recreating social order should have a built-in mechanism whereby *some innovative structuration practices are introduced (system change) and others are rejected (system stability)*.

Changing focus from the creation and recreation of structure to the subject of power, there is a certain parallel between Giddens' critique of structuralist conceptualisations of structures and my criticism of his theory of power. Within Giddens' structuration theory structures only exist in time-space in the instant of action. As the unintentional effect of action, structures do not exist in time and space outside of action. Any attempt to postulate that they do is a belief in the existence of the non-visible 'metaphysical' entities of radical/determinist structuralism. Taking structures as 'out-there' given entities introduces an unsatisfactory dualism between agency and structure. In structuration theory, structures only exist as p.c. and d.c. memory traces which are actualized in time-space through praxis. Outside of structuration, structures exist in potential form as p.c. and d.c. rules. Consequently, Giddens has replaced dualism with duality through the theorization of structures as inherently ephemeral entities which are recreated in structuration. Any conceptualization of structure which posits an enduring 'out there' time-space ontological, non-emphemeral, existence to structure is driving a conceptual wedge into the process whereby it is possible to replace dualism by duality. Consequently, in structuration theory, it is an analytical prerequisite not to conceptualize structures as 'out-there' entities.

I would argue that this position is not only a theoretical necessity for the theorization of the re/creation of structure but it is equally essential for an explanation of the process whereby power is produced. As observed by Giddens, the central concept of agency is the ability 'to do'. *Qua* agents, actors are the producers of social power and the recreators of structure in the moment of social action. Central to the concept of agents as the creators of power, must be the hypothesis that power exists only in the moment of 'doing'. Agents draw upon structures, and their 'ontic' embodiment as resources, in order to act. In so doing they become agents by 'doing' or realizing power. The ability to act is actualized through the production of power in the moment of action. In short, in the moment of social action, structure is recreated and power produced as the realization of agency. When theorized as such, neither structure nor power can be conceptualized as having a time-space existence outside of the moment of social action. Any theoretical perspective which attributes the re/creation of structure and the production of power to praxis is inherently precluded from postulating that either phenomenon can have an 'out there' existence.

While Giddens does take the position that power is the realization of agency in action (see previous chapter) he also argues that it has a continuous existence over time and space outside of action. The theoretical fusion between power as the realization of agency and power as 'out there' is expressed in an analytical formula whereby it is argued that power is manifest (not produced) in action: "Unlike the communication of meaning, power does not come into being only when being 'exercised', even if ultimately there is no other criterion whereby one can demonstrate what power actors possess. This is important, because we can talk of power being 'stored up' for future occasions of use." (Giddens 1976 p. 111-2). Postulating the hypothesis that power can be stored means it has an existence prior to the action through which it is manifest. Consequently, "...power is logically *prior to subjectivity,* to the constitution of the reflexive monitoring of conduct." (Giddens 1985 p. 15 emphasis not orig.). Commenting upon such a formula, I would say that it is as unsatisfactory as arguing that structure exists in time and is only manifest in social action. Such a position leaves the recreation of structure in social action as untheorizable. Similarly, a theoretical position, which premises the creation of the social on agency and praxis, cannot provide theoretical space for 'out-there' power. In other words, the premises of structuration theory demand that Giddens either drop the concept of power outside of action or that he abandon the structuration perspective. I recommend the former rather than the latter.

Central to Giddens' project was a commitment to the thesis that any theorization of social reproduction is inherently rooted in agency and praxis. Not only is the postulated existence of power outside of action inconsistent with such premises but it also weakens the conceptual borders which divide power from power resources. Developing Giddens' conceptualization of power as an 'out there' entity, the existence of 'stored up' power presupposes a place to store it. As already stated, *qua* storable entity, power must have an enduring existence in time-space. Consequently, it must follow that it cannot be 'stored' in structures which (as theorized in structuration theory) do not have continuous existence over time-space. However, the social system does have continuity over time-space. Hence, the social system becomes the 'storage container' of power. This concept of power as manifest in action but existing outside of it is presented as an aspect of the fusion of 1-D, Parsonsian and Foucauldian perceptions (see Giddens 1985 p. 15). The obvious question begged by such an analysis of power is: how is this power stored in the system? Or to put differently: 'given the ontological status of structure and system, what is the ontological status of power?' It would appear that it is an unseen thing which flows smoothly inside the system: "The existence of power presumes structures of domination whereby power that 'flows smoothly' in processes of social reproduction (and is, as it were, 'unseen') operates." (Giddens 1984 p. 257).

The adoption of power as a storable systemic flow, from Parsons and Foucault, made Giddens able to provide conceptual space for such phenomena as Foucault's Panopticon or Mumford's city power container: power can emanate from architecture to control social agents. However, if power can be stored, what is the theoretical status of resources? Is this storage of power, as distinct from resources, part of its existence as a 'flow' in social system? Exactly, how is the 'flow' 'stored' in the system? etc. In short, the 'out there' 'metaphysical' power which flows in the system rears its head as something which can be stored, the normal attribute of resources.

The consequent theoretical confusion which exists between power and power resources becomes manifest in Giddens' sometimes inconsistent use of the concept of power resources. In particular this becomes clear in certain formulations of his concept of authoritative resources. Resources in general "... are the media whereby transformative capacity is employed as power in the routine courses of social interaction..." (Giddens 1976 p. 92). More specifically authoritative resources can be classified as follows:

"1) Organization of social time-space (temporal-spatial constitution of paths and regions).
2) Production/reproduction of the body (organization and relation of human beings in mutual association).
3) Organization of life chances (constitution of chances of self development and self-expression)."
(Giddens 1984 p. 258).

In what sense can the above be described as resources? For example, imagine that in the thought experiment it was observed that an actor A told Jane to stand in front of a machine for so and so long (resource one). In so doing A is exercising authoritative power over Jane. The effect, or the extent of Jane's level of compliance, indicates to the observer whether or not A has power over Jane. If Jane changes her time-space paths whereby she stands in front of the machine for the length of time specified by A, it would appear that A has power over Jane; that is, unless Jane would have stood in front of the machine regardless of A telling her to do so. If A has power over Jane, the change brought about in Jane's time-space 'paths' is the *effect* of A's exercise of power. It tells us nothing about the power resources available to or used by A to ensure Jane's compliance. To describe Jane's change in time-space 'paths' as A's power resource is to confuse the effects of an exercise of power with the authoritative resources which made that exercise of power possible. Resources are what enable a person to exercise power. They are what the exercise of power draws upon. (see Giddens 1979 p. 91). Agents have resources at their disposal which, as non-passive beings, enable them to act. To refer to Giddens against himself: "It is mistaken...to treat power itself as a resource as many theorists do." (Giddens 1979 p. 91) What gives A the ability or power to change Jane's time-space 'paths' is that A has resources, authoritative and/or allocative resources, at his/her disposal. These resources are not power in the abstract (even if it exists as a 'flow' in the system) nor are they the effects of an already constituted exercise of power. Any attempt to describe them as such is a treatment of power as a resource. Turning to authoritative resources two and three, these supposed resources are also typological categories of the effects of exercises of power. An individual actor A has power over Jane if he/she can affect her patterns of reproduction and/or life chances. However, the resources which enable actor A to exercise this power must be something other than this observed ability. In essence, Giddens' classification of authoritative resources is a description of possible (authoritative?) exercises of power.

Earlier in the chapter, I mentioned that Giddens attributed some forms of social change to the expansion of levels of power resources. It has already been argued that Giddens' actor-based theorization of social change runs into trouble on a praxiological level. These praxiological problems also manifest themselves as an inability to provide conceptual space for theorization of the expansion of power resources.

In structuration theory, social resources are analytically distinct from purely natural things by virtue of being socially systemically constituted. As such, "[r]esources are structured properties drawn upon and reproduced by knowledgeable agents in the course of interaction." (Giddens 1984 p.15) Consequently, there can be no such thing as unstructured power resources. Things/objects are only power resources to the extent to which they are systemically structured. Hence, the creation of new power resources is inherently linked to the creation of social structures. As a structured systemic entity, a social resource must be drawn upon by actors according to specific rules. Hence, the expansion of power resources is subject to the same forms of structural constraint as the creation of new 'pure' structures discussed earlier. As such, the attempt to theorize the expansion of power resources must inherently fall foul of Giddens' inability to theorize the praxiological basis for social change. If actor A perceives that a given object has tremendous power potential, it is necessary that B accepts *and* understands *both* the power potential of that resource *and* the *structural* elements 'carried' by it. The act of 'inventing' or introducing a new power resource is an act of innovative structuration. New resources are the ontic embodiment of novel structures. In an unsophisticated social theory where the 'motor' of social change is pure technological efficiency, it could be postulated that society would accept all new resources with high power potential and reject those without it. In short, power potential could represent the sole criterion for the theorization of social change or continuity. However, within structuration theory, where resources are structured entities, it is also necessary to be able to attribute such change or stability to structural factors. Within structuration theory, new resources may be accepted or rejected for the praxiological structural content of that act of introduction. A common 'real life' example of this phenomenon is the rejection of potential power resources for cultural reasons (see chapter 11). However, due to the inability to provide adequate conceptual space for praxiological structural change, there is not sufficient theoretical space for the invention of new power resources.

It is possibly worth observing that the inadequate theorization of the praxiological re/creation of structure would also appear to render the relationship between structural constraint and structurally constituted inequalities of power untheorizable. Both allocative and authoritative power resources are structurally constituted. This implies that the maintenance of a given inequality of resources is inherently linked to the continuation of structural systemic configurations of resources. To the powerful and powerless this means that structural constraint is fundamental to continued maintenance of what counts as a power resource and what does not. If the sole source of structural constraint is a barrier which is constituted through the recursive force of habit, it would appear that existing distributions of power could be changed whenever the less powerful overcome internalized lack of structural imagination. In reality, to challenge existing inequalities in power resources, the individual actor is both constrained by his/her lack of knowledge of 'new' resources *and* the necessity to get others to accept these resources as part of a different legitimately structurally ordered reality. At this level, structural change becomes linked to the issue of vested interests. Those who are powerful will attempt to reinforce the set of structural constraints which are fundamental to existing unequal distributions of power resources. On the other hand, the less powerful will attempt to break existing barriers of structural constraint through the introduction of new resources which tip balances of power in their direction.

The inability to theorize changes in the structural configuration of power resources and the conceptualization of power as a storable flow combine to result in the emergence of an uncomfortable feeling of duality within Giddens' account of historical change. As already stated, described as a storable flow, power becomes an almost metaphysical force that is conceptually divorced from individual action. When this is combined with the absent theorization of the praxiological nature of the creation of new power resources, the expansion of the powers of society is not described in terms of distinct acts by agents but instead becomes a more 'macro' phenomenon. Rather than explicable in terms of individual structuration practices, the historical expansion of systemic power is analysed in such terms as, for example, moves from cities as 'crucibles' of power to nation states as 'power containers'. While the latter is fascinating and convincing on an analytically descriptive level, it is inherently discomforting to read such an account without being provided with the necessary conceptual tools for explaining the process by which agents contribute to such historical changes. The net result is that one is left with a history of power where the expansion of power is an assumed given. It is almost as if power expands 'on its own'. In short, it is as if Giddens' framework exists on two levels. There is structuration theory, where the subject is 'centred'. Then there is also the history of the expansion of systemic power.

In conclusion, I would argue that Giddens' perspective is conceptually fundamentally incomplete with regard to a number of the key goals of structuration theory. In particular, these goals include the theorization of the relationship between agency, social structure, constraint and power. At the level of agency and structure, Giddens offers a conceptualization of the praxiological production of structure which fails to distinguish between rüle-governed habitualized recursive patterning of an individual acting singly and the necessary interactive conditions inherent to the creation of socially systemic structures. In terms of the academic context of the agent-structure debate, if the Jessop/Poulantzas solution can be placed at the structural extremity of the spectrum, with respect to the same continuum, Giddens' position can be located at the agent-centered end. The centrality accorded to the individual fails to take account for the fact that the structuring of action, through the use of p.c. and d.c. rules, is not the same as the creation of systemically meaningful structures. Actor A may intend to create a new structure through the recursive ordering of action according to rule $a_n = n^4 - 22 + n^6$. However, this is not the same as actually creating a new systemically meaningful structure. In terms of constraint, structure only manifests itself as an internalized set of rules which preserve the barriers between levels of consciousness and, consequently, prevent ontological insecurity. The equally (if not more) fundamental structural constraints derived from the interactive dimension of structural reproduction are left untheorized. With regard to structural change, it must be inherently true that actors *do* have the imagination to create new rules and are psychologically able overcome ontological insecurity. If this were not the case structural change would either be impossible or completely haphazard. In order to take account of this phenomenon theoretical space must be provided for external structural constraint.

With regard to power, loosely speaking, Giddens' position suffers from a problem which can be described as analytically opposite to that found with respect to theorization of the re/creation of structure. Giddens has introduced an unnecessary duality into his framework. Rather than being too agent-centred, it is a duality which precludes an agency based account of the production of power. Power is given a transcendental 'out there' time-space existence which has more than a passing similarity to a structuralist perception of structure. It is a position which inherently precludes an adequate explanatory theorization of the praxiological production of power. On an analytical level, it is a dualism which also renders the conceptual boundaries between power and resources inherently problematic.

As asserted in the beginning of the chapter, this is intended as a positive critique of structuration theory. In other words, it is meant to pinpoint problematic issues for a constructive purpose. In this particular case, it means a change of perspective whereby it is possible to theorize: 1) the inherently systemic essence of structures as rooted in their recreation, 2) the praxiological nature of social change, 3) the production of power in action, 4) the relationship between such power and structured power resources, 5) the emergence of social change through the introduction of some new power resources and 6) the maintenance of continuity by the rejection of other resources. These six points will form recurrent themes in the next section. The latter will constitute an alternative explanatory theoretical formulation of the process whereby structures are re/created and power is produced through praxis. It is a position which will involve a fundamental change of focus away from individual actors A and towards actors B. It will also include the development of a host of new conceptual tools including restructuration, destructuration and non-restructuration.

Section Three
RESTRUCTURATION
AND POWER

8 Interaction and restructuration

In this chapter I will examine the creation of social structure. It will be within a restricted focus in the sense that I shall methodologically 'bracket' many dependent and interrelated phenomena associated with the overall concept of structure. However, many of these points will be dealt with in later chapters. The present one will be divided into two sections: the first is a general introduction concerned with 'stage setting' for what follows and the second an analysis of the praxiological production of structures.

In his attempt to overcome the dualism of sociopolitical theory, Giddens made agency the central 'binder' between action and structure. It was through this analytical core notion that he replaced a dualism with a duality. However, by placing the agent at center stage, he failed to theorize the inherently systemic essence of structure into the process by which structures are created. It is a lack of theorization which manifests itself with regard to the provision of adequate conceptual space for praxiologically based social change: the creation of new social structures through innovative structuration practices. In the previous chapter, I suggested that one of the first steps necessary in order to resolve this problematic would be to make the basic building block, out of which social structures are produced, inherently different from the unit from which non-socially-systemic structures are created. In

Giddens' analysis of the process of structuration, social action is the basic theoretical unit used for the explanation of the re/creation of structure. In social action, actors draw upon certain rules in order to order their behaviour in a particular manner with respect to others. In the p.c. and d.c. consciousness of the actors, rules exist both as a facility enabling socially ordered action and as a constraint preventing him/her from using new rules. For example, it is this duality which enables an actor to use $a_n = n^2 + n - 1$ and simultaneously constrains him/her from substituting a new rule $a_n = n^4 - 22 + n^6$ for the usual one. However, if he/she were to overcome this source of constraint he/she would be free to initiate change. What is left untheorized, in such a conceptualization, is the imposition of structural constraint by others. Because of outside systemic constraint, A's new rule can only constitute a source of social change *if* this rule is *understood and accepted* by another actor B. Implicit in this is the necessity to substitute interaction as the basic building block out of which structure can be created. Interaction embodies the systemic aspect of a simple dyadic social system. It has another actor present as a representative of external rule-governed constraint.

Before embarking upon an analysis of the interactive praxiological production of structure, I wish to preempt three possible misunderstandings. Firstly, as should be evident, in my emphasis upon the systemic qualities of structure, it is not being maintained that Giddens was not fully aware of this aspect of the essence of structure. Instead, it is argued that this facet of structure is not inherent in the process by which structures are created through structuration. Secondly, it should be observed that in replacing social action by interaction, I am not making the claim that Giddens did not conceive of social action taking place interactively. Obviously he considered social action as 'taking account of other' and as realized in an interactive context. However, the structuration perspective does not theorize the interactive dimension into the praxiological production of structure. Thirdly, as will become evident, I am not putting forward the hypothesis that all forms of interaction necessarily result in the reproduction of structure. Drawing these points together into a positive formulation: I am looking for the interactive theoretical apparatus which will facilitate the analysis of the praxiological production of structure, as a systemically constituted entity, while providing conceptual space for social continuity and change. It is this project which will from the central theme of what follows.

In order to uncover how structures are created through interaction, I will focus on structured aspects of every-day life; how every-day interaction is ordered according to structuring principles. These are structured elements which, for the most part, exist as part of the p.c. of social actors. The particular example of structured interaction which I have chosen for analysis can broadly be analysed as routinized greeting behaviour. An example of such interaction might run as follows:

Case 1

(A) Hello, how are you?
(B) Great, How are things with you?
(A) Fine, did you hear about...?
(B) Ya, but....

In this hypothetical example, A's question is action which is "...meaningful orientation to the expectation that others will act in a certain way, and to the presumable chances of success for one's own action resulting therefrom." (Weber, on the definition of social action, 1968 p. 1375, see also p. 4). The response of B is action which is specifically oriented to take account of the behaviour of A. Both these criteria are what go to make A's and B's action inherently social as distinct from action more generally conceived. "When I dip my pen in the ink or turn on my study lamp, I am acting meaningfully." (Schutz 1972 p. 15). The latter is action in the general sense. However, when such action is directed towards other (by other I mean any other agent, person acting, as distinct from a material thing) in a meaningful way then the action is usually defined as social action. "Accordingly, the fundamental requirement for social behaviour is its meaningful relatedness to the conduct of others." (Freund 1968 p. 103). Hence, "Social action does not occur when two cyclists, for example, collide unintentionally;..." (Weber 1968 p. 1375). What makes action specifically classifiable as social action is an orientation toward the probability that other will behave in a particular fashion and a consequent taking account of that probability in ordering of your action. "Thus, if at the beginning of a shower a number of people on the street put up their umbrellas at the same time, this would not ordinarily be a case of action mutually oriented to that of each other, but rather of all

123

reacting in the same way to the like need of protection from rain."
(Weber 1968 p. 23). This is action in the general sense but not
social action. The action of A and B (this time members of the crowd
putting up umbrellas) is meaningful all right with respect to the
rain. As such, it may draw upon A's and B's rules governing how to
deal with rain and consequently reproduce those rules. However,
these rules do not pertain to other as a social actor. When two such
social acts are combined and mutually related then social
interaction can be conceptualized as taking place.

In case 1 both actors are clearly acting socially and interactively.
Neither actor is acting as a person putting up an umbrella nor are
they behaving as if they were on a desert island. In effect A is
drawing upon the rule whereby 'Hello, how are you?' constitutes a
form of phatic communion eliciting a specific response. When B
replies "Fine, thanks.....' this constitutes a fulfilment of the
expectations according to the rule whereby A ordered her
behaviour. In contrast to this case I will now focus upon an instance
of interaction where a violation of the rule used by A takes place.
For this purpose I will look at Garfinkel's breaching experiments.

As a word of caution, it should be observed that, for the moment,
my intention is not to analyse the experiments as part of a
phenomenological interpretation of what constitutes the *verstehen*
intersubjectivity of actors but rather the 'mechanics' of how
structures are produced in interaction. In this sense my analytical
use of the experiments is different from that of Garfinkel. The
particular cases I have chosen are numbers six and two (renamed
here two and three respectively) from *Studies in
Ethnomethodology*, beginning with the latter:

Case 2

The victim waved his hand cheerily.
(A) How are you?
(B) How am I in regard to what? My health, my finances, my
school work, my peace of mind, my...?
(A) (Red in the face and suddenly out of control.) Look! I was just
trying to be polite. Frankly I don't give a damn how you are.

(Garfinkel 1984 p. 44)[1]

Case 2 begins as a typical example of an everyday greeting. As such, A's action is social action as in case 1. B's reply is also meaningful orientation towards A: B asks A which criteria of assessing well-being A had in mind. Consequently, interaction took place. However, when A says "'How are you?'" she does not intend what the words literally mean. This point is made by A: "'Look! I was just trying to be polite. Frankly, I don't give a damn how you are.'" Hence, B's act of interpreting the remark literally (and, consequently, asking for specific criteria by which to interpret A's greeting) was inherently inappropriate. It was this inappropriate behaviour on the part of B that made A angry. In short, B violated the rule whereby A structured her behaviour. Other possible reactions by A could have been changing the subject or expressing concern for B. Case 3 illustrates this point:

Case 3

(A) Hi,...[B]. How is your girlfriend feeling?
(B) What do you mean, "How is she feeling?" Do you mean physical or mental?
(A) I mean how is she feeling? What's the matter with you?
(...[She] looked peeved.)
(B) Nothing. Just explain a little clearer, what do you mean?
(A) Skip it. How are your Med. School applications coming?
(B) What do you mean, "How are they?"
(A) You know what I mean.
(B) I really don't.
(A) What's the matter with you? Are you sick?

(Garfinkel 1984 p. 42-3).

Here the dialogue has two parts. The first is ended by A changing subject ("Skip it.") and the second by A expressing concern for B's (mental) health ("Are you sick?"). However, as in the previous case, B's responses are not considered appropriate by A. Yet, both are acting meaningfully with respect to other i.e. it *is* an instance of two mutually related social acts which, together, constitute an instance of interaction. Despite the presence of active and reactive social action, there is a clear difference between the successful every-day greeting and the Garfinkel experiments. In the former social action meets with social action which is appropriate reciprocal action as defined by A. It is appropriate because it is a fulfilment of the expectations inherent in the rule used by A. In an every-day greeting, *B's reply is a verification of the rule used by A to structure his/her action.* In the Garfinkel experiments, A is also structuring according to social rules pertaining to other. However, when B replies 'How am I..', *B is falsifying the expectation inherent in the rule of phatic communion.* Communication breaks down because B's action is not perceived of as appropriate - hence the display of anger by A. B's action is inappropriate from a *certain perspective and according to a specific rule.* This is the perspective whereby the rule inherent in 'Hello, how are you?' is an opening to an interaction which is meaningful as a form of phatic communion. In other words, B's violation of the rule by which A structured inherently changed the systemically constituted meaning of their joint interaction. It is only when B's response is a verification of the rule used by A that the phatic communion meaning 'Hello,..' greeting behaviour is reproduced. On a socially systemic level it is the structuredness of an interaction which confers meaning. Consequently, it is in the moment of verification by B of the rule used by A that social structure is reproduced. In other words, rules have to be converted into structures through interactive affirmation by other. *Rules do not become structures purely through orientation towards other or through recursive application in structuration. Rules become structures in the moment that rule governed expectations are fulfilled.* When A said 'Hello, how are you?' she was drawing upon her p.c. knowledge of rule governed behaviour. As social action, this rule was a guide whereby A meaningfully oriented herself towards B. The unintentional effect of such action should have been to reproduce a certain social order, as in case 1. However, B failed to react in a certain, highly specific, way and consequently neither reinforced A's expectations or knowledge of a rule nor contributed to the structuredness of the phatic communion interaction surrounding greetings.

In case 1, the inherent lack of arbitrariness of A's question and B's answer is representative of the mutual labour necessary in order to produce social order through social interaction. As phatic communion, they are two social acts which have the unintentional effect of reproducing a certain rule-governed social order. Viewed on a systemic level, A's social action and B's reaction are contributing to the structuredness of social order. They are reproducing the structures of an ordered social world. Their ability to do this is partly determined by the prior structuredness of this world which predated their act of reproducing it. In case 2, A acts initially and says, "Hello, how are you?" She is drawing upon her knowledge of how she expects B to react. A may believe this expectation to be a certainty. Hence, she is angry when B does not behave according to expectations. Case 2 demonstrates that appropriate reciprocal action is not a certainty but a probability. Prior to the reaction of B, it is only highly probable that her action will contribute to the structuredness of social order. This implies that the opening remark "Hello, how are you?" only contributes to social order in a specific form of interaction. Both cases one and two are interaction but only in the former are the structures of phatic communion reproduced.

Prior to saying "Hello how are you?", A has knowledge with respect to the probable reaction of other. Based upon that knowledge she says, "Hello, how are you?" However, it is an act which will only contribute to systemically defined structural features if B fulfils rule-governed expectations. With B's appropriate reciprocal action (as defined by a given rule) the social structures of greetings are reproduced. Structures are not reproduced in the moment of the recursive reproduction of a rule through structuration. They are reproduced by the fulfilment of the expectations inherent in a rule through the actions of others. I will retain the concept of structuration to signify A's initial rule governed social act. The actual reproduction of structure, through rule affirmation by B, will be referred to as restructuration. *It is with the act of restructuration that social structures are reproduced.* Without restructuration there are no social structures only rules. Consequently, it is only with a specific form of social interaction, which affirms a shared perception of a rule, that structure is reproduced. The reproduction of structure through restructuring interaction can be represented as follows in fig. 8.1 (see over).

In the example of putting up umbrellas in the rain neither A's nor B's action was intended to be social. Neither was taking account of other. To reiterate, this should not be taken to imply that all action or interaction which takes account of other ipso facto contributes to the reproduction of social structures. In a framework which attributes the production of structures to social action or interaction, as generally conceived, this would be the case. However, as observed, with the introduction of the concept of restructuration this is no longer so. In case 2, the probability that B will respond appropriately is high. Possibly A assumes it to be a certainty (see

Fig. 8.1

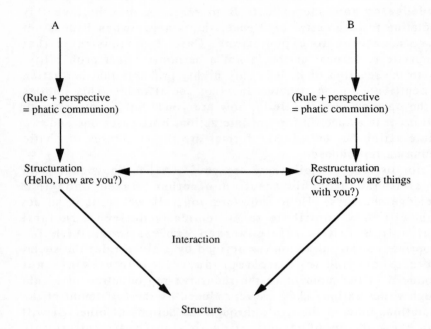

next chapter) because it is a structure which is a highly familiar part of the every-day-world. It is experienced by A with a 'natural attitude' where there is suspension of doubt. As a structuration practice it has possibly never failed to meet with restructuration and, consequently, contribute to the structuredness of the social world. However, in this case what exists as a certainty, as part of the 'natural attitude', turns out to be a probability. A's action was social action, intended to take account of other, which failed to contribute to the reproduction of social structures. It was also behaviour which was structured by A, with respect to her previous experience, and yet its subjective structuredness proved irrelevant to the reproduction of the structures of the social system in question. In addition, B's reaction was meaningfully oriented towards A. In other words, there were two mutually related social acts: interaction took place. Yet, social structure was not reproduced as an unintentional effect. In short, through the absence of restructuration *by B*, A's act of structuration has failed to contribute to the recreation of structure.

128

In assessing the failure of the breaching experiments to reproduce social structures, it should be observed that A was fully aware and understood the rule by which B was responding. B's reaction to A was meaningfully and intelligibly directed towards A. It was not total chaos as in the following imaginary example:

Case 4

(A) How are you?
(B) Pink, blue or yellow ?
(A) Are you nuts? Why are you wasting my time?...............

In the 'breaching experiment' (case 2), B's reaction is a literal interpretation of the question 'Hello, how are you?' as a request for information. A is fully aware of this and expresses it: "Look! I was just trying to be polite. Frankly I don't give a damn how you are." In other words, with respect to a certain interpretation (perceived by A) of 'Hello, how are you?' B's response could have been wholly appropriate. This means that reciprocal action is only appropriate as defined with respect to a *specific* point of view. Actor A understood the rule by which B was attempting to reproduce structure, but she defined B's affirmation of such a rule as inappropriate. In short, the structuration and restructuration reproduction of social structures is not a simple question of action and reaction. What constitutes a restructuration practice can be, and often is, contested by actors participating in the reproduction of structure. When A refuses to accept B's act of reaction as appropriate he/she was rejecting the validity of converting a specific rule into structure. To put it another way, as the labour of two or more actors, structural reproduction is an intensely political act (a point which will be explored more fully in chapters 12 and 13). It is political in the sense that, instead of reproducing structures passively as 'carriers' of structure, actors constantly monitor and contest what should constitute the 'correct' structured interpretation of action. Through not restructuring with respect to the phatic communion perspective, B has both prevented the reproduction of 'Hello, how are you?' as the 'carrier' of specific structures and violated the rule by which A structured her action. Due to the high level of intentionality inherent in such a violation of rules, I will refer to to such reactions as *destructuration*. This is to distinguish them from responses where rules appear as either unintelligible or absent. The latter I will call *non-restructuration*. The commonest manifestation of non-

129

restructuration is where B does not know how to affirm the rule used by A. As a limiting case, *absent restructuration* will be used to describe the complete absence of a reaction to a rule. For example, A's act of structuration elicits no response because B is deaf. Summarizing this difference I am left with a four-fold typology of social interaction, which can be represented graphically in figs 8.1, 8.2, 8.3 and 8.4. (fig. 8.1 has been repeated for comparative purposes).

In case 2, A refused to accept B's request for criteria of well-being as valid. Both actors are reacting according to different rules and both have refused to recognize the appropriateness of the rule used by other. This implies two things: 1) both actors' social action has been rendered 'private' by other and 2) the same act by B can be interpreted as either structuration or restructuration depending upon the rule applied to it. Developing the latter point, according to the rule of 'phatic communion' the reply 'How am in..' is an act of destructuration. However, according to B's rule concerning well-being it calls for a reply by A. In short, it is also an act of structuration. As such, it fails to meet with restructuration from A: 'Frankly I don't give a damn how you are'. In other words, A's reply is an act of destructuration which renders B's act of structuration 'private'.

The ability of the same act to be both structuration and destructuration, according to different rules, can be interestingly illustrated by a reinterpretation of fig 8.4. Imagine for a moment that A were to decide that B's absence of a reply were not due to deafness nor any other inability to respond. Imagine instead that B's failure to return a greeting *is* a deliberate withholding of reciprocity and A were to recognize it as such. In such a case, B's absent reply is not a non-event but a social act according to the rules concerning snubs (see McHugh et al 1974 p. 115-19). As observed by McHugh et al there are two crucial elements in the interactive reproduction of snubs. Firstly, B's reaction to A is ordered according to the rules governing snubs whereby the absence of a reply constitutes a deliberate denial of other. Secondly, it is crucial that A recognize B's action as a reaction which violates the rules of phatic communion and accords with the rules for snubs (McHugh et al 1975 p. 131). Hence, for the structures pertaining to snubs to be reproduced, A's act of recognition constitutes the act of restructuration by which snubs are reproduced. This can be represented in fig. 8.5.

In addition to the rather novel terms of restructuration and destructuration, I also wish to introduce another distinction. In the

130

Typology of Interaction

Fig. 8.1

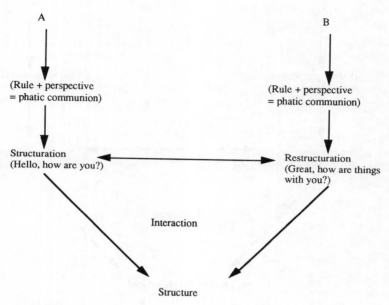

Fig. 8.2

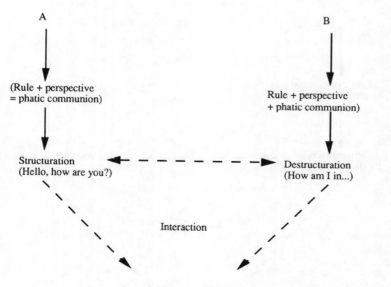

Fig. 8.3

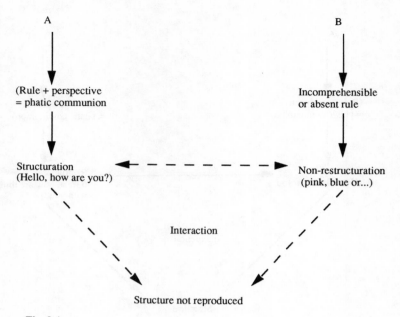

Fig. 8.4

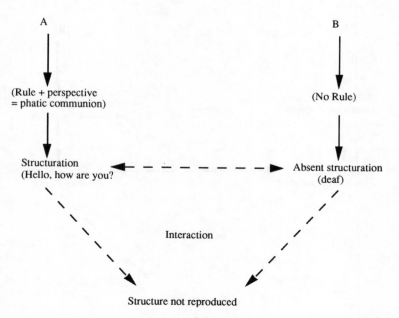

132

Fig. 8.5

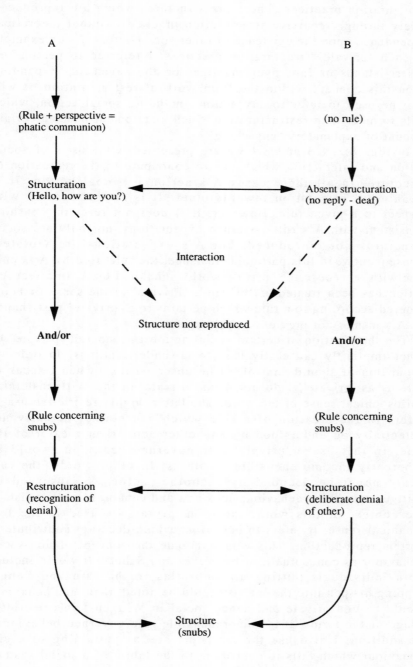

A   B

(Rule + perspective =
phatic communion)   (no rule)

Structuration   ◄─────────►   Absent structuration
(Hello, how are you?)   (no reply - deaf)

                              Interaction

                    Structure not reproduced

And/or   **And/or**

(Rule concerning   (Rule concerning
snubs)   snubs)

Restructuration   ◄─────────►   Structuration
(recognition of   (deliberate denial
denial)   of other)

                              Structure
                              (snubs)

previous chapter I briefly alluded to the idea of 'private' structuration practices. These are structures which are reproduced solely through recursive structuration practices without theoretical dependence upon the existence of other social actors. As an example of such 'private' structuration practices, I referred to persons on desert islands or Jane avoiding lines on the pavement. Expanding upon this concept within the framework of restructuration, it will also be used to refer to any action, including social action, which fails to meet with restructuration. Such a statement needs a certain amount of explanatory 'unpacking'.

In Figs 8.2, 8.3 and 8.4 we are presented with forms of social action and interaction which fail to contribute to the recreation of structure. In all these cases A's action is social action. It is meaningful orientation towards other. It is also structured with respect to a given rule. However, if B does not react in a fashion consistent with A's rule-governed expectations, not only are social structures not reproduced, but A's expectations are violated. Consequently, in this particular instance, the rule used by A is only true with respect to the 'private world' inhabited by A. In effect A's action has been treated as 'private'. 'Private' in the sense of being ordered according to a rule which pertains to a 'private' past shaped by A's memory of previous social experience.

The theorization of certain social action as rendered 'private' by other implicitly can easily lead to misunderstandings. In order to avoid this, it should first of all be observed that, when I speak of actions as 'private', I do not mean 'private' in the Wittgensteinian philosophical sense of the word. The latter, highly restrictive usage, refers to the creation of a rule which can neither actually nor potentially be understood by any other actor than creator of the rule. In this usage 'private' rule-governed behaviour would be inherently incomprehensible to others. In other words, the rule could never be decoded by a another actor. As observed by Wittgenstein, such behaviour does not, and cannot, actually exist. In the context of this work, the term 'private' is used in the less technical sense. It refers to behaviour which does not contribute to system reproduction. This would include the concept of non-social behaviour as conceptualized by Weber and Schutz. It would include both individuals putting up umbrellas in the rain and Schutz dipping his pen into the ink (it should be noted, that such behaviour would be non-private and hence social in Wittgenstein's restricted usage of the term - it is comprehensible rule-governed behaviour). In addition, I also use the term 'private' as pertaining to social behaviour which fails to contribute to the fabric of a social system.

The need to extend the usage of the term, to social behaviour which fails to feed into systemic reproduction, is derived from the addition of the concepts of restructuration, destructuration and non-restructuration. The introduction of restructuration means that it is no longer the individual actor who decides if his/her action will contribute to system reproduction. Hence, it is possible for an actor to act according to rule-governed behaviour which takes account of other - structuration - but that fails to reproduce social structures. Through the absence of restructuration by other, a given form of systemically meaningful interactively created order has not been recreated. In other words, while structuration is a necessary, it is not a sufficient, condition for structural reproduction. This means that, while inherently social in subjective orientation, in the absence of restructuration the rule governed behaviour of A has been treated as if it were 'private'. It is treated as meaningful only with respect to the 'private' realm of A. By not being defined as systemically meaningful, A's action fails to contribute to the fabric of the larger social system. It is social action which has become treated as 'private' through the violation of the expectations inherent in the rule by which the social action was ordered. This can be represented as in fig 8.6.

Not only does the concept of restructuration provide a necessary interactive dimension to the reproduction of social structures, but it also provides a new praxiological method of dealing with the initial creation and demise of social structures. In this context I will analyse the creation and demise of structures through restructuration while methodologically bracketing the 'invention' of new power resources (see chapter 10).

When A interacts with B, the structuration practice of A only potentially contributes to the reproduction of social structure. If B fails to restructure, a systemic structure is not reproduced praxiologically. Suppose we were to imagine that A 'invents' a new structuration practice and as such introduces 'private structuration practices' into the 'public realm'. In such a case actor A can be said to have overcome his/her internal p.c. and d.c. sources of structural constraint. For example, despite his/her knowledge of rule $a_n = n^2 + n - 1$ he/she has decided to structure according to rule $a_n = n^4 - 22 + n^6$. In this case, the probability that B restructures will tend to be low. B's knowledge of $a_n = n^2 + n - 1$ will represent an outside systemic source of structural constraint. B may either destructure (if he understands but rejects the rule) as in fig. 8.2 or, alternatively, B may non-restructure (if he does not know how to

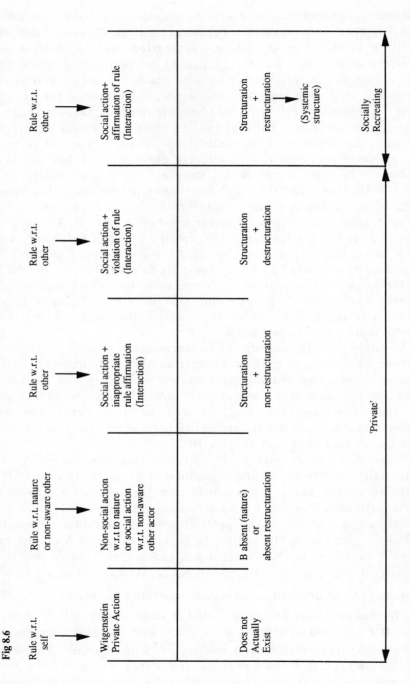

Fig 8.6

| Rule w.r.t self | Rule w.r.t nature or non-aware other | Rule w.r.t. other | Rule w.r.t. other | Rule w.r.t. other |

Wigenstein Private Action | Non-social action w.r.t to nature or social action w.r.t. non-aware other actor | Social action + inappropriate rule affirmation (Interaction) | Social action + violation of rule (Interaction) | Social action+ affirmation of rule (Interaction)

Does not Actually Exist | B absent (nature) or absent restructuration | Structuration + non-restructuration | Structuration + destructuration | Structuration + restructuration → (Systemic structure)

'Private' | | | | Socially Recreating

* (w.r.t. is an abbreviation of 'with respect to'.)

136

affirm the new rule) as in fig. 8.3. However, there is a possibility that B will restructure. If B understands and accepts $a_n = n^4 - 22 + n^6$ as a valid rule for restructuring interaction then a new structure will be created. When this structure is purely confined to the interaction of A and B it is a structure of minimal social systemic significance. However, if further actors C, D,E,F,G,H,I,J,L,............... were all to structure and restructure according to rule $a_n = n^4 - 22 + n^6$, the 'new' social structure would be of greater systemic significance.

With the production of new social structures it is usually difficult to assign them to specific actors. Social structures are simply noted to change or occur. However, there are notable exceptions: "[t]he urge to greet relatives and friends at Christmas, the homeliest holiday of the year, and to wish them happiness in the coming year is so general and deeply imbued that it is difficult for many to realize that our pleasant and convenient method of doing so was invented not much more than 100 years ago." (Bunday 1954 p. 16). The convenient method to which Bunday is referring is to the invention of the first Christmas card, which was designed in 1843 by John Calcott Horsley on the initiative of his friend Henry Cole (Bunday 1954 p. 6). The Christmas card is now so much a structural feature of social interaction, in most 'Western' societies, that when Bunday did a survey on the topic he found that " the majority thought that Christmas cards and the invention of book printing coincided. Many others believed that Christmas cards date back to the time of the introduction of engraving." (Bunday 1954 p. 16-7).

The inventor of the Christmas card, Henry Cole was known as eccentric: "...the columns of the respectable *Art Journal*, would label him 'a man of wild theories and vague speculations which are Utopian in their character',..." (Bunday 1954 p. 7). Possibly the Christmas card was another of his eccentricities. One thing that is certain is that in 1843, and for several years later, no-one had any idea that this inherently trivial act would have such a profound and lasting effect on social patterns surrounding Christmas. "To the early manufacturers, Christmas cards appeared to be a merely ephemeral business. As they experienced a positive reaction to and growing demand for them, they were quick to follow up their chances in the most expedient manner. These early manufacturers considered Christmas cards only a temporary vogue which would pass as unostentatiously as it began, and so concentrated on a quick turn-over 'while the craze lasted.'" (Bunday 1954 p. 37). By 1880 the 'craze' had built up to 11.5 million or 4.5 tons of Christmas cards sent during Christmas week through the G.P.O. in London (Bunday

1954 p. 6).

When, in 1843, Cole decided to have 1000 Christmas cards printed he was acting as an individual who had no reliable or certain way of knowing if people would react favourably to his idea. The success or failure of the Christmas card was dependent upon others. People could have regarded the Christmas card as a manifestation of Cole's 'eccentricity'. As it happened, people responded with appropriate reciprocal action. Cole's initial act of structuration met with restructuration and new social structures surrounding the ritual of Christmas were created. Not only did this initial act meet with restructuration but the early manufacturers in general experienced "a positive reaction to and a growing demand for them." In other words, the early acts of structuration met with restructuration and have, by and large, met with restructuration ever since. Consequently, they have remained as a permanent structural feature of society.

The demise of social structures can happen either through the absence of structuration or restructuration practices. Beginning with the latter, since every act of structuration is dependent upon restructuration, in order to contribute to the reproduction of social structures, social structures are inherently continuously potentially subject to demise. As figs 8.2, 8.3 and 8.4 demonstrated, even the most apparently permanent structures are not always successfully reproduced in interaction. What makes some structures inherently more permanent than others is linked to probability of restructuration. In fig. 8.2 an act of structuration by A, with a high probability of meeting with interactive restructuration, failed to contribute to the reproduction of the structures of phatic communion. Obviously, in that specific case it would be absurd to speak of the overall demise of a given social structure on a systemic level since that particular structure was simultaneously being reproduced by millions of other actors over the globe. In other words, important structural features are not going to disappear because of relatively contingent events, such as a specific experiment carried out by a given sociologist. However, it does illustrate the point that even the most permanent structural features of a society are potentially subject to demise over time. It is not at all inconceivable that continued non-restructuration and destructuration practices could, over time, result in the demise of the phatic communion perspective as a systemic feature.

It should also be observed that, aside from the absence of restructuration, the demise of structures can take place through the absence of initial structuration practices. Structures are recreated through structuration plus restructuration as properties of interaction. Structuration is not sufficient for the creation of a social structure and restructuration can't take place in the absence of structuration. Consequently, both are necessary for the reproduction of structure.

The theorization of the interactive dimension of the production of structure implies a reconceptualization of the process whereby structures are carried outside of interactive reproduction. As yet, I have not shown how actors know how to structure and restructure. In other words, if social structures only exist in the moment of interaction, how are the same structures recreated again and again? Since structures do not have an 'out-there-existence', except in the moment of restructuring interaction, how are they 'carried' outside interaction so as to be reproducible again and again in a social system? While Giddens' analysis of p.c. and d.c. provides excellent conceptual tools for analysing this phenomenon, the introduction of restructuration necessitates a certain reformulation of these concepts. This will form the central theme of the next chapter.

9 Paradigms and interaction

In the previous chapter I showed how structures could be represented as produced in interaction through restructuration. If, as described, structures only 'exist' in interaction when they are reproduced or produced the obvious next question must be: how is such reproduction possible? Arising from that, what is the nature of what is constantly being reproduced?

As already explained, Giddens' answer to the first question is that: outside the moment of action, they are carried as memory traces retrieved through d.c. and p.c.. While there is a continuous flow between d.c. and p.c. there is a negative bar between them and u.c.. This bar is necessary in order for an actor to maintain ontological security by controlling motives and drives which derive from u.c.. Ontological security is maintained through 'trust' built up by the routinization of day-to-day existence. Routinization is the conceptual bridge between ontological security on the one hand and social structures on the other. Like Giddens does, I would wish to argue that social structures are 'carried' outside their moment of creation. However, because of the replacement of the centrality of action with interaction and the introduction of the concepts of restructuration, destructuration and non-restructuration d.c., and especially p.c. have to be reinterpreted to a certain extent.

The ability to 'go on' is fundamentally linked to Husserl's concept of the 'natural attitude'. The fundamental prerequisite of the natural attitude is the suspension of doubt. "The reverse of the natural attitude is radical 'Cartesian' doubt which skeptically denies the objectivity of perception, the adequacy of knowledge or the utility of past experience." (Heritage 1984 p. 41). Specifically this involves suspension of doubt with respect to others and the 'reality' of the 'world-out-there' and simultaneously placing an epoche upon the possibility that others 'inhabit' a different 'reality'. In other words, the actor assumes that, 'there is an objective world out there which others perceive in more or less the same way that I do'. Taking the analogy of Wittgenstein's duck-rabbit picture:

The picture can be seen in two entirely different ways (Wittgenstein 1968 p.195). The change is the result of a visual gestalt. However, in the 'natural attitude' an actor does not see things as things. When I see a knife and fork I don't see pieces of metal which appear as a fork and as a knife. I see knife and fork (see Kuhn 1970 p.85 for similar point). Hence it would make little sense for me to say 'Now I am seeing this as a knife and fork.' (Wittgenstein 1968 p.195).

If A 'inhabits' a subjective reality where the duck-rabbit picture appears purely as a duck and B one where it is only rabbit and if A and B were to interact with respect to the picture, appropriate reciprocal action would not take place. The dialogue might be as follows:

A: That picture would be better if there were water and fish in the background.
B: What! I don't get the idea, is this some attempt at surrealism? Who has ever heard of a rabbit drawn against a background of water and fish!

Returning to dialogue two, what B replied made complete sense with respect to a reality, or view of the world, where 'Hello, how are you?' is not phatic communion but an inquiry about B's state of well-being. This is brought out by A when she says, "Look! I was

141

just trying to be polite. Frankly I don't give a damn how you are." This implies that for appropriate reciprocal action to take place A and B must perceive the same, or a broadly similar, subjective reality.

Aside from 'inhabiting' the same/similar subjective world, B must also believe in the existence of the 'objective' out-there-world. This is the suspension of Cartesian doubt referred to already. With the 'natural attitude' an actor "...brackets...the doubt that the world and its objects might be otherwise than it appears to him." (Schutz 1971 p. 229). Moreover, the ability of A to expect rule affirmation is dependent upon the idea that the world is ordered in a relatively static fashion. The past must be able to serve as a guide to the present and future. If this were not the case appropriate reciprocal action would have no meaning. It is appropriate with respect to the previous experiences of A and B. Things will continue more or less as they were. "Fundamentally governed by pragmatic considerations [to 'go on'], the natural attitude involves the suspension of doubt that things might not be as they appear or that past experience may not be a valid guide to present and future experience." (Heritage 1984 p. 41).

In the case of dialogue one, the reciprocal action of B can be repeated again. At some future point this in turn will constitute experience upon which another interaction can be constituted. The experience of past greetings can be used as a guide for future action. Of course, that presupposes that greeting situations are recognized as similar. B may see a rabbit in the field and see a similarity between it and Wittgenstein's duck-rabbit picture (see Wittgenstein 1968 p. 197). B looking at the same landscape will not see any similarity and consequently there will be no repetition of experience involved at any level. Thus there "...are repetitions only from a certain point of view. (...) But this means that, for logical reasons, there must always be a point of view - such as a system of expectations, anticipations, assumptions, or interests -before there can be any repetition; which point of view, consequently,cannot merely be the result of repetition." (Popper 1963 p. 44-5). In this sense every social action presupposes a set of expectations or theories about the world (Popper 1972 p. 21). Actor's subjective reality constitutes a framework with respect to which the repeated actions of others constitute part of an ordered totality. The nature of the future reproduction of that reality is consequently reproduced against the 'horizon' of that subjective reality. It is the sharedness of the subjective perception of social order which constitutes the root of the assumption of objectivity. This assumption is so strong, in every-day action, that whatever the subjectivity pertaining to a particular moment it will always be seen as objective. This is even the case when 'outside reality' changes due to reflection against a different subjective perspective. Substituting the word paradigm for subjective reality: "Looking at the moon, the convert to Copernicanism does not say, 'I used to see a planet, but now I see a satellite.'....Instead, a convert to the new astronomy would say, 'I once took the moon to be (or saw the moon as) a planet, but I was mistaken.'" (Kuhn 1970 p. 115).

If subjective reality is a horizon against which to interpret, this implies a rejection of a theory of knowledge based upon induction where the mind is a blank sheet or 'empty bucket' filled with facts through repeated exposure to them. This in turn means that "[w]ithout waiting, passively, for impressions to impress or impose regularities upon us, we actively try to impose regularities upon the world. We try to discover similarities in it, and to interpret it in terms of laws invented by us. Without waiting for premises we jump to conclusions. These may have to be discarded later, should observation show that they are wrong." (Popper 1963 p. 46). In short, the observation of regularities presupposes a deductive process based on a given frame of reference and expectations (Popper 1963 p. 47). Relating this to the concept of the natural attitude: "...it is characteristic of the natural attitude that it takes the world and its objects for granted until counter proof imposes itself. As long as the once established scheme of reference, the system of our and other people's warranted experiences works, as long as the actions and operations performed under its guidance yield desired results, we can trust these experiences. We are not interested in finding out whether this world really does exist or whether it is merely a coherent system of consistent appearances. We have no reason to cast doubt upon warranted experiences which, so we believe, give us things as they really are. It needs special motivation, such as the eruption of a 'strange' experience not subsumable under the stock of knowledge at hand or inconsistent with it, to make us revise our former beliefs." (Schutz 1971 p. 228).

The eruption or strange experience which makes social actors revise their expectations could be interpreted as either Popper's test of falsification or Kuhn's anomalous experiences. If the former, the subjective reality is like a scientific theory for Popper. If the latter, the natural attitude is a paradigm which is resistant to change, though not impervious to overthrow. An anomalous experience may simply present itself as a puzzle within the existing paradigm or contribute to provoking a crisis which will in the long term lead to the overthrow of the paradigm in favour of another paradigm (Kuhn 1970 p. 146-7). Possibly the best way of deciding in favour of one option or the other is by examining Garfinkel's breaching experiments.

In 8.2, B did not change his views on how greetings 'should' be constituted. However, this constitutes only one anomalous experience within a context of an often repeated form of social interaction. Consequently, it does not constitute sufficient evidence on which to base an assessment (unless Popper were interpreted very literally). The 'student counselling experiment' is a better test case in that the subjects of the experiment were subjected to multiple inconsistencies in a social situation which they were not that familiar with.

In this experiment students were asked to take part in an alternative form of psychotherapy. "In each case, the subject was asked to describe the background of his problem and to ask the 'counsellor' at least ten questions about it. Each question was to be designed so as to permit a 'yes' or 'no' answer. The subject and the experimenter-counsellor were situated in adjoining rooms connected by intercom. The subject was required to tape-record his reflections on each answer after disconnecting the intercom 'so that the counsellor will not hear your remarks'. Unknown to the subject, the experimenter-counsellor predetermined his sequence of 'yes' and 'no' answers with a table of random numbers. At the completion of the questions and answers the subject was asked to summarize his impressions of the exchange as a whole." (Heritage 1984 p. 90).

Case 1

S: Ok,....I happen to be of the Jewish faith and have been dating a Gentile girl now for two months. My dad is not directly opposed to the situation, but I feel at the same time that he is not exactly pleased with it....he has never said don't date her, but at the same time he will come up with digs.... My question is, do you feel under the present circumstances that I should continue or stop dating this girl? Let me put this in a positive way. Do you feel that I should continue dating this girl?

E: My answer is no.

S: No. Well that is kind of interesting. I kinda feel that there is no great animosity between Dad and I, but perhaps he feels greater dislike will grow out of this....

Should I have further discussion with Dad over this subject about dating the Gentile girl?

E: My answer is yes.

S: Well I feel that is reasonable but I really don't know what to say to him. I mean he seems to be not really too understanding....

If after having the conversation with Dad and he says to continue dating her, but at the same time he gives me the impression that he is really not, he really does not want me to date her, but he is only doing it because he wants to be a good dad, should under these conditions, should I continue dating her?

E: My answer is yes.

S: Well I am actually surprised at the answer. I expected a no answer on that. Perhaps this is because you are not quite aware of my Dad and his reactions....

E:......

S:........

Do you feel that I should tell the girl that I am dating the problems that I am having at home over her religion?

E: My answer is no.

S: Well once again I am surprised. Of course,....

(Garfinkel 1984 p. 80-2).

While the subjects in these experiments all found the answers given surprising, they all considered them useful answers to the questions asked (Garfinkel 1984 p. 89-90). "When answers were incongruous or contradictory, subjects were able to continue by finding that the 'adviser' had learned more in the meantime, or that he had decided to change his mind, or that perhaps he was not sufficiently acquainted with the intricacies of the problem, or the fault was in the question so that another phrasing was required." (Garfinkel 1984 p. 91).

This means that when the reciprocal reply deviated from the calculated one it was explained away by postulating that things were not quite as they appeared: "Perhaps this is because you are not quite aware of my dad and his reactions..." The analogy holds with the physicist who in the pre-Einsteinian era, based on Newtonian mechanics, calculates that the planet Uranus will move in a particular orbit. When Uranus fails to move as predicted the scientist in question does not reject the paradigm of Newtonian physics, instead "[h]e suggests that there must be a hitherto unknown planet p' which disturbs the path of p [Uranus]." (Lakatos

1978 p. 17). In short, the 'natural attitude' is a paradigm which can continue to maintain itself in a permanent ocean of anomalies. (see Lakatos 1978 p. 6).

In the experiment, this paradigm was based on the permanent assumption of a pattern. This assumption was there even with the first advice given. "Throughout there was a concern and search for pattern. Pattern, however, was perceived from the very beginning. Pattern was likely to be seen in the first evidence of the 'advice'." (Garfinkel 1984 p. 91). In other words, in the paradigm within which the answers were interpreted there was a fundamental assumption of order. However bizarre the answers were, not only was the paradigm left in tact but randomness was never postulated as a possibility (Garfinkel 1984 p. 91). Not only do actors not have any reason to move into cognitive, social or linguistic disorder but order is assumed to exist (see Barnes 1988 p. 38).

The paradigm of p.c. is based on an inherent assumption of order. It is an assumption which is necessary for social action (see Popper 1972 p. 21). If this were not the case the concept of rule affirmation would be meaningless. Furthermore, it is also necessary to assume that others perceive this order with respect to the same paradigm. The literal interpretation of the question,'Hello, how are you?' is not random. It constitutes part of an order with respect to a paradigm within which such requests are interpreted literally.

The assumption of order is also based on a further presupposition. It is a basic expectation that it is possible to reason from particular instances in the past to future instances. If the correct reply to 'Hello, how are you.' is 'Fine thanks,...' this will remain true in the future. If this were not the case, and the future were only contingently dependent upon the past, appropriate reciprocal action would be impossible. However, as observed by Popper when commenting on Hume, there is no logical necessity for this to be so. It is not logically justified to reason from repeated past experiences to other instances of which we have no experience (Popper 1972 p. 4). Moreover, it is not justified to reason inductively from individual instances to a general principle. A general principle concerning a given order cannot be logically induced from repeated instances. People only do so because of psychological predisposition. This conclusion led Hume to conclude that "Our 'knowledge' is unmasked as being not only of the nature of belief, but of rationally indefensible belief - of an irrational faith." (Popper 1972 p. 5). Kant's resolution of the problem was that "'Our intellect does not draw its laws from nature but imposes its laws upon nature,'..." (Popper 1963 p. 48). This position has a

146

certain plausibility in the sense that knowledge is deductively derived and based on an assumption of order. However, as argued by Popper, it goes too far in claiming "...that these laws are necessarily true, or that we necessarily succeed in imposing them upon nature,..." (Popper 1972 p. 48). In other words, the existence of an assumed order in the mind of the beholder does not necessarily imply that the natural world is so ordered or operates according to the natural laws attributed to it as a causal explanation for that order.

Unlike the natural world the social world is a human creation produced through interaction. This means that while Kant's solution to Hume's problem of induction may not work for the natural world it does for the social. The orderedness of social life is produced in interaction by actors who through their assumption of order create and recreate order. While the laws of nature are not created by observers of that order, in the social world they are.

This social orderedness presupposes a grammar of mutual intelligibility based on a shared symptomatic grammar of the social world. To take an example from Wittgenstein: "When we learnt the use of the phrase 'so-and-so has a toothache' we were pointed out certain kinds of behaviour of those who were said to have a toothache. As an instance of this behaviour let us take holding your cheek. Suppose that by observation I found that in certain cases whenever these first criteria told me a person had a toothache, a red patch appeared on the person's cheek. Supposing I now said to someone 'I see A has a toothache, he's got a red patch on his cheek.' He may ask me 'How do you know A has a toothache when you see a red patch?' I should then point out that certain phenomena had always coincided with the appearance of the red patch. Now one may go on and ask: 'How do you know that he has got a toothache when he holds his cheek?' The answer to this might be, 'I say, he has toothache when he holds his cheek because I hold my cheek when I have a toothache.' But what if we went on asking: 'And why do you suppose that toothache corresponds to holding your cheek?' You will be at a loss to answer this question, and find that here we strike rock bottom, that is we have come down to conventions." (Wittgenstein 1969 p. 24).

I would argue that the reason for being at a loss how to answer is that the person asking these questions is clearly working from a different paradigm. It is a paradigm within which the symptomatic reading of the social world must be inherently different. In this sense, the choice between two "...paradigms proves to be a choice between incompatible modes of community life." (Kuhn 1970 p. 94).

As such, a shared paradigm of p.c. is a common community of meaning and rules: we know A has a toothache from the commonly shared rule that holding your cheek means that someone has a toothache. Similarly when we meet someone, we know that 'Hello, how are you?' is phatic communion because of a shared paradigm. In order for two actors to be able to interact successfully it is necessary for them both to see the duck-rabbit picture as either a duck or a rabbit.

Taking an example from Marx, an object or a thing can be classified as having two values: use value or exchange value. "The coat is a use-value that satisfies a particular need." (Marx 1976 p. 132). It keeps a person warm, a quality attributable to its specific physical qualities (Marx 1976 p. 126). This coat could be made by one individual (good at sewing) for another. This scenario would hold true in a feudal society, in an Indian village or a capitalist society (Marx 1976 p. 131-2). However, unlike in a feudal society or in an Indian village, in a capitalist society coats can also be commodities and, as such, be a source of virtually limitless wealth (Marx 1976 p. 149). The reason for this is that in capitalism the coat is perceived as exchange value. Interaction within capitalist relations of production presupposes a paradigm within which the concept of exchange value makes sense. Exchange value is not branded into the cloth of the coat but is a social hieroglyphic (Marx 1976 p. 167). Hence, interaction between actors with the coat as a commodity presupposes a common practical consciousness (see Marx 1967 p. 166-7) paradigm within which the coat is perceived as exchange value.

The natural attitude paradigm is not only a common way of perceiving things but also a set of shared examples and a way of behaving with respect to those examples or situations (see Kuhn 1970 p. 181-91). As a paradigm it is more than a view but also a shared ability to 'go on'. As emphasized by Giddens, it is also a set of rules. An actor's knowledge of these rules is shown both in their ability to apply them, as manifest through their ability to 'go on' in social practice, and by their ability to verify rules used by other.

At the level of p.c., knowing a rule means applying it in varying circumstances. Taking an example from Kuhn, let us say a sociologist were to observe a scientific community with a shared paradigm. A component of this paradigm is a commitment to Newton's Second Law of Motion. This law is generally written as $f = ma$ (Kuhn 1970 p.188). The latter is of course a d.c. formulation of the rule. However, as such, this would tell us little about what it was like to be a member of this community. To know a rule is more than to utter it. The student who wishes to 'join' this community has first of all to learn how to analyse a set of examples shown to him/her using $f = ma$. He/she has to see that these examples have something in common which makes them analysable using $f = ma$. After being shown these examples he/she must understand the meaning of the phrase 'and so on' and from the examples given 'go on' to examples 'beyond' (Wittgenstein 1968 § 208). Because of the infinity of future examples, "...we might imagine rails instead of a rule. And infinitely long rails correspond to the unlimited application of a rule." (Wittgenstein 1968 § 218). This means viewing other examples as similar. However, since not all examples prove identical it means not only applying the rule but transforming it. "For the case of free fall, $f = ma$ becomes $mg = m$ (d^2s/dt^2); for the simple pendulum it is transformed to $mg \sin0 = -ml(d^20/dt^2)$;... and for more complex situations, such as the gyroscope, it takes still other forms, the family resemblances of which to $f = ma$ [sic] is still harder to discover." (Kuhn 1970 p. 188-9). Part of the paradigm is not only to see a family of resemblances but also to transform the relevant rules accordingly.

When parts of the paradigm become promulgated they form part of d.c.. As p.c., this paradigm can be described as a set of subjective 'assumptions' which constitute the deductive basis upon which to act. D.c. is an objectivisation in the sense of being faced critically as something other which can be 'faced' as a hypotheses: "..subjective knowledge becomes criticizable only when it becomes objective. And it becomes objective when we say what we think; and even more so when we write it down, or print it." (Popper 1972 p. 25).

While it is possible analytically to separate p.c. knowledge from d.c., it is important to note that d.c. is an articulation within an overall framework of p.c.. Even a scientific rule such as $f = ma$ is embedded in a p.c. paradigm. As such, it is dependent for its applicability upon a myriad network of tacit assumptions (Kuhn 1970 p. 190-2). As such, $f = ma$ only has meaning with respect to the non articulated p.c. paradigm which enables actors to apply and adapt the rule appropriately.

As emphasized by Giddens, not only are d.c. and p.c. inextricably intertwined but the move of knowledge from one to the other is highly fluid. The level of this flow changes with circumstances. Anomalous behaviour by self or other is when this is most likely to happen. A sociologist subjecting him/herself to phenomenological *epoche* - "...the suspension of our belief in the reality of the world..." (Schutz 1971 p. 229) - would be an example of anomalous behaviour of self contributing rapid movement of knowledge from p.c. to d.c.. Another different example of the same phenomenon is the social actor who feels uncomfortable with his/her behaviour. Garfinkel's study of Agnes is a case in point. Agnes was a nineteen year old girl who had a penis and testicles. She regarded herself as female and behaved as a 120 percent female (Garfinkel 1984 p. 129). However her possession of normal male sexual organs made her behaviour a continuous trial where she had to prove her femaleness. This made her an acute observer of the behaviour of other women. Due to her anomalous position "Agnes was self-consciously equipped to teach normals how normals make sexuality happen in commonplace settings as an obvious, familiar feature, recognizable, natural, and serious matter of fact. Her speciality consisted of treating the 'natural facts of life' of socially recognized [sic], socially managed sexuality as a managed production..." (Garfinkel 1984 p. 180). In other words, she treated what is normally p.c. knowledge as d.c.. It is this move from p.c. to d.c. which made her able explain to 'normals' how sexuality is managed in day-to-day life.

The transfer of knowledge from p.c. to d.c. can occur in everyday life when an actor A asks actor B 'what do you mean?' If A takes for granted what he/she means then making him/herself accountable will involve a d.c. articulation of what is assumed at the level of p.c.. On a more general level it occurs in a situation of anomalous behaviour of others. When B told A that the question 'Hello, how are you' was not a request for information on a person's well being, there was a transfer of knowledge from p.c. to d.c.. When B initially said 'hello', more likely than not, he/she had not formulated to him/herself this piece of information as d.c. knowledge.

Aside from the transfer from p.c. to d.c., in the case of anomalous behaviour of other, there is often also anger. Indeed the extent to which the victims of Garfinkel's breaching experiments reacted with rage to apparently trivial incidents is striking. Giddens postulated that Garfinkel's experiments caused such deep anxiety because they broke down the barrier between p.c. and u.c.. Due to this break, the unconscious came flooding through. While it is possible that someone not responding appropriately to "hello" or a simple question will cause psychological distress from the unconscious, this is only one possible interpretation. Ontological insecurity can be described as happening when someone mentioned homosexuality or transvestism to Agnes: she became highly uncomfortable with respect to self as a gendered social actor. The discovery of a person's 'back region' by forcing them to defecate in public would be another example. However, most of Garfinkel's experiments were not of this nature: there was no flooding through of repressed drives from the unconscious. Rather they constituted examples of anomalous behaviour by other. They contribute to a *crisis in the paradigm of p.c.*. This crisis of paradigm meant an undermining of certain rules. The rules used to order an act of structuration became violated through the act of destructuration by B. This implies a violation of an actor's *knowledge* of rule-governed behaviour. It is not necessarily an ontological issue linked to the flooding through of u.c. Destructuration and non-restructuration place a question mark on an actor's paradigmatic social knowledge. Hence, in theorizing the reproduction of social structure, as carried in the p.c. and d.c., what is fundamental is an actor's paradigmatically constituted knowledge of social rules. It is this knowledge which the Garfinkel 'breaching experiments' call into question. Consequently, the doubt which actors experience in these experiments can better be conceptualized as epistemological insecurity rather than ontological security. In essence, epistemological insecurity is a doubt placed upon the validity of past knowledge as a guide for future rule-governed action. While I do not wish to negate the existence of ontological insecurity as a phenomenon, I am essentially arguing that epistemological insecurity is of primary consequence when wishing to theorize the process by which structures are reproduced. The concepts of restructuration, destructuration and non-restructuration highlight an uncertainty of expectations which can best be theorized through the concept of epistemological insecurity. Outside their recreation in structuring interaction structures exist potentially as a p.c. and d.c. knowledge of rules. As such, the recreation of structure is first and foremost an epistemological issue not an ontological one.

Epistemological insecurity is experienced within a social world where order is the creation of social actors fulfilling their assumptions concerning the orderedness of the social world. Actors constantly use knowledge of past order to create rules by which to structure their own social practices. This ordering of practice constitutes an act of structuration. However, when an act of structuration stimulates an unforeseen act of destructuration or non-restructuration in B, the knowledge inherent in the act of structuration has been violated. In such a case, the absence of restructuration inherently implies a certain level of epistemological insecurity for the structuring actor A. Actor A can respond in a number of ways to his/her insecurity. Among these possibilities can be a decision to learn new rules or change paradigmatic perception of social order. This would constitute an example of an actor's socialization process. Alternatively, A can ignore B's act of destructuration or non-restructuration and inform him/her of 'correct' restructuration practices - 'Look! I was just trying to be polite. Frankly I don't give a damn how you are.' When actor A decides not to be socialized, he/she is in a fundamentally different position to an astrophysicist observing an anomalous planet. Unlike in the natural world, in the social system order is the responsibility of others through restructuration practices. In Garfinkel's breaching experiments the epistemological insecurity experienced by A is the responsibility of B. Hence, epistemological insecurity manifests itself as rage with respect to other - there is no point in getting angry with Uranus or gravity but there is with B.

10 Restructuration and consensual power

In the previous chapter I showed how the paradigm of p.c. constituted a necessary predispositional backdrop for the spontaneous production of social structures through action. As such, the social paradigm constituted away of interpreting, recognizing, and anticipating rule affirmation and, hence, contributing to the creation of social structures in the act of restructuration. In this chapter, I want to develop these themes in the context of theorizing the process by which the praxiological production of consensual power takes place. In order to do this, I shall begin with a stage-by-stage analysis of some of the main elements which I wish to draw together to form such a theorization. These stages will be presented as, to a certain extent, disparate elements which will slowly be woven together. The chapter will also include some illustrative and explanatory examples of this process.

In the chapter on Parsons' theory of consensual power I concluded by drawing attention to the manner in which Parsons' concept of power could be used as an analytic tool to interpret some of Hannah Arendt's observations on power and violence. Hannah Arendt argued that "[r]ule by sheer violence comes into play where power is being lost..." (Arendt 1970 p. 53). According to a Parsonsian interpretation, this is because power is like money in the sense that both have value which is systemically created based on trust. Like monetary metal, violence is an ultimate substitute for power when confidence is collapsing in it as a systemic attribute. In many respects, this concept of power and violence can be interpreted as consistent with the distinction drawn by Giddens between social power and physical power. When a given actor is subjected to violence they are treated as a body, not a social actor. Physical force is the action of one upon another as if that other were no different than a stone. In short, in all three theories, violence is not classifiable as a form of social power. Inherent in this argument is the analysis of power as a socially relational concept. The logical extension of this argument must be that for an exercise of power to draw upon socially systemic resources that action must in some respect be interactive. However, as analysed in chapter 8, there are many forms of interaction of which restructuring interaction is only one type. Consequently, it is necessary first of all to establish which form of interaction is necessary for the production of structure.

When A exercises power over B, the behaviour of B is a manifestation of whether or not A exercised social power over B. If B responds as desired by A, the exercise of power constitutes successfully exercised social power. Let us imagine that A wishes to produce power with respect to issue a. As observed by A. Goldman, an actor A is only powerful with respect to issue a "if and only if: 1) If A wanted outcome a, then a would occur, and 2) If A wanted outcome not-a, then not-a would occur." (A. Goldman 1986 p. 159) In other words, if A were to engage interaction with B in order to produce the desire effect a or not-a, an outcome z would not constitute an exercise of power - though z might be an effect of their interaction. In other words, causal effect in general is *not* what is analytically fundamental to the theorization of the production of power. If A desires a or not-a the fact that outcome z may have a devastating effect upon B is theoretically irrelevant. What is central is the level of control over the outcome of interaction. If A has an unknown or unpredictable effect upon B, then A will not have the possibility of achieving a and/or not-a as he/she desires. In short, the exercise of power involves initiation of *controlled* causal effect. It is not just the production of any effect whatsoever. This points to the key role played by the fulfilment of expectations in the classification of an interactive effect as an exercise of power. For A to achieve a or not-a through interaction with B the rule by which he/she structured must be affirmed in the reaction of B. Hence, an interaction of the type represented in figs 8.2, 8.3 and 8.4 could not lead to the production of power, though they could produce other causal effects. Only in the restructuring interaction, as represented in fig 8.1, are expectations actually fulfilled with any level of accuracy. Consequently, social power is inherently produced through an interactive process where restructuration takes place.

Returning to the distinction between power and violence, in interaction between A and B, where B responds through destructuration or absent restructuration, A will effectively have lost control of the situation. In the case of absent or destructuration, if A finally resorts to physical manipulation of B then B is no longer a social actor but a physical body. In this case the action of A is ordered according to rules which do not take account of other qua social actor. A's action is not a social act of structuration. This distinction is also summed up well by Michel Foucault: "In effect, what defines a relationship as power is that it is a mode of action which does not act directly and immediately on others. Instead it acts upon their actions... A relationship of violence acts upon a body or upon things; it forces, it bends, it breaks on the wheel, it destroys, or it closes the door on all possibilities. Its opposite party can only be passivity. On the other hand, a power relationship can only be articulated on the basis of two elements which are each indispensable... that 'the other'... be thoroughly recognized and maintained to the very end as a person who acts...." (Foucault 1982 p. 220). In many instances such an act of violence represents the inability of A to comply through the verification of rules.

In order to preempt any misunderstandings concerning this power/violence distinction, it should be observed they are analytically scalar concepts. In actual 'real life' situations many acts of violence happen in conjunction with interactive exercises of power. Within observable social life, possibly the most common act of 'pure' violence upon other is the removal of other as a recalcitrant social actor by destruction of his/her body (e.g. shooting him/her). The latter *often* has no interactive content and is perceived to be a highly effective method of removing other when an exercise of power has failed. In contrast to the latter, there are also many exercises of violence which occur in conjunction with exercises of power. For example, torture always occurs interactively. In such a context, violence can used to force a desired form of compliant interaction from actors refusing to engage in specific forms of interaction. As observed by Richard Rorty, a fundamental facet of sadistic torture is the ability to use physical pain to induce patterns of behaviour which an actor will be unable to cope with having engaged in (R. Rorty 1989 p. 178). In the language of restructuration, violence is used to force an actor into patterns of behaviour which cannot be rationalized with respect to

155

that actor's paradigm. However, despite the frequent occurrence of power and violence together, it is analytically important to theorize the concept of violence in its 'pure' or ideal form as a limiting case. Such a limit case conceptualization is of consequence in delimiting the analytical borders occupied by the phenomenon of social power. Consequently, it is a distinction which is given importance in most theoretical work on power.

From the hypothesis that power and violence are opposites, Arendt and Parsons argued that power is an inherently consensually based communicative medium. As such, power is essentially a systemic property which is perceived as the ability 'to do'. Extending and reinterpreting Parsons argument, within the framework of interaction and restructuration, a number of points can be made. Taking the analogy of language as used by Giddens, when a social actor speaks English, he/she is acting intentionally while simultaneously unintentionally contributing to the reproduction of the English language. When a given actor uses a word or a sentence he/she knows, with relative accuracy, how other will react based on a 'natural attitude' confidence in a shared perceived meaning. In using the English language an actor is using it as a facility to stimulate a relatively predictable action by other. Money operates on the same level. When B decides to sell an object of utility to A, both know the approximate parameters of the mutual interaction. There are only so many ways in which A and B can act or react to the units of paper-money changing hands. It is in this sense that Parsons maintains that power, money and language share communicative content which define the parameters of social action[1]. In addition, unlike language, power and money also have an inherent prescriptive content.

While existing as prescriptive communication on an actor level, as a systemic property, power is conceived of in terms of a circulating medium or force. In the chapters on both Parsons and Giddens I take them to task for, in this act, contributing an unduly 'metaphysical' concept of power to the theoretical framework of analytical political theory. Aside from the inherent inability to theorize the praxiological production of 'out there' power, the concept of systemic power which circulates tends to lead to a notion of power as a resource - an analytical problem which Giddens and Parsons appear to share. An actor A who contains or 'stores' this flow is 'powerful'. Hence, his/her power is not a product of resources but rather this undefined 'thing', current or flow, which he/she 'has'. In other words, a confusion of power and power resources takes place.

Having rejected the idea of power as analytically equal to systemic resources, it must be pointed out that it does appear as though power has a communicative content. If actor A has power over B it means that, on some level or other, A can control the behavioural patterns of B according to a desired preconceived pattern. Not only can A change the behaviour of B but he/she can do so in a relatively determined and predictable way. To deal with this point I will, for a moment, return to the concept of social interaction in general. When A interacts with B, what enables B to act with appropriate reciprocal action is the general systemic structuredness of certain forms of interaction. If reactions were inherently random there would be no social system nor would there be social structures. Ordered each with respect to other, restructuring interaction is a contribution to the reproduction of the systemic whole. While an interaction may be intentional, the recreation of a structured system is not necessarily so. As explained, what defines the action of A and B as structurally significant interaction is the act of restructuration by B. In the case of restructuring interaction, it is structures which contribute to the orderedness of the interaction. Hence, it is the structuredness of an interaction which gives A the ability to predict, with relative accuracy, the reaction of B. It is these structures existing as rules in the minds of actors which give exercises of power an inherent communicative content. If a mutual communicative content were not part of the praxiological production of power actors would not have the ability to read the rule-governedness of other's action: structuration and restructuration would not take place. Communication is not part of the essence of power itself but part of the process through which social power is created. In attributing communicative content to power, Parsons and Arendt are confusing the structural component of the exercise of power, as a social phenomenon, with the concept of power itself.

When an actor exercises social power it takes place through intentional interaction which unintentionally contributes to the production of the social structures. It is this structuredness which makes interaction ordered as opposed to random. Power is purely the ability to do or to affect something (see Oxford English Dictionary 1989 vol. 12 p. 259) and, as such, should not be confused with the resources used in the effecting or doing. Power does not exist as a resource nor does its exercise contribute to ordered social reproduction of a 'thing' which has similar characteristics. As social interaction, social power is ordered through the reproduction of social structures: structuration and restructuration. Power is the

157

ability to achieve a future apparent good through the restructuration of other.

It is structures which contribute the orderedness of an exercise of social power. It is an orderedness which is systemically defined. However, on an actor-based level, a necessary prerequisite for the production of this order is a shared ability to symptomatically read the social world in a similar fashion. If A sees Wittgenstein's duck-rabbit picture as a duck and B sees it as a rabbit then interaction will be unsuccessful. The production of social structure is premised on a shared social paradigm. For B to react with appropriate reciprocal action through restructuration, A and B must have a shared paradigm. Consequently, a common social paradigm is a necessary prerequisite for social power.

When discussing Parsons, I mentioned the importance of trust to his theoretical perspective. If power is like money, which has no intrinsic worth, it is 'trust' which defines value. Not only do both derive their systemic value based on trust but both perform a similar function based on confidence. When a person parts with an object of use value for a unit of money, he/she does so because of a belief that others will behave in a similar fashion. He/she has confidence in the ordered and predictable behaviour of others with respect to units of currency. In this case the value of money is a case of 'operation bootstrap'. Everyone accepts paper money because everyone else does so. Parsons argues that power, as a circulating medium, is similarly based on the trust that others will behave in a particular manner. On a descriptive level Parsons is correct that trust is associated with power. However, I would argue, that trust appears as part of the process of production of power as a restructuring phenomenon. It is not inherent in the concept of power as some abstract entity. This point needs some developing.

In chapter 9 I argued that social structures are carried outside the moment of their re/creation in d.c. and p.c.. Fundamental to this process is a paradigm within which there is suspension of doubt. In the 'natural attitude' there is the assumption that there is an objective world-out-there. This world is inherently ordered and within this order past experience is similar to future. In these terms a key aspect of Garfinkel's breaching experiments is that they shatter or prove inconsistent with the epistemological security implied in this attitude. In these experiments the social world is not ordered as defined within an actor's social paradigm. There is irregularity in an otherwise ordered world. Actor A is in a similar position to the Newtonian physicist on the discovery of Uranus. The law which should have enabled him/her to predict a future regularity failed to do so. However, as pointed out, the social and natural world are in one important respect unalike: society is created by those who predict its regularities. The orderedness of social life is produced in interaction by actors who through their assumption of order create and recreate social order. In the form of 'operation bootstrap', the trust implicit in the assumption of order functions to create order. Both the assumption of order and the creation of order are mutually self-fulfilling prophesies. Through the expectation of order, social actors create the structuredness of interaction which makes it possible for similar interaction to be reproduced over different spans of time and space.

If a chemical 'a' is placed in combination with element 'b' then reaction 'c' will occur according to law 'z'. In accordance with the structures governing phatic communion in Anglo-Saxon culture, when actor A says 'Hello, how are you?' to actor B then B will react 'Fine thanks,...'. In both cases reaction x and 'Fine thanks' constitute affirmation of rules. If appropriate reciprocal action were not to occur they would constitute anomalous experiences within their respective paradigms. Reaction x constitutes another case of non falsification of law 'z' and 'Fine thanks' is a recreation of the structures concerning phatic communion through restructuration.

In other words, I am arguing that it is social structures which are analogous to money, not power. It is social structures which make it possible for the same social practices to be repeated over time and space; for the regularities of the past to be a guide to those of the future. In short, communicative meaning and trust are associated with power as social interaction based upon restructuration. It is a restructuration which is facilitated through consensus upon a paradigmatic reading of the rule-governed order of social interaction.

I have consistently maintained that power is not 'in' the social system as some form of separate phenomenon. As distinct from physical power, *social power is the ability 'to do' or to affect which an actor gains through systemically meaningful social interaction.* Such social interaction contributes to the re/production of social structures and hence to the recreation of the social system. The social actor is a member of that system to the extent to which he/she contributes to its reproduction through such interaction. In this dual act of drawing upon and re/creating structure through interaction, what is the power that the social actor produces? The answer to this question is an answer to the question: what is the enabling aspect of social power?

If A and B are members of the same social system they will also share a common paradigm concerning the orderedness of the social world. When A draws upon his/her knowledge of social structures he/she can feel relatively confident that B will restructure. The act of restructuration contributes to the reproduction of the social system as a structurally defined assembled set of regularities. The latter enables social actors to predict future action based upon past restructuration practices. While the social actor does not necessarily have a d.c. understanding of the causal relationships at work in constituting this order, he/she does have a p.c. knowledge whereby it does not appear as formless. The action of others is not perceived as arbitrary and, consequently, epistemological insecurity is relatively rare. However, equally importantly, the social actor can use the social system to realize goals which were otherwise unrealizable. What enables A to gain an otherwise unattainable goal in collaboration with B is the knowledge that B's behaviour will not be inherently arbitrary. That is to say, power 'to do' can be realized through restructuring interaction with others. Hence, social power is derived through the structuredness of the social system reproduced in restructuration practices. This can be expressed as follows:

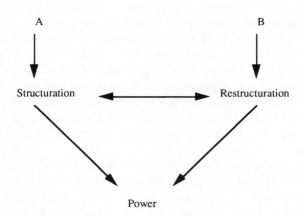

In this case the power realized by A and B is dependent upon restructuration. B restructures intentionally in order to facilitate the creation of power which will enable A and/or B 'to do' something. The unintentional effect of B's restructuration is to re/create certain social structures. This re/creation is a contribution to the orderedness of the social system as a whole. In other words, the intentional effect of restructuration will be the realization of social power and the simultaneous unintentional effect will be to

160

re/create a system the existence of which is the necessary prerequisite for the production of future power. This implies that restructuration provides both the key to the creation of social structures and also to the production of social power. This can be represented as as follows:

Restructuration and Social Power (fig. R.C.P.):

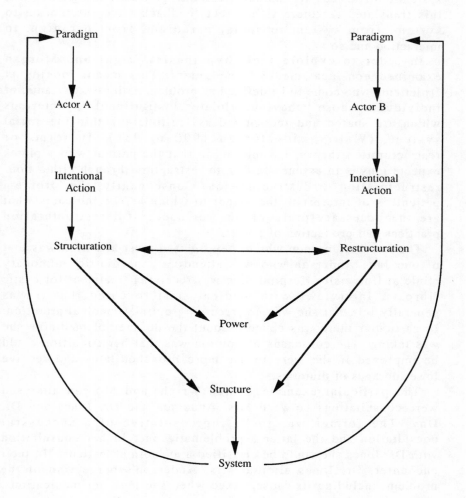

The method by which the one act of restructuration intentionally provides consensual power and unintentionally re/creates structure can be illustrated or elucidated using an example derived from medical sociology. The example in question is derived from an attempt by Wright and Morgan (1990) to analyse the frequently encountered concept in medical discourse of the 'problem patient'.

One of the fundamental theoretical premises upon which Wright and Morgan based their analysis was the hypothesis that the hermeneutics of a medical encounter and the surrounding wider systemic influences are mutually sustaining. Within my framework, this translates as: there is a direct feedback from interaction to system, from system to social paradigm, from paradigm to interaction and so on.

In order to explore their hypothesis Wright and Morgan examined non-ideal medical encounters. This meant looking at "[p]atients who come to be defined as problem patients...deviants, or individuals whose behaviour violates institutional expectations which are shared and recognized as legitimate within the social system" (Walter and Morgan 1990 p. 951). In terms of restructuration theory, I would argue that the patient who violates expectations is in essence failing to restructure through either non-restructuration or destructuration. Consequently, the 'problem patient' is of interest to the extent to which he/she indicates what are the necessary prerequisites for successful restructuration practices and production of power.

The interaction upon which they focused most attention was that of one Jane Anderson who was attending a paediatric pulmonary clinic at University Hospital. She was receiving treatment for cystic fibrosis. Interviews with medical staff revealed that it was generally felt that she was not receiving optimal medical attention. In particular there was concern about the dosages of medicine she was taking. The consensus of opinion was that her condition could be improved if she were to use more bronchodilates and receive lower dosages of diuretics.

The particular examples which Wright and Morgan analysed were consultations between Mrs. Anderson and Dr. Jones and Dr. Day. The former was to be representative of a successful consultation and the latter a problematic one. In her consultation with Dr. Jones she could be classified a as 'normal' patient: "In their encounter, Dr. Jones elicited Mrs. Anderson's perception of the problem, including its cause, asked when she took her medications, and gave credence to her beliefs by explaining the medical model and drug effects in her terms. In response, Mrs. Anderson phrased one question in terms of 'you would know more about this' and was generally cheerful and open with Dr. Jones." (Wright and Morgan 1990 p. 954). For both parties concerned the consultation was a success. Mrs. Anderson learned about her condition. Dr. Jones obtained information on the condition of her health from which her medical dosages could be adjusted.

In the second interaction Mrs. Anderson became a 'problem' patient. The consultation began by Dr. Day giving her a physical examination in silence. Then he defined her condition for her purely within the terms of professional medical discourse. He also generally ordered her about. "Mrs. Anderson's response was defensive and *involved breaking several unspoken rules*:

'Dr. Day stated: 'we need to check your electrolytes. I think that you're taking too much diuretic at the one time.' Jane said that she didn't agree. Dr. Day felt that after checking the electrolytes, the best solution would be to skip one dose of diuretic.'

'At this point the patient said 'No'. She planned to take a small dose in the morning and the rest in the afternoon as before. In fact, she stated, the cardiologist had said it was best that way.'

'Dr. Day said that he was uncomfortable with that solution and that he was not convinced that she needed a diuretic. The patient contradicted him, saying 'I need it.' The physician said 'I'm quite sure you are dried out; you're overdoing it.' The patient stated, 'Well, I do seem to have thin ankles.' Again the physician stated 'You need to cut down on the amount.' But Jane insisted she needed 100 mg.'" (Wright and Morgan 1990 p. 954 emphasis not orig.).

Commenting on the consultation between Mrs. Anderson and Dr. Day, Wright and Morgan analysed her role as a problem patient as follows:

"Jane became a problem patient by *violating the rules of appropriate behaviour*. First, she volunteered unsolicited information which made sense in terms of her concerns and explanatory model but which were *irrelevant* to the medical modes. She frequently interrupted and contradicted Dr. Day, countering his suggestions with her own, which she supported with statements from other subspecialists. During part of Dr. Day's examination she chatted with the fellow. Through all her actions Mrs. Anderson became a 'bad' or ungrateful patient, since 'good patients' follow doctor's orders without question." (Wright and Morgan 1990 p. 954-5 emphasis not orig.).

Later, when the two consultations were compared and analysed for the source of their difference, it turned out that "Dr. Day was trained during a time when 'the trust of the patient in the complete competence of the doctor and the dependent desire to be "taken care of " by the doctor...(were) considered essential aspects of the relationship.'" (Wright and Morgan 1990 p. 954). In contrast to this position "...*societal expectations of a doctor's demeanour have changed dramatically*..." (Wright and Morgan 1990 p. 954 emphasis not orig.). Within the wide range of beliefs concerning what constitutes an 'ideal' doctor patient relationship "...there has been a great deal of pressure for doctors to provide more information and form a partnership with their patients,... Mrs. Anderson herself stated that she likes to be treated as an equal, to participate in decision making." (Wright and Morgan 1990 p. 954). Unlike Dr. Day, Dr. Jones was a younger doctor who was as yet learning on the job.

It is interesting to note that subsequently Dr. Day realized that his consultations with Mrs. Anderson were proving unsuccessful due to the form they were taking. He decided to change his approach by asking her for her perception and interpretation of her symptoms. The result was not only a more pleasant consultation, where more information could be obtained but, "[f]or the first time they negotiated the timing of her diuretics." (Wright and Morgan 1990 p. 955). As a general observation on this change Wright and Morgan commented on the aptness of the observation that "'...knowledge that determines medical behaviours is constituted from a flow of intention, observation and expectation; it is continually reformulated as the actor monitors his own behaviour and its effects.'" (Wright and Morgan 1990 p. 955).

I will now reinterpret this information within a restructurationist framework. Aside from a general commentary I have also summarized my analysis in figurative form. Each is an application of Fig R.C.P.. Fig 10.1 represents the successful encounter between Dr. Jones and Mrs. Anderson. Fig 10.2 is the encounter between Dr. Day and Mrs. Anderson, where no power is realized. Fig 10.3 is the final interaction between Dr. Day and Mrs. Anderson, where restructuration does take place. Fig 10.4 is a hypothetical unsuccessful encounter with Dr. Jones.

In fig 10.1, both Dr. Jones and Mrs. Anderson have a relatively recent paradigm of how a medical encounter is constituted. Both believe that interaction between doctor and patient should be an exchange of information which leads to a consensually derived decision as to the best course of treatment. As a consequence, Dr. Jones considers himself to be a fellow actor. Mrs. Anderson perceives herself as an equal to Dr. Jones. As is consistent with their shared paradigm, the first thing Dr. Jones does is to request Mrs. Anderson's assessment of her condition. Mrs. Anderson responds appropriately with a general description which is meaningful with respect to her frame of reference. As an elicitor of general information, his act of structuration has met with restructuration with respect to a specific formulation of rules according to a certain perspective. Dr. Jones then uses the information contained in her appropriate reciprocal action in order to frame a medical analysis. Dr. Jones is drawing upon the rules which define the doctor as a re-interpreter of 'layman's' analysis. Mrs. Anderson accepts this and restructuration takes place in accordance with this paradigmatic reading of social order. Noting Mrs. Anderson's confidence, Dr. Jones decides to provide information on correct medical dosages. In doing so he does not set himself up as an 'untouchable' expert but, instead, does it in the form of a discussion. Mrs. Anderson says that he knows more than she does, thus restructuring Dr. Jones' act of structuration. In short, all Dr. Jones' acts of structuration meet with restructuration. From a given interpretation of what constitutes an ordered medical interaction, the intentionally desired result is the creation of power to treat Mrs. Anderson's condition. It is power which neither actor could have created singly. Power `to do' was produced as a consequence of successful interaction.

Aside from the intentional result of social power 'to do' there are also the unintentional effects resulting from the interaction. On a general structural level, social structures are reproduced whereby, in medical encounters, restructuring interaction is based on joint eliciting/analysis of information and decision making. More specifically, structures have been reproduced according to rules whereby it is appropriate for: a) the doctor to ask for a general description of symptoms and for the patient to furnish such; b) the doctor to reinterpret the information given in a medical framework and for the patient to accept such an analysis; c) the doctor to prescribe a course of medication in the form of a discussion and for the patient to see this prescription as a jointly derived decision.

On a systemic level the unintentional effect of the encounter between Dr. Jones and Mrs. Anderson is to contribute to the reproduction of the ordered system of clinical interaction at University Hospital. The reproduction of the social system of interaction at University Hospital has the additional unintentional consequence of reinforcing Dr. Jones' and Mrs. Anderson's paradigm of social action. For both, it was a structured interaction which once again proved correct their paradigm of what constitutes the order of the social world. The social system is exactly as they both thought. In short, the interaction represented in fig 10.1 is of the same type as 8.1.

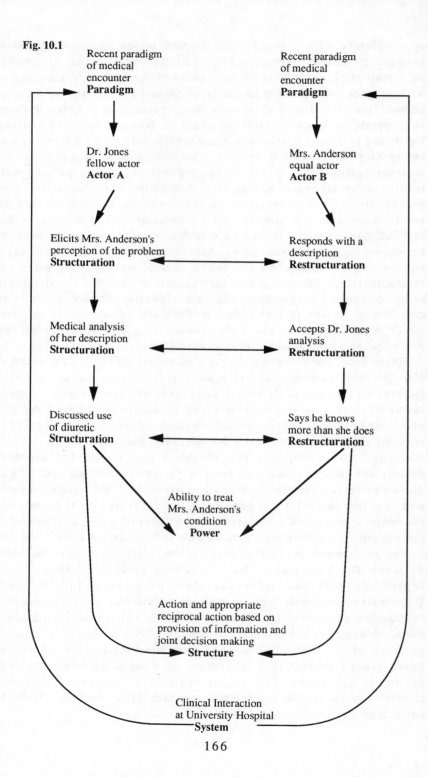

Fig. 10.1

Recent paradigm
of medical
encounter
Paradigm

Recent paradigm
of medical
encounter
Paradigm

Dr. Jones
fellow actor
Actor A

Mrs. Anderson
equal actor
Actor B

Elicits Mrs. Anderson's
perception of the problem
Structuration

Responds with a
description
Restructuration

Medical analysis
of her description
Structuration

Accepts Dr. Jones
analysis
Restructuration

Discussed use
of diuretic
Structuration

Says he knows
more than she does
Restructuration

Ability to treat
Mrs. Anderson's
condition
Power

Action and appropriate
reciprocal action based on
provision of information and
joint decision making
Structure

Clinical Interaction
at University Hospital
System

The interaction between Mrs. Anderson and Dr. Day is in many respects a complete contrast. Mrs. Anderson has the same paradigm as in the previous interaction. However, Dr. Day is an older doctor with a paradigm which was constituted many years previously. Dr. Day is the medical expert attending his consultancy. Mrs. Anderson is the object upon which he must exercise his medical expertise. As such he begins with a silent examination. She is the 'body' whose social interaction is limited to responding to orders given. On her part, Mrs. Anderson considers herself a social actor on an equal footing with Dr. Day. Consequently, rather than react as a compliant other, resentment builds up. As medical expert, Dr. Day decides that the best course of action would be to test her level of electrolytes. From the evidence of the test he concludes that she is taking too much diuretic. In these prescriptive acts he is structuring his behaviour relative to rules whereby other is expected to react compliantly based upon trust in the expertise of the doctor. Rather than restructuring with trust in his assessment of the evidence, Mrs. Anderson directly challenges Dr. Day's structuration practices by contradicting his verdict. To reiterate the words of Wright and Morgan, she is *"violating the rules of appropriate behaviour."* (1990 p. 954). Mrs. Anderson does this by drawing upon a *different set of rules* which are incompatible with Dr. Day's act of structuration. Because Mrs. Anderson inappropriate reaction is clearly meaningfully shaped with respect to a given paradigm and is consistent with given rules it is not classifiable as non-restructuration ("she volunteered unsolicited information *which made sense in terms of her concerns* and explanatory model but which were *irrelevant* to the medical modes." (Wright and Morgan 1990 p. 954 and above, emphasis not orig.)). Mrs. Anderson is engaging in destructuration as represented in fig 8.2. In response Dr. Day again draws upon the structures of medical interaction as he knows them: he *tells* her to skip one dose of diuretic. Mrs. Anderson *refuses* to accept his advice and destructuration again takes place. Twice more Dr. Day's acts of structuration do not meet with appropriate reciprocal action as predicted according to specific rules viewed within a given medical paradigm. Ultimately, Mrs. Anderson insists that she is going to continue taking the same doses of diuretic as usual. The overall result is an inability to realize the goal for which the consultation was intended: viewed from the perspective of improving Mrs. Anderson's condition, there is no power 'to do'.

With respect to the older paradigm and more recent medical paradigms, all of Dr. Day's acts of structuration meet with non-restructuration and, as a consequence, no social structures are reproduced. Framed with reference to his role of medical expert taking care of a helpless patient, his acts of structuration are not met with restructuration. Instead of passive trust he encounters unsolicited irrelevant information and outright contradictions. In terms of classification fig 10.2 takes the same form as 8.2. The analytical similarity between 10.2 and 8.2 illustrates the fact that destructuration is a relatively common part of every-day life. It is *not* confined to the rather esoteric example of a sociological 'breaching' experiment. Destructuring interaction is a frequently encountered phenomenon. Consequently, a very large proportion of interaction does not contribute to structural reproduction. With regard to fig 10.2., on a structural and systemic level the interaction fails to contribute to the reproduction of the system of social interaction at University Hospital. Neither the authoritarian nor the egalitarian method of interaction are recreated.

As a note of qualification on this interpretation, it should be observed that both the failure to recreate structure and to produce of power only take place with respect a specific paradigm and with regard to certain rules. There was not total interactive breakdown. For example, there is no mention of either Mrs. Anderson or Dr. Day disputing the rules which other employed with regard to the usage of the furnishings of Dr. Day's office. Consequently, the structures 'carried' by such furniture were reproduced. Similarly, if it were supposed that the purpose of the interaction were *not* to cure Mrs. Anderson's condition, then it could plausibly be argued that Dr. Day and Mrs. Anderson were highly successful in producing power *not to* help her ailment. It is a point which highlights the fact that the structuration, restructuration, destructuration and non-restructuration interpretation of any piece of social interaction takes place with respect certain analytical criteria which are derived from a postulated analysis of actors' social paradigms, use of rules and motivational intentionality. From the perspective of social and political theory, this implies that the analytical interpretation of social action must take place within a framework where certain conditionals and a limitation of focus are assumed as given.

If it is assumed that both Dr. Day and Mrs. Anderson wish to realize power in order to deal with her ailments, this highlights the fundamental role played by paradigmatic consensus in the realization of power. While there is consensus between Mrs. Anderson and Dr. Day, with respect to the issue of realizing power, there is not consensus on shared paradigmatic perceptions. As a

Fig. 10.2

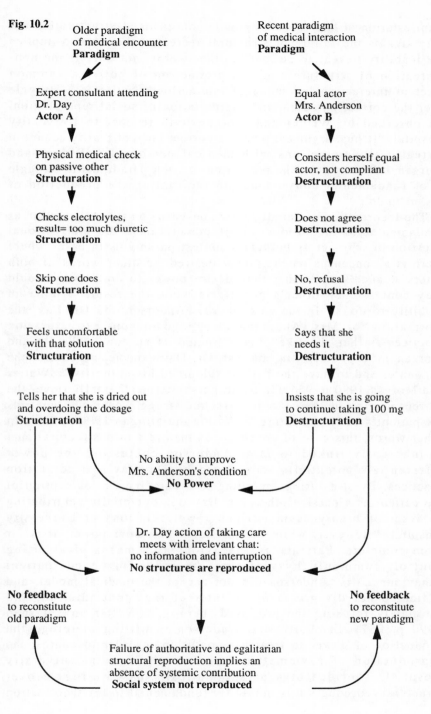

Older paradigm
of medical encounter
Paradigm

Recent paradigm
of medical interaction
Paradigm

Expert consultant attending
Dr. Day
Actor A

Equal actor
Mrs. Anderson
Actor B

Physical medical check
on passive other
Structuration

Considers herself equal
actor, not compliant
Destructuration

Checks electrolytes,
result= too much diuretic
Structuration

Does not agree
Destructuration

Skip one does
Structuration

No, refusal
Destructuration

Feels uncomfortable
with that solution
Structuration

Says that she
needs it
Destructuration

Tells her that she is dried out
and overdoing the dosage
Structuration

Insists that she is going
to continue taking 100 mg
Destructuration

No ability to improve
Mrs. Anderson's condition
No Power

Dr. Day action of taking care
meets with irrelevant chat:
no information and interruption
No structures are reproduced

No feedback
to reconstitute
old paradigm

No feedback
to reconstitute
new paradigm

Failure of authoritative and egalitarian
structural reproduction implies an
absence of systemic contribution
Social system not reproduced

169

manifestation of lack of paradigmatic consensus, destructuration not only signals the failure of structural recreation but it also implies the inability to realize power. In other words, not only is the non-recreation of structure and non-production of power a common facet of interaction but much of interaction constitutes a struggle over the correct paradigmatic interpretation of social reproduction. As observed by Wright and Morgan with respect to University Hospital, "[t]hus, argument over the correct view of reality occurs in virtually all interactions with medical personnel." (Wright and Morgan 1990 p. 956). The resolution of such paradigmatic struggle is of fundamental consequence in facilitating the production of power 'to do'.

The theorization of paradigmatic consensus on rule affirmation as fundamental to the production of power raises the motivational question of why actors bother to contest paradigms in cases where there is a consensus on the power desired. In other words, if both actors A and B agree that they desire power to do X, why would they contest each other's paradigms when the result will be an inability to do X? In the case of Mrs. Anderson and Dr. Day, the motivation for Mrs. Anderson to engage in non-restructuration practices is that she liked to be treated as an equal (Wright and Morgan 1990 p. 954). "In contrast, Dr. Day expected to control the encounter and to have the patient submit to his authority." (Walter and Morgan 1990 p. 954). In paradigmatic terms, "..conflict over the correct version of reality objectifies the struggle over who controls the patient's body and future." (Walter and Morgan 1990 p. 956). In other words, this case of conflict - as manifest in destructuration - is inherently linked to Mrs. Anderson contesting the power differentials potentially reproduced by Dr. Day's structuration practices. By structuring according to a paradigmatic perception of the patient as a passive other, Dr. Day was potentially contributing to a set of highly asymmetrical power relations in University Hospital. "However, while the physician has more power, it is far from complete. Patients use behaviour as a means of asserting control, commonly by violating the *rules* for 'good' patient behaviour....Mrs. Anderson did not accept the medical model, and indicated her disagreement by interrupting, contradicting, and ultimately refusing the proposed therapy." (Walter and Morgan 1990 p. 957). In short, Mrs. Anderson is willing to forego the production of power to treat her condition in order to contest the reproduction of asymmetrical power relations in University Hospital. The idea of a paradigmatically based struggle over structural reproduction is implicitly fundamental to the theorization of Lukes' concept of 3-D. However, these are themes which I methodologically bracket for the moment - the phenomenon of 3-D will be examined in chapter 13.

For both Dr. Day and Mrs. Anderson the experience fails to reinforce their respective paradigmatic perceptions of the orderedness of the social world. Mrs. Anderson wants to maintain her paradigm. She wishes to be considered an equal and deems Dr. Day out of step. She considers him out of step or insists on her interpretation of reality because she desires a more egalitarian form of interaction with her doctor than Dr. Day offers. For her the experience constitutes an anomalous experience which does not change her paradigm. However, unlike Mrs. Anderson, Dr. Day appears to evaluate failure of the interaction to realize social power to help her condition. As a consequence, he decides to experiment with a new paradigm in his next interaction with Mrs. Anderson. The latter is represented in fig 10.3.

In fig 10.3, due to his change of paradigm, Dr. Day now conceives of himself as a fellow actor. His request for Mrs. Anderson's perception of her condition is met with restructuration. The intentionally desired outcome is the realization of power. On an unintentional level the social structures which define the nature of their interaction are reproduced. In turn, these are part of the ordered whole which constitutes the system of social interaction at University Hospital. For Dr. Day it also means reinforcement of his newly acquired paradigm of social interaction.

With respect to Dr. Day, figures 10.2 and 10.3 are illustrative of how paradigms are changed and then, in turn, reinforced. Dr. Day is not coerced into changing his structuration practices (as stated previously, some of these are themes will be taken up again in chapter 13 in the context of a discussion of the concept of false consciousness). Unlike Mrs. Anderson, who is willing to forego the production of consensual power, Dr. Day changes paradigm and uses new rules out of a desire to realize consensual power in interaction; that is, although such a paradigmatic change implies a socially interactive context where he is less powerful than previously. His previous paradigm is inconsistent with the social order which he encounters when interacting with Mrs. Anderson. To use the language of chapter 9, Dr. Day experiences epistemological insecurity and as a consequence decides to use different rules and change his paradigmatic perceptions. Dr. Day overcomes epistemological insecurity by reading and interpreting the unexpected order correctly. His next interaction with Mrs. Anderson is met with restructuration. The net result is a successful creation of

Fig. 10.3

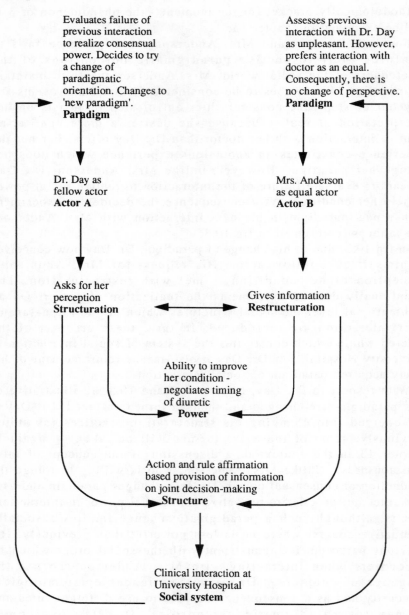

Evaluates failure of
previous interaction
to realize consensual
power. Decides to try
a change of
paradigmatic
orientation. Changes to
'new paradigm'.
Paradigm

Assesses previous
interaction with Dr. Day
as unpleasant. However,
prefers interaction with
doctor as an equal.
Consequently, there is
no change of perspective.
Paradigm

Dr. Day as
fellow actor
Actor A

Mrs. Anderson
as equal actor
Actor B

Asks for her
perception
Structuration

Gives information
Restructuration

Ability to improve
her condition -
negotiates timing
of diuretic
Power

Action and rule affirmation
based provision of information
on joint decision-making
Structure

Clinical interaction at
University Hospital
Social system

power 'to do'.

In assessing Dr. Day's paradigm change, it should be borne in mind he was taking a risk in structuring the way he did. The risk is much higher than that taken by the average actor in routine structuration practices. In normal, often repeated, structuration practices restructuration is almost certain. In everyday interaction structuration is a repetitive act based on the actor's experience of past structuration practices. In this case Dr. Day's risk is analytically, to some extent, similar to that taken by Henry Cole in printing the Christmas card. In both cases the structuration practices attempted were derived from a new reading of social order. Dr. Day's risk is lower than Henry Cole's because Dr. Day was not the first doctor to treat his patients as an equal. As such, Dr. Day's social action involved new structuration practices for *him*. On the other hand, Henry Cole's act of structuration implied the creation of systemically new structures. In essence, Dr. Day's changed perception can be described as typical of an actor's everyday socialization process. In contra-distinction, Henry Cole's action constitutes innovative structuration based on a paradigmatically insightful reading of possible future social praxis.

I have constructed a hypothetical fig 10.4 in order to illustrate the risk involved in all structuration practices. In this case Dr. Jones is part of an unsuccessful interaction. I have chosen Dr. Jones as the actor A to make the point that Dr. Day did not do something inherently 'wrong' in fig 10.2. In Wright's and Morgan's handling of the material there is a certain prescriptive content. Consequently, aside from illustrating the 'risk' of most social interaction, fig. 10. 4 is also intended as a counter-weight to any implied normative bias which could be read into my reinterpretation of the material. I have not included a commentary on fig 10.4 as I consider it self-explanatory.

In the interaction between Mrs. Anderson and her doctors there was very little explicit mention of power resources. The following were inadvertently referred to: a) a machine for measuring electrolytes; b) the knowledge of both doctors; c) the medicines that Mrs. Anderson should or should not be taking. In fig 10.2 all of these are rendered useless as power resources through absence of restructuration. Mrs. Anderson even refuses to accept the evidence of the electrolyte machine. The information it gives is made valueless by her insistence on continuing to use diuretic.

Implicit in the interaction between Dr. Day and Mrs. Anderson is the hypothesis that social power resources are only power resources if, and only if, they are structurally embedded. For this to

173

Fig. 10.4

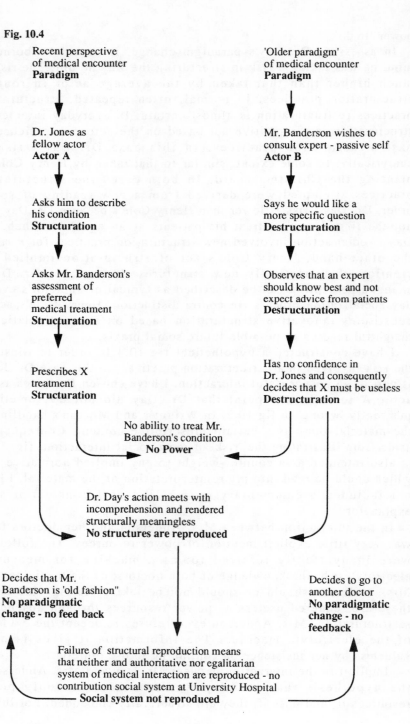

174

happen two prerequisites must be fulfilled: firstly, to be drawn upon initially by actor A, in structuration, the resource in question must be perceived as a potential power resource and; secondly, it must be also similarly perceived by B who is responsible for restructuration. In the act of being perceived as a resource and meeting with restructuration, the resource in question becomes a carrier of social structures. In the moment of restructuration an object becomes a social resource which is part of a system of interaction. As such, the resource is transformed into a part of the order of a social system.

This concept of resources, placed within restructuration theory, facilitates theorization of the praxiological creation of resources - a phenomenon which was inherently untheorizable within the structuration perspective (see chapter 7). As 'carriers' of social structures, resources have the same lack of permanence as social structures. Drawing upon resources in social action is an act of structuration which depends upon the restructuration of other in order to re/create social resources. This means that the usefulness of a resource in interaction is inherently dependent upon the restructuration of other. Consequently, on the one hand, social resources are continually potentially subject to demise. On the other hand, resources can be created for the first time through new structuration and restructuration practices. The success of an attempt to introduce new resources will be dependent upon a subjective assessment of two variable factors: a) the power potential of the new resource, b) the likely systemic implications of the structures carried by the resource in question. For an object to be constituted as a resource, both actors A and B must perceive it to contain desired potential consensual power and to entail structuration and restructuration practices which are paradigmatically acceptable. The dependence of power resources upon restructuration practice can be well illustrated from the annals of failed technological innovations. I have picked one such to illustrate the interrelationship between resources, perceived potential power and willingness to restructure.

For the purposes of domestic cooking, there is an acute fuel supply crisis in many parts of the Third World. In Africa and parts of Asia, the main source of cooking fuel traditionally has been wood. However, due to massive deforestation, recently there have developed firewood shortages in these regions. The main carriers of the burden posed by this shortage have mostly been women (Dankelman and Davidson 1988 p. 68). In order to meet household needs, it has not become uncommon for women to carry loads of up

175

to 35 kg distances of 10 km and/or to attempt to supplement fuel supplies with dried animal dung (Dankelman and Davidson 1988 p. 69). In order to alleviate this problem there have been many, mainly unsuccessful attempts, to introduce new stoves into the traditional village household. In addition to being cheap in fuel consumption, many of these cookers were also designed to improve safety standards and lower levels of indoor pollution (for the dangers of indoor pollution see Dankelman and Davidson 1988 p. 72).

Yet surprisingly, despite these objectives, "...most of these stoves were rejected at a village level." (Carr 1988 p. 133). One such stove was a solar reflexive cooker. It had the great advantage of using no fuel at all, combined with complete absence of pollution and very high safety standards. Superficially, it appeared to have tremendous potential as a new resource for the African women to whom it was given. However, being solar powered it needed direct sunlight. This meant that instead of cooking inside the house, as is traditional, it had to be done outside. In addition, the stove could only be used during daylight hours. This would have meant changing the main meal from the evening to the afternoon or making it earlier than was normal practice. In short, the solar stove 'carried' structuration practices which were foreign to the society into which they were introduced. They were structures which, if accepted through restructuration, would have had profound implications for the social system into which they were introduced. Consequently, despite their potential power to make life easier, the solar powered stoves were rejected as a resource. As Marlin Carr summed it up: "It is somewhat unrealistic to think that rural women could change the whole *pattern* of their day just to accommodate a new technological device." (Carr 1988 p. 133-4 emphasis not orig.).

Potential power resources are resources which implicitly have power potential and which, if drawn upon, would carry systemically compatible structures. If drawn upon by actor A they would meet with restructuration by actor B. Potential power resources are inert and passive (Dahl makes much the same point about what he calls power bases 1957 p. 203). Hence, groups can have resources at their disposal which, due to an initial lack of structuration, have never been used to realize power. The conversion of potential power resources into actual power resources is dependent upon a double conditional: if actor A structures and actor B restructures then power will be realized and new resources created. The latter will have the unintentional effect of creating new structures, changing the social system and in turn creating the new rules within the shared paradigm of the social actors involved.

As developed so far, this analysis is based on the idea of resources as 'carriers' of structures reproduced in the moment of interaction. In my critique of Giddens' classification of power resources I found fault with what appeared to be a tendency to sometimes confuse power and power resources. In particular I singled out for criticism his analysis of the organization of the time-space paths of others as a resource rather than as an effect of the exercise of power (see chapter 7). I will now extend the implications of the restructuration theory of the production of power to an analysis of control over time-space as a form of consensual power.

By way of general comment, it is important to distinguish two aspects of time. There is the general horizon of time against which social order can be perceived. Then there is a specific ontic concept of time which is contingently defined in terms of the manner in which it is perceived at any given historical conjuncture. One such ontic concept of time is clock-time.

As emphasized by Mumford and Giddens clock-time is a vital element in the development of an industrialized method of production. Using measured time, an actor A is able to know with precision exactly how B will act in the future. This enables him/her to use highly mechanized methods of production where the exact future positioning of B is a key element. The activities of actor B can be controlled with the precision required by the capitalist modes of production. As such, clock time is a vital structural link between the modes and relations of production within the capitalist system of production.

As a material object, the clock is used to constitute a constant measure of time. When actor A says to actor B, 'See you at six ', he/she knows with relative certainty when he/she will see B. B's behaviour becomes ordered rather than random. B knows what will constitute an appropriate reciprocal action with respect to A. Exact measured time is a social structure which is carried by time-keeping devices, watches and clocks, as social resources. (or tools for creating structure) *which are resources that enable actors to organize the social time-space paths of others*. The latter is an exercise of power. The materials of which a watch is constituted, in combination with the social structures, make it a resource. Measured time is 'carried' by a watch and recreated, as a structure, in the moment that social actors draw upon it to order their activities. This act of recreating measured time in turn feeds back to reconstitute the social system as ordered in time. When actor A meets actor B at a given time, they are recreating the social structure of time and simultaneously reconstituting the watch as a power resource which enables them to meet. The power produced is the ability to organize each other's time-space paths.

In addition to recreating the structure of clock-time, the act of using clock-time, to order social interaction, also has the unintentional effect of reinforcing a particular paradigmatically defined concept of time. This concept of time has two aspects: time is both an abstraction which can separated from things or action and it is synonymous with a succession of measurable 'nows'. I will concentrate on each of these in turn.

As emphasized by Heidegger, the concept of time as an abstraction is a particular and peculiar feature of Western social development. This unusual paradigmatic conceptualization is a key factor in enabling social actors to order the social system with respect to time. The point is not that the concept of time is specific to the capitalist relations of production. As Bourdieu puts the same point slightly differently: "It is true that nothing is more foreign to the pre-capitalist than representation of the future as a field of possibilities to be explored *and mastered by calculation.* But it does not follow from this, as has often been supposed, that the Algerian peasant is incapable of fixing his sights on a distant future, since his distrust of any attempt to take possession of the future always coexists with the foresight needed to spread the yield from a good harvest over a period of time, sometimes several years. The fact that the peasant sets aside for future consumption a proportion of his direct goods (...) presupposes that he is aiming at a 'forthcoming' future implicit in the directly perceived present. By contrast, the accumulation of indirect goods which, without being the source of any intrinsic satisfaction, can help to produce direct goods, is only meaningful in relation to a future constructed by calculation." (Bourdieu 1979 p. 22) (emphasis not orig.). The Algerian peasant can observe time-based order but he/she does not try to abstract time in an attempt to create a new imposed order. Time is perceived to be part of nature. It is inherent in nature. Hence, the idea that it can be abstracted from nature to constitute a social structure is foreign.

The distinction between natural resources and social resources is fundamental here. For the Algerian farmer, time is perceived *in* nature and, as such, is a criterion by which the order of the natural world is perceived. In a preclock-time society, time is a resource for interpreting the natural world as an ordered totality. It is perceived that seasons follow each other in an ordered way according to certain rules. This knowledge constitutes a power resource with respect to the natural world. What is not paradigmatically understood is that time can be abstracted as an entity in itself which can then be used to create order in the social world. In other words, time gains an existence of its own as an ordering device. Rather than being inherent in the order of things it can be used as an abstraction to impose order from the outside.

Moving on to the second aspect of clock-time, as emphasized by Bergson, Heidegger, Schutz, Giddens and many others, there are many non-clock based realities of time coexisting simultaneously with clock-time. There is the time of an actor's being-unto-death, there is the durée of an encounter and there is the durée of a set of social institutions. All these have in common that they are not constant. As a consequence, they are not suitable for an exact linear ordering of a social system even though they may be central to many aspects of the actual general orderedness of a system. To take an analogy from Wittgenstein: "The procedure of putting a lump of cheese on a balance and fixing the price by the turn of the scale would lose all its point if it frequently happened for such lumps to suddenly grow or shrink for no obvious reason." (Wittgenstein 1968 §142). It would be as "...if rule became exception and exception rule; or if both became phenomena of equal frequency - this would make our normal language-games lose their point." (Wittgenstein 1968 p. 142). Non-constant weights[2] and similarly different non-specific notions of time, because of their unclear, unpredictable nature, cannot form social structures since restructuration practices could not be set up around them. The inconsistency of these measures of time makes them inherently unsuitable as structuring elements for framing social order. In other words, clock-time is a unique cultural phenomenon whereby time can be perceived as an abstraction and divided into exact units for the purposes of ordering systemic reproduction.

This unique cultural perception manifests itself in an interpretation of the future upon which exact calculable order can be imposed. An expression of this is the concept of the future as a series of possibilities which can be time-tabled (See Giddens 1985 p. 174-5). Similarly the past can also be ordered. The latter manifests itself through the writing of chronologically based histories. This chronologizing of past and future in turn feeds back to constituting the paradigmatic consciousness of social actors whereby time becomes synonymous with measured time. Hence, as a discipline, History becomes a form of chronography where past social action is ordered according to the criterion of clock-time. Taken to its logical extreme, all social order becomes perceived in terms of clock- time. This can be represented as in fig. 10.5.

Fig 10.5

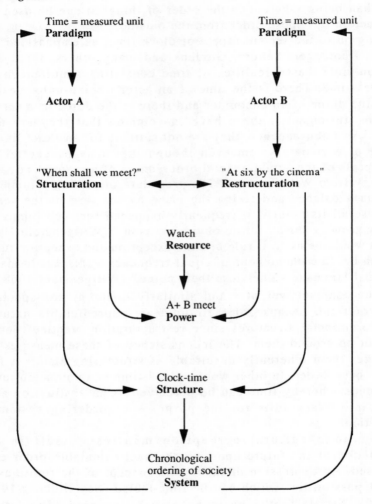

In the chapter on Parsonsian consensual power, I drew attention to the perceived analogical connections between power and money. In this chapter, I have argued that it is the social structures inherent in the creation of social power which give rise to this illusion. Having asserted that clock-time is a social structure carried by the resource of time-keeping devices, I will now assert what is implicit in my assessment of the Parsonsian analogy. As a valued object within social relations, money is in essence a social structure. When actor A gives actor B a unit of currency, the act of accepting the note in exchange for an object of use-value is an act of restructuration: the social structure of money is reproduced. The physical piece of paper or coin is a social resource which carries a social structure. The two in combination constitute money. Since the creation of social structures takes place through restructuration, Parsons is perfectly correct to stress the centrality of 'trust' in the creation of value in money. As already explained, all acts of structuration are a risk where the ultimate base for security is simply the 'trust' that others will restructure. As a social structure, money has systemic significance relative to the probability that others will restructure. When others refuse to restructure the structure in question 'dies' or, in the case of money, the currency becomes valueless and ultimately rejected. Because money is so much part of the twentieth century paradigm it is relatively stable and hyper-inflation is an anomalous experience with respect to our paradigm[3].

When actor A exchanges a commodity for money the intentionally desired outcome is to facilitate an ordered market exchange. The unintentional effect is the reproduction of a money-based economic system and a reinforcement of the conceptual paradigm which is a necessary prerequisite for the capitalist economic system. The sale of an object reinforces the paradigm within which an object exists not only as use value but also as a commodity with embodied exchange value. Hence, in the transition from feudalism to capitalism the same commodity becomes the carrier of another social structure. It is as if an object, like a coat, were a duck-rabbit picture. It can be either seen as use value within the medieval paradigm or as embodied exchange value within the capitalist paradigm. This can be expressed as in fig. 10.6.

The ability to see a coat as exchange value constitutes an additional systemic social structure. The coat becomes a carrier of the structure of monetary exchange value. Similarly, with respect to time, while the Algerian farmer is familiar with the concept of time in nature, he/she cannot perceive it as measured abstraction which can order interaction. Both clock-time and money constitute contributions to the widening of the structural scope of the social system. The introduction of new structures creates new ways of ordering social interaction. For the social actor, this implies a new set of possibilities for producing social power through interaction. In other words, the addition of structures to the system means an increase in the total amount of power which can be derived from the social system. Consequently, the total quantity of systemic power is a non-zero-sum amount which can be expanded through an enlargement of the number of structures contained within the social system.

Fig. 10.6

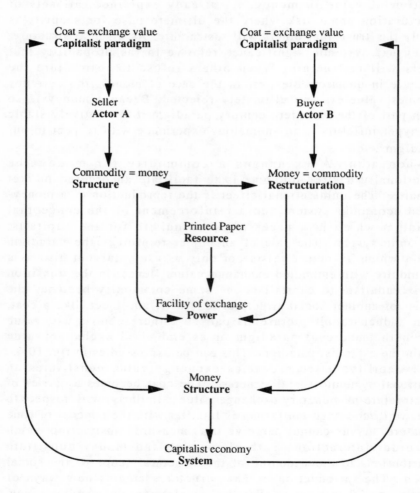

Throughout this work there has been an emphasis upon the idea of positive critique. In such an approach, a core element must be an orientation towards the ability to reconstitute core insights from one perspective into a new framework in such a manner that problematic elements associated with the former perspective can 'left behind'. By way of conclusion to this chapter I wish to take up this theme in an overt manner. In essence this will involve concluding by pointing to, in summary form, some of the insights from the Parsonsian consensual tradition which restructuration has made conceptual space for and taking note of the areas of theoretical difficulty that have been 'left behind'.

Central to Parson's contribution to the concept of power must be the following: that it is a *non-zerosum* phenomenon which is *created* through a process of production based upon *communicative* content and levels of mutual *trust*. It is a consensual trust, which precludes the image of power as an inherently negative blocking mechanism, instead power exists primarily as the ability *'to do'*. It is an ability 'to do' that implies an interactively shared project which drives a fundamental conceptual wedge between power and violence. Violence being an inherently non-interactive action by actor/s A upon a passive B. It is an act which is brought about by an inability of A to influence B through consensus either at the level of trust or at that of a shared project.

While these insights into the essence of power are of analytical consequence, they are accompanied by a number of theoretical difficulties. On the negative side are Parsons' theoretical dependence upon the analogy between power and money and the development of the concept of trust based upon normative legitimation derived from consensus on system goals. It is a formulation which is made more problematic by precluding the ability to provide conceptual space for conflictual power; an absence which is particularly noticeable within a theory where a central element is the concept of leadership as defined in terms of power 'over'.

Through the attempt to overcome the theoretical lack in structuration theory - with respect to the interactive dimension of structural reproduction and the analysis of praxiological social change - I made restructuration a vital element in the production of structure. As developed in chapter 9, the ability of actors to restructure is fundamentally linked to actors' capacity to symptomatically read social order in a common manner derived from a shared social paradigmatic reading of the rules governing social praxis. The shared p.c. and d.c. social knowledge/perception is a fundamental prerequisite for creation of structure through restructuring interaction. While structures are an unintentional effect, this shared p.c. and d.c. epistemological base enables actors *'to do'* something which they otherwise couldn't do. Actors produce power in social interaction which enables them to achieve something which, without restructuration, would be unavailable to them. As implicitly observed by Parsons, the creation of consensual power is not of trivial consequence (see Parsons 1967a p. 316). Within restructuration theory, it is *the fundamental social phenomenon which enables actors 'to do' anything qua* social actors. When an actor orders a cup of coffee in a cafe he/she is drawing upon consensual power arising from an immensely long chain of structuration and restructuration practices crossing national frontiers. As a facet of social systems, it is not power which exists outside of action as a mysterious flow or other metaphysical entity. It is power that is produced in the moment of interaction as the ability *to do*. Yet, it is still a systemically-linked entity: the process through which power is created is theoretically dependent upon the creation of structure as a systemically meaningful entity. In other words, it is structures which constitute the systemic factors which enable actors to derive any facilitative power from interaction.

This ability 'to do', social power is dependent upon a shared reading of the rule-governedness of social praxis. It is these rules which give social action the requisite *communicative* content so that each actor can symptomatically read another's action in such a manner as to facilitate restructuration. With respect to an actor's social paradigm, this means a dual interrelated level of trust. There is trust pertaining to the ability of self to interpret past interaction as a guide for future action and there is a fundamental trust that other will act in accordance with this interpretation of social rules. In other words, there is a trust that other will restructure to an act of structuration. These levels of trust are both necessary for epistemological security and the ability to create consensual power. In short, trust based on others' ability to restructure becomes a vital link for the production of power as *a created non-zerosum* phenomenon.

While restructuration theory has conceptual space for core Parsonsian insights into the nature of social power, the different theoretical premises/perspective make both the money analogy and the necessity for consensus on system goals redundant. While it is a core element for the production of power, the concept of restructuration is analytically quite separate from power. This implies that the consensus required for production of structure (as an unintentional effect) and power (as a desired ability 'to do') does not depend upon system goals. Instead, it is consensus manifest in the ability to structure and restructure derived from a shared p.c. and d.c. knowledge. In other words, it is a consensus upon the p.c. and d.c. substance of rules whereby restructuration can take place, structure re/created and power produced. It is a social power which exists in the moment of interaction. It does not circulate. The passing resemblance with money is derived from a confusion between the structuredness inherent in process of the production of power and the structures which are 'carried' by money. These structures are reproduced through communication, trust etc. and are an essential element in constituting money as a power resource. In fact, they are the systemic prerequisites for the existence of anything as a power resource. Outside of action, resources can only be termed systemically constituted resources with respect to their potential to stimulate restructuration when drawn upon in structuration. However, the theoretical necessity for conceptualizing resources as 'carriers' of structure in no respect implies a blurring of edges between the attributes of structure and those of power. Neither does the consensus inherent in restructuration imply an inability to theorize the production of power for the purpose of conflict. The praxiological level of consensus necessary for the creation of power does not necessarily preclude A prevailing over B. The consensus which I have theorized is one of socially paradigmatic perceptions of rule verification. It is *not* one which pertains to the nature of the power produced. This is achieved by by distinguishing between the consensus necessary for the production of power and the use to which the power is put. Consensus is a key element at the level of unintentional effect - the reproduction of structure. This does not necessarily imply consensus on an intentionally facilitative level. However, because the Parsonsian model is unable to provide conceptual space for conflictual power, I will now turn to Dahl to base the development of a theory of the production of conflictual power. For the sake of clarity I have represented the distinctions and convergence between Parsons and consensual power in restructuration in figurative form (fig 10.7).

Fig. 10.7

Parsons Problem Areas	Consensual Power	Restructuration
	Power implies ability to do.	
Money analogy		Structuration/ restructuration
	Power produced/ created + non-zero-sum	
Power 'out there' circulating medium		Facility in moment of interaction
	Communicative content	
Consensus based on system goals		Consensus on p.c. + d.c Paradigm
	Trust	
Confidence in ability Other to 'invest'		Confidence in other (epistemological sec. + restructuration)
	Power - violence distinction	

Untheorizable (Parsons)	Theorizable (Restructuration)
Absence of conceptual space for conflictual power	Conflictual power examined: Dahl (next chapter)

11 Conflictual power and restructuration

I began the first chapter on conflictual power by observing that it was written with two purposes: firstly, as a measure of the type of phenomena upon which to focus and, secondly, as a way of showing where the conflictual power debate drifted into the analysis of phenomena such as structural constraint. In this chapter I will deal the with the former theme concentrating specifically on 1-D power. This analysis will be extended to 2-D and 3-D in the chapters which follow.

In chapter one, I argued that there is a core conflictual view of power. This perception is intrinsically causally based. It is linked to the ability of A to affect B. This means a relationship between the two actors where the counterfactual claim can be made that if it were not for the action of A, B would not have acted in the manner he/she did. This assertion is qualified by the thesis that A's affecting of B must in some way be significant. Significance is assessed either with respect to the concept of 'key decisions' or the 'interests' of B.

I will start my conceptualization of conflictual power by analysing the idea of 'significant affecting' within the framework of restructuration theory. What does it mean to say that A 'significantly' affects B? If a father affects his daughter so that she always drinks Coke instead of Pepsi, is that significant? Or are only the actions of Mayor Lee of New Haven significant?

I would accept that significant affecting can be a useful yardstick for distinguishing power from other causal relationships. However, who is to decide what is significant? I would argue that significant affecting is ultimately linked to the subjective intentions of actors A and B. Take the following type of example: actor A is standing on the pavement. Actor B is walking along and has to change his/her path in order to avoid bumping into A. In this case, if A was staring vacantly into space oblivious of B's existence, A has affected B in a manner which is non-significant. However, the same actions could also be analysed as a form of power if A were deliberately standing in a given position on the pavement in order to make B change his/her direction. In such a case A would conceive of his/her position producing an affect upon B of significance. In this case A would be exercising power over B. I would argue that, at the analytical core, the criterion of significant affecting highlights the fact that the relationship between A and B must be one where rules are used to predict the action of other. The significant point about A's intentionality, as a criterion of 'significant affecting', is that he is using a given rule to predict the action of other. Going back to the earlier example of A staring vacantly into space, even if B believes that A is deliberately blocking his/her path, this belief is not sufficient to enable the political theorist to say A was exercising power over B. The central point is that A was not drawing upon a rule which could be used to affect B. In other words, A was not affecting B through the use of social resources because no structures were reproduced. While it could be argued that restructuration took place, structuration did not. While B thought he/she was responding to a rule (restructuration) A was not structuring according to any rules pertaining to the behaviour of B. Consequently, the central ingredient of structural reproduction was absent: they were not engaged in repeatable interaction. It could happen that A might be staring vacantly into space the next week and B might by chance come along and think 'there is A blocking my path again.' However, such an instance is purely contingent. What is of central theoretical consequence is that, as an instance of interaction, the absence of structuration means that as interaction of A and B *does not constitute a precedent for repeatable patterning of interaction*. With regard to the rules of language this is similar to what Wittgenstein is arguing when he writes that it is not possible that there exists a rule which has been obeyed only once because '[t]o obey a rule,...to play a game of chess, are *customs* (uses, institutions).' (Wittgenstein 1968 § 199). In broader conceptual terms, it must be emphasized that, in the restructuration perspective, not only are the structures of a system a set of repeatable rules - a position consistent with Giddens - but in addition systemic structures consist of a set of repeatable rules *with predictive content that is actually fulfilled*. In restructuration theory, a structure is more than a rule or Giddens type structure, a structure is the realization of meaning through the reaffirmation of the expectations presupposed by a given rule viewed though a given social paradigm. The p.c. d.c. paradigm provides the subjective 'horizon' against which expectations and repetition can be compared (see chapter 9). It is the convergence of such interpretive horizons that provides the consensus inherent in conflictual power. It is a consensus on the affirmation of specific rules. It is due to necessity for reaffirmation of expectations that the concept of 'private' actions was developed to denote actions which are not 'private' in the Wittgensteinian sense. In restructuration theory it is not possible to reproduce a social structure without another actor fulfilling the expectations in the initial act of rule-following - structuration without restructuration (see fig. 8.4). Neither is it possible for an actor to reproduce structure by fulfilling expectations which are inherent in an imagined rule - restructuration without structuration. Consequently, the reproduction of structure is a much less taken for granted, a more contested facet, of social life than it is in Giddens' structuration theory. Going back to the example of snubs, if an actor A were to tell an actor B that he/she was not snubbing B when he/she didn't say 'Hello,..' three weeks before, the point of this exercise is to redefine the meaning of their interaction by pointing out that he/she (A) was not structuring according the rules governing snubs. In effect, A is arguing that, irrespective of B's restructuration (even if B thought that A was snubbing), the interaction did not reproduce particular structures concerning snubs - the interaction was nonfulfilment of the rule that absence of a 'Hello,..' meant a deliberate denial of recognition. If A wishes to explain why the structures of snubs were not fulfilled (even if B thought they were) he/she can offer an explanation: 'I didn't see you because...' In other words, A is using the fact that structural reproduction necessitates both structuration and restructuration as a resource in order to establish the 'correct' meaning of a past interaction. By telling B that there was no structuration, he is de facto saying that snubbing did not take place.

The idea of restructuring interaction which fails to reproduce structure through the absence of structuration is directly applicable to the pavement incident. In the pavement incident, the reason why social power cannot have been said to have been produced by A over B is that A was not drawing upon structures in order to affect B. What is central here is not how much A affected B. If A was staring vacantly into space and, in the act of avoiding A, B fell off the pavement and under a bus, A is still not exercising social power over him/her. The point is not that something has happened that would not otherwise have happened or that what has happened is of or over a certain magnitude. The point is that what happened has happened because social power was produced - that would not otherwise have been there - using resources which yield power due to their structural embeddedness. In other words, the production of social power involves the production of abilities through the structural reproduction of the networks of meaning that constitute the essence of social life. What is of interest to the political theorist is not that actors can do things or prevail over others per se, what is theoretically significant is that it is possible to do so through the production of power derived from systemically constituted resources. This is inherently different from any affecting which could take place in a Hobbesian state of nature.

What is being argued for is an analysis of power which is not a typology of all the various causal factors which effect social life. It is theorization of the process by which we can realize an ability to do things, prevail over others, through the use of socially structured resources. This is the point which Stewart Clegg missed when he argued that the rat was an historically significant social agent in the fourteenth century. Yes, it is true that the rat had a profound effect upon a large number of people. However, that causal effect was not achieved through the reproduction or based upon any of the social resources which were intrinsic to life in the fourteenth century. As observed, if the fourteenth century had been a Hobbesian state of nature, made up of individual actors acting singly, the rat would still have had a theoretically similar effect.

The theoretical necessity for structuring and restructuring interaction in the production of power is consistent with the argument, developed by Bachrach and Baratz, that power is an inherently a relational concept. Consequently, it links into the hypothesis developed by them, in a tentative form, that power is a creation of both actors A and B. It also provides a good explanatory account of Dahl's core causal notion of conflictual power. In the pavement incident I gave an example of interaction with absent structuration practices. It was an example with direct applicability to the many analytical power debates concerning actor A and his/her paranoid neighbour B (for an example of such, see Clegg 1989 p. 67-8). The main point of this type of analysis is to develop

190

analytical criteria which can be used as conceptual tools to see if it makes sense to speak of A exercising power over B when A's effect upon B is actually a manifestation of B's paranoia. In restructuration theory, what is significant is that A is not structuring. The fact that B is restructuring is a reflection of his/her psychological condition. B is affirming imagined rules. Consequently, as in the pavement incident, it is a limiting instance of interaction with absent structuration practices. Consequently, the effect that A has upon B is not derived from an ability produced through the reproduction of structure. Analytically this is also similar to Dahl's example of Senator B who regularly votes the way he/she thinks would be most pleasing to President A who is unaware of his/her influence upon B's voting patterns. (Dahl 1968 p. 412). For Dahl, as it is here, the central point is that President A is not doing anything. Consequently, it would be inappropriate to argue that A is exercising power over B (Dahl 1968 p. 413). As observed by Dahl, if such a situation were analysed as an exercise of power, "...one would in principle need only study B's perceptions, the intentions B imputes to A, and the bearing of these on B's behaviour. Carried to the extreme, then, this kind of analysis could lead to the discovery of as many different power structures in a political system as there are individuals who impute different intentions to other individuals, groups, or strata in the system." (Dahl 1968 p. 413). With regard to the absence of action by A, for the restructuration theorist, what is analytically fundamental is that power has not been produced through a systemically significant route of structural reproduction.

What is central to Dahl's analysis is the interactively participatory nature of conflictual power. With respect to this issue, what is of particular interest to him is the development of a set of criteria which can distinguish relations of power from other interactive forms. In this regard, I have already shown how the absence of structuration gives an explanatory content, in terms of the production of power, to Dahl's descriptively analytical formulation of the inadequacy of analysing an interaction as an exercise of power purely with respect to the perceptions of B. The restructuration theorization of the production of power also gives explanatory content to Dahl's early 1957 'intuitive' notion of power. To repeat (see chapter 1) this example: "Suppose I stand on a corner and say to myself, 'I command all automobile drivers on this street to drive on the right side of the road'; suppose further that all the drivers actually do as I 'command' them to do; still, most people will regard me as mentally ill if I insist that I have enough power over

191

automobile drivers to compel them to use the right side of the road. On the other hand, suppose a policeman is standing in the middle of an intersection at which most ordinary traffic moves ahead; he orders all traffic to turn right or left; the traffic moves as he orders it to do." (Dahl 1957 p. 202). This particular example is of great theoretical interest because structuration and restructuration *is* taking place. Yet, structures are not recreated and power is not produced because structuration and restructuration is taking place with respect to different rules. Actor A (Dahl) believes that he/she has rules at his/her disposal which, when drawn upon, will cause a specific reaction in drivers B. Possibly A waves his/her hand in a manner which he/she thinks will be interpreted by B to mean 'drive on the right'. In restructuring, the reaction by B should constitute a rule-governed response to A's gesture of waving his/her hand. It should be a rule-governed response which reinforces the expectations inherent in the rule-governedness of A's act of structuration. This would then have the effect of reproducing the structures of meaning whereby a hand wave by A means 'drive on the right'. In short, through verifying the content inherent in A's hand wave rule, social structure would be reproduced. However, B's reaction is a p.c. or d.c. act of obeying or verifying the predictive content of the rules of the road. As such, it has the effect of reproducing the rule whereby drivers drive on the right. It is not an act of restructuration which reproduces structures concerning a citizen's ability to direct traffic through a wave of the hand. It is an act of restructuration which reproduces the rules of the road. However, the rules of the road are a different set of rules than those used by A in his/her structuration practice. Consequently, A's structuring wave of the hand constitutes a 'private' language act which, when introduced to the social world, does not meet with restructuration as defined by the rules which give meaning to A's hand wave. That is, despite the fact that A believes that restructuration has taken place.

For social interaction to contribute to structural reproduction, the causal relationship between A and B must be based upon structuration and restructuration with respect to the same rule. Restructuration must be appropriate reciprocal action with respect to the rules inherent in A's act of structuration. Unlike in the case of Dahl, in the case of the police-officer, this is exactly what is happening. The police, qua police-officer, structures using rules with a predictive content that certain signals by him/her will meet with a certain appropriate response. In the act of driving in accordance with the signals given by the police a driver obeys the police-officer's command and fulfils the rules he/she used in structuring. Essentially, the driver is recreating the structures which the police-officer is drawing upon. In the latter act of restructuration, the driver is contributing to the creation and/or recreation of social structures whereby a particular signal by a man/woman, in a given uniform, means a command to drive in a particular way. These acts where restructuration is absent (with respect to Dahl) and restructuration (with respect to the police-officer) contributes to the reproduction of a social system within which police can direct traffic, using certain signals, but private individuals cannot. This contribution will also feedback to recreate a certain paradigmatic reading of social order. A refusal by social actors to accept this feedback would constitute social deviance. Hence, Dahl's remark "...most people will regard me as mentally ill if I insist that I have enough power over automobile drivers to compel them to use the right side of the road". In this context, mental illness is made equivalent to the persistence in maintaining a different paradigm from others in spite of anomalous experiences as manifest in the non-fulfilment of rules. The contrast between Dahl and the police officer can be represented as in figures 11.1 and 11.2 (over).

In many respects the fig 11.2 successful exercise of power, by the police-officer over a driver, is a good example of 1-D. As such, I wish to use it to analyse some of the many phenomena associated with conflictual power.

One of the first things which can be observed is that, as in consensual power, the success of the interaction is dependent upon a shared paradigmatic reading of symbols. Hence, Bachrach's and Baratz's point (which is similar to Parsons' with respect to consensual power) that the exercise of power is an inherently communicative act (see chapter 1). In other words, the production of conflictual power is premised upon the same form of p.c. and d.c. consensus on rule affirmation as is found with respect to consensual power. However, appropriate reciprocal action is also linked to another related factor. Even if Dahl had used exactly the same hand movements as the police officer restructuration would not take place. A shared 'language' of restructuration practices is not enough to give power over B. It is A's role, qua traffic police, which gives him/her the legitimate 'right' to draw upon the structures which he/she does. The police-officer's act of structuration implies drawing upon rules which meet with restructuration *only if* drawn upon by the police. In this case, unlike A2 (Dahl), A1 (police) has the authority to draw upon certain social structures. Hence, B's

Fig 11.1

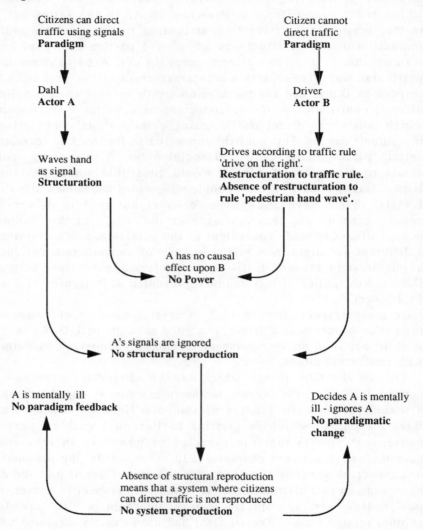

Citizens can direct
traffic using signals
Paradigm

Citizen cannot
direct traffic
Paradigm

Dahl
Actor A

Driver
Actor B

Waves hand
as signal
Structuration

Drives according to traffic rule
'drive on the right'.
**Restructuration to traffic rule.
Absence of restructuration to
rule 'pedestrian hand wave'.**

A has no causal
effect upon B
No Power

A's signals are ignored
No structural reproduction

A is mentally ill
No paradigm feedback

Decides A is mentally
ill - ignores A
**No paradigmatic
change**

Absence of structural reproduction
means that a system where citizens
can direct traffic is not reproduced
No system reproduction

Fig. 11.2

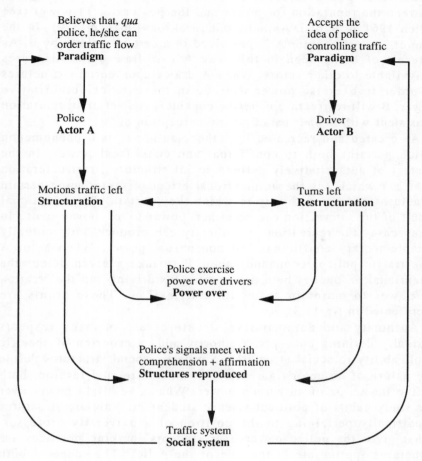

compliance is both communicatively and authoritatively based. When B restructures, the unintentional effect of his/her compliance is to reproduce both the symbols used and the authority of the police. The authority reproduced is a role-specific social phenomenon which is structurally defined and constantly reproduced through the restructuration of 'other'. In this act of restructuration 'other' is implicitly legitimating A's 'right' to draw upon certain role-specific social structures.

The recreation of authority through restructuration by B is a self-perpetuating process. It is analogous to Parson's 'operation bootstrap'. It is also similar to the hypothesis developed by the reputational power theorists that there is an inherent connection between the reputation for power and the possession of power (see Erlich 1961 p. 926; D'Antonio and Erickson 1962b p. 370). In the case of authority, actor A is perceived in a certain manner by B. As a result of being seen in this way A can draw upon structures unavailable to other actors. When A draws upon certain structures in order to exercise power over B, in the case of authoritative power, B will restructure if he/she considers A's act of structuration consistent with his/her paradigmatic perception of A.

As created and recreated by 'other', authority is a phenomenon which pertains both to conflictual and consensual power. In the context of authoritatively defined social structures, restructuration is an act which has the unintentional effect of reproducing certain structures and the authority to which they pertain. The intentional result of the interaction can be either 'power to' or 'power over'. In many cases the recreation of authority can produce both mutually complementary conflictual and consensual power. When actor A (the traffic police) commands actor B to take a given detour the intentional product is both power *over* B's driving and the creation of power *to* maintain a smooth traffic flow. These points are represented in fig 11.3.

Authority and authoritative structures are in many respects mutually defining concepts. Authority adds a criterion of specific applicability to social structures. Similarly, social structures define the nature of an actor's authority. In an interrelated fashion, both define the scope of an actor's power. What gives Dahl power over the study habits of political science students at Yale are structures specifically pertaining to the position of a university professor. What gives the police power over students' parking practices are structures appropriate to the role of the police. The scope of both the power of Dahl and the New Haven police is constituted by the structures which they can draw upon and expect restructuration through compliance.

Authority gives the police access to social structures which are unavailable to Dahl. It is this availability, as manifest in the restructuration of other, which makes the police more powerful than Dahl with respect to the issue area of traffic. As already emphasized, this power is an ability 'to do' which is derived from social interaction in the moment of restructuration. Like social structures, power exists only as the facility *produced* in the moment structures are *recreated*. In the moment of restructuring interaction power is an intentional product, the creation of which has the unintentional effect of re/creating social structures. If A is more

196

Fig. 11.3

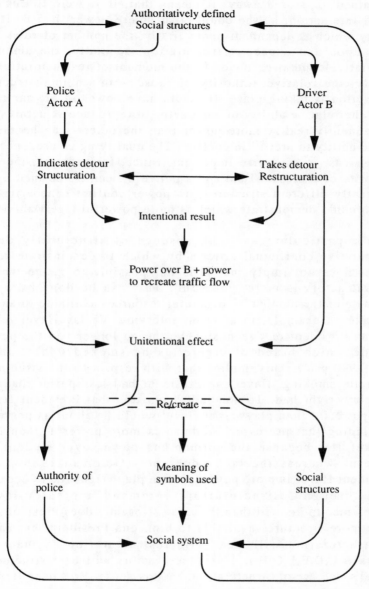

powerful than B this does not imply that he/she has power 'contained' or stored away. It means that, if A were to engage in social interaction, he/she could create more power than B. It is an ability which is dependent upon: firstly, the number of rules A can draw upon and expect restructuration, secondly, the amount of facilitative content produced in the moment of restructuration and, thirdly, the relative authority of those with whom restructuring interaction is taking place. If actors have power in the same issue area, the relative ability of each actor to reproduce structures - and consequently realize more power than the other - can be assessed by the ability to prevail in conflict. The qualifying clause, specifying issue areas, is of course important. Since, for example, the actual authority of professor Dahl and a police-officer are defined by such inherently different structures, no power conflict can be imagined which could demonstrate which is more powerful (see Dahl 1957 p. 206).

In a particular case, the absence of structurally defined comparative conflictual criteria by which to demonstrate relative power does not imply that it is not possible to gauge which of several actors is more 'powerful'. This can be done by a rough estimate of the number of structural resources available to an actor. To take an example, in a recent interview Vaclav Havel revealed that as President of Czechoslovakia he no longer had the power to decide which brand of cigarettes he smoked (The European 11/5/1990 p. 4). This implies that with respect to the issue area of cigarette smoking, Havel the President had less power than Havel the playwright had. To conclude from this that President Havel is less powerful than playwright Havel would be about as perverse as concluding that professor Goldman is more powerful than Nelson Rockefeller because the former has power over student study patterns whereas the latter does not (Goldman 1986 p. 157). President Havel is more powerful than playwright Havel because he can, through restructuration, command a greater level of compliance to his will than the latter. Not only does President Havel have more structures available to him, qua President, but each act of structuration will meet with restructuration by many more actors B,C,D,E,F,G,H,I,.... All these actors will be restructuring to Havel's one act of structuration. In this sense, President Havel can exercise power over a multitude of actors by engaging in social interaction with all of them at once. In addition, his power is further magnified by an ability to prevail over actors in positions of authority, actors who, due to their authority, have more social structures at their disposal than the average citizen of

Czechoslovakia. Through a command system, Havel's initial act of structuration will meet with restructuration by powerful actors. If this restructuration takes place through commands to other less powerful actors, then the act of restructuration by these powerful actors will in turn constitute structuration for other actors. Potentially, this process could be continued throughout Czechoslovakia. This implies that one act of structuration could have have a ripple effect throughout an entire command system of the politically defined social system of Czechoslovakia.

Giddens describes authoritative resources in terms of an ability to control the time-space paths of 'other'. In my critique of Giddens' position, I argued that he was confusing the effects of A's exercise of power with the resources which A used in order to exercise power over B. If the police orders a driver to take a turning left, the compliance of other is a manifestation of the production of power over B. What gives A the power over B is B's willingness to restructure. The authoritative resources available to A are recreated through this act of restructuration and conflictual power is produced. These resources are described as authoritative because they pertain to actor A qua police officer. In the example of the traffic police, what gives A power over B is linked to a whole series of factors among which is B's ability to recognise A as a police officer. In such a case A's clothes carry within them social structures in much the same manner as a clock carries the structure of time. The police officer's clothes are material objects which carry within them authoritative resources - a police officer without his/her uniform has as much power over car drivers as Dahl.

The above implies the hypothesis that allocative and authoritative resources are only social power resources to the extent to which they carry social structures. In effect, I am extending the argument concerning resources already made in the context of consensual power. Developing this point further: within the capitalist relations of production, for an actor A to gain power over others through wealth derived from selling coats, it is a necessary prerequisite that a coat carries structures which define it as exchange value. The same argument can be applied to the ability of the owner of an acre of land to use his/her ownership as a resource to prevent people trespassing. The success of such an action is inherently linked to the social structures carried by the land within a system of social relations where actors B understand the concept of private property[1]. It is an agreement which has the same analytical status as the p.c. and d.c. consensus theorized with regard to consensual power. If B complies with A's command not to

199

trespass, then B is reproducing structures pertaining to the capitalist system. Hence, private property only becomes realized as a resource in the moment of the production of power through restructuration. What makes the owner of private property more powerful than another propertyless actor, is his/her access to social structures which are unavailable to the latter. They are social structures pertaining to a system of which A and B are a part but to which only A has access.

Within the system, social structures give a specific *meaning* to a given area of soil. They are what makes that soil an inherently social resource which is systemically meaningful. These social structures define the land in question as pertaining to a given individual, as distinct from ground which is owned by another or no-one. The structures 'carried' by the land make it different to other areas of soil in a manner analogous to the Paris to Geneva train example used by Saussure. The difference conferred upon the land, by the structures it carries, makes it a resource which a specific actor can draw upon in order to prevail upon another actor.

The comparison between the propertyless and propertied actor is in many respects similar to that between Dahl and the traffic police. With respect to the issue of trespassing, the owner of land has more power than the propertyless individual because the structures, carried by the ground in question, define his/her unique relationship to it as a piece of property. His/her ownership means that if he/she structures, by commanding another to leave his/her land, restructuration will follow. Similarly, with respect to the issue of traffic flow, the police officer has more power than Dahl because he/she has an authoritatively defined ability, through the restructuration of other, to gain compliance.

Having argued that the traffic police have more power than Dahl, with respect to the issue of traffic flow, the next question is to explain why Dahl has more power than the police with respect to study patterns. What are Dahl's power resources? I would argue that his power resource is knowledge. I have already argued that paradigmatic social knowledge can exist both at the level of d.c. and p.c. Dahl's knowledge of political science exists at the level of d.c.. In chapter 9, based on Popper and Giddens, I argued that d.c. knowledge is knowledge which is objectified through promulgation. Consequently, unlike p.c., it has an existence 'outside' the mind of a specific actor. In terms of interaction this means that it can exist as a resource. *It can exist as an object which carries social structures.* As a social resource it can also pertain to a specific individual. A police-officer is an actor with authoritatively-defined access to structures pertaining to the direction of traffic. Similarly the 'expert' has unique recourse to d.c. social knowledge. As an expert, Professor Dahl can pronounce upon or create specific areas of d.c. knowledge. If Dahl draws upon knowledge within the discourse of political science, it will meet with a different reaction from students than it will if stated by a police-officer. Dahl's 'expertise' gives certain information or ideas a structured content by which he can expect compliance through restructuration. The traffic police's authority makes a certain uniform a power resource whereas Dahl's expertise makes information/ideas into a resource. It is this d.c. knowledge which gives him (and Professor Goldman) power over student study patterns.

In the context of analysing the structuredness of power resources, it is important to point out that while objects are systemically defined as resources by the structures they carry, the material characteristics of which a resource is constituted are a necessary prerequisite for creation of power. As I implicitly observed, with respect to Dahl's example of the traffic police, once a police officer's uniform is systemically structurally constituted as a resource, the perceived physical characteristics of silver buttons and blue cloth enables an actor to direct traffic. The possession of such a uniform makes a police officer more powerful than Dahl in certain issue areas. Similarly, my emphasis on the structures carried by an acre of land should not obscure the fact that it is the possession of land, within a system characterized by the structure of private property, which makes certain individuals more powerful than others. In the context of Dahl, it should also be observed that the structured knowledge which he, as political scientist, draws upon also exists as information. While this information carries different structures, depending upon who draws upon it, the actual objectified informative content is a prerequisite for its constitution as a power resource. In short, a powerful individual not only has access to structures but also to the materials which carry these structures.

Inherent in my conceptualization, of power resources as the carriers of structures, is the hypothesis that the creation of power over B is inherently dependent upon rule affirmation by B. It is B's act of restructuration which gives A social power over him/her. This applies even in cases where A can threaten severe sanctions. The traffic police example can be extended to illustrate this point.

Imagine a situation where the threatened sanction for non-compliance with the traffic police is a fine of £20. At a particular intersection police officer A directs driver B to turn left. Instead of driving as directed, B turns right. A then imposes a £20 fine upon B. In this case case payment of the £20 is an act of compliance, through restructuration, with respect to A's authority to impose fines. According to the rule of law one would expect B to pay £20. However, B does not pay the fine and A has again failed to exercise power over him/her. As a result A takes B to court where a £100 fine is imposed upon him/her for not payment of the initial £20 fine. If B pays the £100 this means a recreation of the structures carried by the court. However, B can again fail to restructure and the process can go on ad infinitum. In sum, it is B's act of restructuration which ultimately gives another social power over him/her. Eventually, in the case of continuous destructuration, the only way in which the compliance of B can be realized is through non-social power: violence is inflicted upon B's body - he/she is handcuffed and physically confined to a prison.

In many respects, the central theoretical position of the above example is consistent with Parsons' hypothesis that physical coercion is only an ultimate base for power. It is simultaneously also in agreement with Arendt's observation that where power ends violence begins. In this context, violence is an ultimate base which defines certain borders of restructuration practices. It is ultimately restructuration, not violence, which is the source of power in a system.

Returning to the example of President Havel, what gives him power is the ability to gain compliance through appropriate reciprocal action. As Arendt would have observed, it was Ceausescu's inability to exercise power that made him resort to violence. Of course, it is true that Havel also has a massive administration at his disposal which is occupying/using an enormous amount of material resources. The image of Mill's power machine immediately springs to mind. However, the point is that such an organizational machine can only generate power if it carries within it social structures so that it can command restructuration. This point is well illustrated by the comment made by the sovietologist Seweryn Bailer when questioned on the attempt by old guard communists (in the USSR) to hold on to power through continued occupation of the traditional command posts: "They may have control over buildings, telephones, cars - all the paraphernalia of power - but if there is nobody to obey the commands any longer there is no longer a command system." (BBC Newsnight 29/6/1990). To use Mill's image, actors may have 40,000 phone switchboards or fifteen miles of pneumatic tubing at their disposal. However, this does not make them inherently powerful unless they also have access to systemically meaningful social structures. A Mosca, Michels or Mills type organizational power machine, or Leviathan, is only a power resource if it carries structures which make restructuration likely. The latter is systemically determined by those over whom power is to be exercised. However, the dependence of a Leviathan upon restructuration should not obscure the fact that, when managed efficiently, it can generate massive amounts of power. Even though inherently dependent upon other, a well-managed organization is a very effective tool for the mobilization of power. If managed by an individual who uses his/her authority well, it can also be used to create new systemic and authoritative power. In other words, through the skillful use of organizations, it is also possible to be a 'Ceausescu in reverse'. A good example of such an individual is given by Dahl in his description of the political success of Mayor Lee of New Haven - I have included an analysis of Lee's successful use of organizations as an appendix to this chapter (see appendix 2). In short, like any other resource, an organizational Leviathan can be a power resource within one system and not within another.

In conclusion, 1-D conflictual power is power over others realized in the moment of interaction by the compliance of other through the act of restructuration. This means that ultimately it is social structures which determine who is powerful, who has power resources and what constitute systemically defined social resources. However, structures do not just exist 'out there'. They are realized through praxis. This implies that it is possible to manipulate social structures so as to influence the balance of power between actors within a system. However, such a manoeuvre would involve the exercise of 2-D power - the central theme of the next chapter.

12 Destructuration, institutions and powerlessness

In order to preempt misunderstandings, I will begin this chapter by re-emphasising certain aspects concerning the aims and scope of a restructuring approach to the analysis of power and structural phenomena. The primary purpose of such an introductory section is to outline the criteria used in the restructuring interpretation of 2-D power. Since the publication of Lukes' *Power: A Radical View* (1974), it has been generally recognized that there exist core analytical problems in differentiating causal phenomena attributable to power and those ascribable to structure. It was due to the perception of this problem that Lukes developed the conceptualization of an analytical opposition between spheres of contingency and determinism. However, as has been observed, this position only worked on a descriptive level. Clegg interpreted the emergence of the power/structure debate as a manifestation of a modernist paradigmatic crisis and argued for a postmodernist perspective. Another reaction to the theoretical problems posed by the relationship between power and structure was to interpret the emergence of the problematic as a manifestation of a lack of explanatory understanding of the process by which structure and power are brought into existence. As part of this reaction, Jessop sketched the bare outlines of a Poulantzasian Marxist structuralist explanatory theorization. On a more detailed level, Giddens developed the theory of structuration specifically to explain the recreation of structure. This work is, in many respects, a continuation of the latter type of approach. Here the key to the resolution of the relationship between power and structure is perceived to reside in changing the focus of investigation away from the pure analysis of concepts. Instead emphasis is placed on the explanatory theorization of the re/creation of structure and the production of power. In this framework, the analytical reasons for calling a given phenomenon power or structure serve as delineating pointers which tell the political theorist the exact conceptual terrain occupied by the phenomenon which he/she wishes to explain. Consequently, debate on the relative conceptual semantic merit of calling a phenomenon power or structure become perceived as inappropriate. In other words, conceptual problems are not resolved by becoming involved in the intricacies of debates on analytical neatness. These debates are instead used as a guide to highlight phenomena deserving explanation. Once the processes by which structure is recreated and power produced are theorized, this understanding is then used in the explanatory categorisation of a specific phenomenon as either power or structure. Referring to the specific arguments contained in this chapter and chapter 13, it will be argued that the phenomena of 2-D and 3-D are actually facets of the recreation of structure. Such a theorization should not be interpreted as meaning either that 2-D and 3-D are in any respect socially insignificant or that issue has been taken with those who argue it is analytically neater to call them power. Instead, it is intended to convey explanatory information, using the framework of restructuration theory as a theoretical tool, which shows that any manifestations of 2-D and 3-D will invariably be causal phenomena derived from the re/creation of structure. In other words, in 2-D and 3-D the powerlessness of B is realized as an effect of structure not the production of power.

When discussing Bachrach and Baratz's concept of power, I argued that in the move from 1-D to 2-D power there was an inherent conceptual change in emphasis from actor A to B. In 1-D the central focus is upon the power of A as manifest in his/her ability to prevail over B. In 2-D emphasis is placed on the powerlessness of B. It is a powerlessness which is generated through the establishment of organizations. Using the words of Schattshneider (1961 p. 71), Bachrach and Baratz argued that "[a]ll forms of political organization have bias in favour of the exploitation of some kinds of conflict and the suppression of others because *organization is the mobilization of bias.*" (Bachrach and Baratz 1962 p. 949). In other words, they were arguing that organizations are a primary machinery by which the powerlessness of B can be actualized. Bachrach and Baratz were particularly interested in two facets of organizational machinery used to create B's powerlessness: a) the ability of an organization to render B's grievances non-issues and, b) the processes by which this bias could become reinforced through the the reproduction of B's knowledge of anticipated reactions.

On a purely descriptive analytical level, the 2-D phenomenon was considered an intrinsically important part of the analysis power for a number of reasons. For theorists working within the framework set out by Dahl, it was considered analytically significant that 2-D often involves agency. The point of nondecision-making is not that decisions are not made but that a decision is made not to make a decision with respect a specific issue area. This is done by deliberately confining the scope of the decision-making arena. Such acts of nondecision-making do not simply happen but are often attributable to certain actor/s A. Of course, it is equally true that much of the mobilization of organization bias is not attributable to specific agents A. In a perspective which attributes the ability to affect other solely to the exercise of power, this is conceptually problematic. However, it is a problem which does not obscure the fact that the day-to-day non-agent specific reproduction of organizational bias is highly significant in effecting distributions of power. In other words, the absence of given actors A realizing their agency through the exercise of power over B, does not invalidate the observed fact that the day-to day reproduction of organizational bias is analytically fundamental in assessing the powerlessness of B. Consequently, any sophisticated analysis of relations between actors A and B is conceptually incomplete without taking account of both agent and non-agent specific organizational bias. In arguing that 2-D is not a form of power, issue will not be taken with this core analytical argument. Instead it will be used as a conceptual guide for the explanatory application of restructuring theory to the phenomenon of 2-D. Since Bachrach and Baratz considered organizations a fundamental facet of the machinery of 2-D, the theoretical starting point of this chapter will an explanatory theorization of the concept of organizations. What is an organization and how does it create bias?

At the analytical core, an organization is a d.c. intentionally created social order. It is the factor of d.c. intentionality which distinguishes it from a social system. A social system is an order which is created as the unintentional effect of intentional action. It is an effect which is ultimately a product of the nonfalsification of some of the rules inherent in actors p.c. and d.c. perceptions of social order. The verification of this 'natural attitude' is a necessary prerequisite for the creation of both systemically generated conflictual and consensual power. Like a system, an organization produces power through ordered interaction. It is an order which is theoretically more analogous to Hobbes' Leviathan than to a social system. As a whole, an organization is a d.c. attempt at intentionally creating systemically ordered interaction. In broad conceptual terms, the comparative relationship between a system and organization can be understood analogically by comparing a living language - where rules are reproduced and fulfilled spontaneously without actors 'knowing what is going on' at the level of d.c - with an artificial language such as is used in a computer programme or a legal code.

When broken into its constituent parts, a social system is an aggregate of social structures. Through difference, these structures give meaning to each other in the same way as language gives meaning to a word and words meaning to each other. Where these meanings give way to different meanings, or chaos, the social system ends. On a descriptive ontological level, this is what Giddens means by time-space edges. With regard to interaction, once the edges of a system are crossed, an act of structuration will not meet with restructuration. In other words, not only is there a different patterning across time-space, as conveyed in the concept of time-space edges, but recursively used rules will not be fulfilled. For a social system, these edges define the area within which ordered interaction takes place and rules are converted into structures through restructuration. Produced through praxis, the creation of these edges is a spontaneous nonconscious effect of intentional action.

As distinct from a system, an organization is an intentional effect of intentional action. In organizations a given set of rules is devised in order to achieve a preconceived function. When an organization is broken into its related parts, it is found to be made up of intentionally constructed structures. Prior to the creation of an organization, it has been conceived of as a totality consisting of an assembled set of social structures which have been formulated at the level of d.c.. Each of these structures has been created to pertain to a specific organisationally defined function. For the sake of analytical clarity, I will distinguish these intentionally based organizational structures from other social structures, by referring to the former as institutions. Institutions are social structures which, in their creation, were intentionally conceived of as d.c.

guides for future ordered interaction. In short, as scalar concepts, *structures are the unintentional effect of intentional action whereas institutions are the intentional effect of intentional action.*

Once formulated at the level of d.c., social institutions have an important characteristic in common with social structures: they have to be recreated. This means that they must be used as rules to guide structuration and have to be affirmed through restructuration. Just like structures, institutions have the potential to remain in the realm of a 'private language'. In other words, it is not sufficient for certain social actors to conceive of an organization in the abstract for there to actually be an organization. An organization which does not order interaction is only an organization in name. In theoretical terms, this is the effect of structural constraint upon the possibility of creating new institutional orders.

With respect to the creation of new power resources, in chapters 7 and 10 it was argued that it is not theoretically sufficient for actors to perceive that a given object has a specific power potential. To create a new resource it is necessary that other actors accept the structure implicitly carried by that object. In the case of the creation of institutions this process is substantially more overt. The creation of a new institution inherently means a deliberate attempt by actors to introduce new rules for a certain purpose. Ultimately, the achievement of this purpose is dependent upon the willingness of others to verify the rule in question. Since organizations are set up for specific purposes, this will often involve an assessment of the validity of the goals of an organization. In this context, it is theoretically interesting to observe that the Parsonsian theorization of the concept of system goals is theoretically more satisfactory with regard to social organizations than it is with respect to systems. In systems consensus is a p.c. and d.c. paradigmatic perception on the verification of rules. In no respect does such systemic social knowledge imply consensus on systemic goals. However, with regard to organizations, the desire to create institutions is for a specific purpose. Consequently, the d.c. conceptualization of institutional rules does reflect a certain consensus on goals. In particular, this applies to the initial creation of institutions and, to a lesser extent, to their continued reproduction over time. However, the emergence of this second level of consensus should not obscure the central theoretical point which is that institutional reproduction takes place through the p.c. and d.c. paradigmatic consensus pertaining to rule affirmation. The reproduction of institutions can take place without consensus on organizational goals. In other words, the d.c. intentionality with which institutions are created does not alter the need for continuous rule affirmation through restructuration. A traffic light is a series of three lights which carry intentionally created social structures - social institutions. However, in order for the lights to 'carry' these institutions people must react with appropriate reciprocal actions by affirming the rules of the Highway Code. If drivers were to ignore the lights they would lose their organisationally-defined meaning through the non-reproduction of certain institutions. Such non-restructuration or destructuration would in turn have the overall organizational effect of disrupting the d.c. formulated order which was intended to be created by the Highway Code - organizational goals.

Over time the reproduction of institutions will tend to become more and more routine. Routinization will tend to make d.c. reproduction of institutions a more p.c. phenomenon. However, the initial d.c. 'for the sake of' reason, which an institution was originally created for, will tend to make the move from p.c. to d.c. inherently easier than in a social system. Even the slightest anomalous experience will tend to make institutional reproduction a d.c. act. For members of such an organization, the clarity of organizational edges and the institutional smallness of an organization will make an anomalous experience more likely. In short, institutional reproduction will tend to be d.c. and, even when highly routinized, the flow from p.c. to d.c. is very easily triggered. In other words, the d.c. specificity of rules will make the perception of new rule-governed structuration practices more perceptible. When a member of an organization is faced with slightly different structuration practices, destructuration is more likely than in a social system. Higher levels of control over restructuration and destructuration mean that organizational change does not happen in as unmonitored a fashion as systemic change does. Consequently, organizational edges can be better maintained than systemic edges.

In the theorization of the production of conflictual and consensual power, it was argued that the reproduction of social structures is the fundamental facilitative mechanism whereby power can be realized in the moment of agency. As such, social systems exist as a mechanism whereby restructuring interaction enables actors 'to do' something which they could not otherwise do. It is the structures 'carried' by things which make objects social power resources. Without the actual fulfilment of rules resources will have an unpredictable effect upon other. This means that *things are only structurally constituted as resources, with a*

209

potential for the production of power, within a highly specific systemic space. Outside of that space the absence of restructuring practices will empty a given object of its structural content. In the moment of changing structural content the object in question will either cease to be a power resources - it will cease to 'carry' structures - or alternatively it becomes a different kind of power resource - a carrier of new structures. For actors with a paradigmatic perception defined by an old systemic space, the structural reconstitution of an object as a new kind of resource in different systemic space will preclude the use of that object to initiate *controlled* causal change. Alternatively, if the object ceases to meet with any restructuration practices this can be interpreted as a redefinition of it as an irrelevance. Outside specific systemic edges, whether an object meets with inappropriate restructuration, destructuration or non-restructuration, the central point remains the same: systemic edges mark the boundaries beyond which social power cannot be produced.

A social organization can be seen from two commensurable angles. From one perspective it is an artificial d.c. social system specifically set up to produce power. A problem is perceived by social actors and, as a result, specific institutions are set up to produce power with respect to this issue area. Organizations are also confined within certain institutional edges. Outside these edges power will not be produced. Since organizations are usually substantially smaller and less complex than social systems, they will tend to be more confined in scope by institutional edges than social systems are by structural edges. Due to the d.c. origins of institutions, the edges of a social organization are less blurry than the edges of systems. Both the small size and the clarity of definition of institutional edges, make organizational space easily subject to control and maintenance. In terms of the commensurable facilitative and constraining facets of organizations, the well-defined edges inherent in organizations imply that the scope of organizational power will tend to be highly specific both in form and in nature.

Implicit in the conceptualization of an organization producing power of a specific scope and type is also the converse: an organization which cannot produce power in certain areas and of certain types. An organization can be both created to deal with certain issues (create consensual and conflictual power in these issue areas) or an organization can also be designed specifically not to deal with other issues. The d.c. nature of institutions, the smallness of organization and the clarity of organizational edges can all be mobilized to prevent the production of power in certain areas or of certain types. Organizations can be created to produce power with respect to certain issues but not others. When an actor raises an issue which, in order to create power, calls for the creation of new institutionalized practices outside established organizational edges, organizational members benefiting from bias engage in destructuration. Consequently, the less powerful actor's act of structuration gains the status of a 'private structure/institution'. In other words, in organizations there exists the potential to create "...institutional practices that limit the scope of the political process to public consideration of only those issues which are comparatively innocuous to A." (Bachrach and Baratz 1970 p. 7). On an explanatory level, what is theoretically fundamental is that the process by which an organization is controlled and confined to 'safe issue areas' is in many respects the reverse of 1-D. The mobilization of institutional bias is similar to 1-D in the general sense that it presupposes some level of conflict between A and B. Both are conflictual phenomena. However, in 1-D A exercises power over B by prevailing over him/her in an act of decision-making through the production of power. In 2-D, the more powerful actor devotes all his/her energies to preventing conflict from arising in issue areas of significance to him/her by forestalling the production of undesirable power. Inequality of power is maintained through the preservation of institutional edges. It is a preservation which takes place through preventing the creation of new social institutions with a potential to to produce power of a given scope or nature. In other words, once an organization has been constructed, it is the task of the more powerful actors, benefiting from organizational bias, to maintain the form and number of institutional practices contained within the edges of an organization. In this way it is possible to predetermine with relative accuracy areas of decision-making, areas of potential conflict and types of power produced. Alternatively, expressed another way, an "...organization is the mobilization of bias. Some issues are organized into politics while others are organized out." (Schattshneider in Bachrach and Baratz 1970 p. 8).

In 1-D and consensual power, A draws upon structures and B restructures. In 2-D, the more powerful actor is an active nondecision-maker who prevents potential issues from arising. Nondecision-making is a process of preventing new institutions from being created within the parameters of an organization. At this point it is important to stress that there is an analytical conflict between typology of interaction going from A to B and the traditional perception of A as more powerful than B. In theoretical terms, destructuration is an act done by B not A. Consequently, at this point, in the interests of explanatory theoretical consistency, it is necessary to break with tradition and *refer to B prevailing over A*. If A raises an issue which carries potentially new institutions, B must be careful not to restructure. In short, while in 1-D A structures and B restructures, in 2-D A structures and B destructures.

The destructuration practices, implicit in nondecision-making, constitute the 'other side' of an organization. On one level, a set of institutions orders interaction so that both conflictual and consensual power can be produced. However, through the maintenance of organizational edges it can also preclude certain forms of structured interaction. As an intentional creation, an organization could be compared to an artificially created language. As an intentional product it can be specifically created so that it can be used to facilitate communication. On another level, one could imagine a language specifically created so as to prevent the expression of certain ideas. In such a case, when a speaker persists in using the language in order to express these ideas, the speaker will find him/herself speaking a 'private' language. In other words, successful communication will not take place.

Bringing these threads together, 2-D is the intentional control over institutionalized social interaction facilitated by making certain institutions non-available for the purposes of ordering social interaction. The absence of these institutions are a constraint which prevents A from producing power with respect to certain issues. If A wishes to engage in institutionalized social interaction, in a certain issue area, he/she does not have the institutions available to him/her. In the act of nondecision-making and destructuration, B is preventing the creation of institutions and the production of power. By placing A outside institutionalized organizational edges, B is creating A's powerlessness.

The explanation of the phenomenon of 2-D in terms the non-production of power is of great theoretical consequence. In the theorization of conflictual and consensual power I showed how restructuring interaction can be used to produce power. Here I have argued that the monitored recreation of institutions can be used by B to affect A. Not only has conceptual space been made for a causal relationship to exist between A and B based upon the production of power but it has also been shown that B can affect A through the *non-production* of power. In the case of institutional bias what is analytically fundamental is that B is using specific institutional edges to impose constraints upon the behaviour of A. In other words, *the creation of institutional bias can best be described as institutional constraint.*

The theorization of the phenomenon of 2-D, as institutional constraint, implicitly turns the agent/structure problem on its head. Bachrach and Baratz conceptualized 2-D as power because it involved agency and important differentials of power. Here it is argued that 2-D is a special from of structural constraint - institutional constraint. In the introduction it was argued that a restructuring theorization of 2-D should have conceptual space for the fundamental analytical descriptive characteristics of 2-D. Implicit in this there would appear to be inherent theoretical tension between the concept of 2-D as agency and 2-D as institutional constraint. Using Lukes' scalar dichotomy between agency and structure, it would appear that I have precluded agency from institutional constraint. If agency implies levels of contingency and structure belongs to the realm of determinacy it could be interpreted that the theorization of 2-D in terms of institutional constraint actually empties 2-D of one of its core characteristics. When an actor engages in agenda setting he/she could have done otherwise - he/she is realizing his/her agency. In short, the theorization of 2-D as institutional constraint would appear to preclude providing conceptual space for the agency side of 2-D. In other words, it would appear that conceptual space has only been provided for inequalities of power inherent in the non-agent specific day-to-day praxiological institutional reproduction. Actually I would argue that this is not the case. Rather, the restructuration analysis of institutional constraint shows that the traditional perception of the agent/structure dichotomy is misconceived.

When Lukes analysed the existence of a scalar opposition between power and structure in terms of agency and structure or contingency and determinacy, he was arguing that two theoretical perceptions of social order were commensurable. Social life is characterized both by levels of determinacy and contingency or structure and power. As has been argued, he did not provide an overarching explanatory political theory that had conceptual space for both facets of social life. Lukes was simply asserting that both agent-centred views and structuralist interpretations of social order constituted relevant analytic tools for certain aspects of social analysis. The theory of structuration could be viewed as an attempt to provide the necessary explanatory conceptual framework which Lukes' assertion lacked. However, in terms of the development of contemporary sociopolitical thought, the theory of structuration also represents a reinterpretation of Lukes agency/structure scale. Like Lukes, Giddens argued that agency was manifest in power (see Giddens 1984 p. 9) but it was not an agency which was necessarily hindered by structure. Consequently, the association between structure and determinacy became partly modified. Power was realized in praxis through structuration practices. It was the ability of agents to draw upon structures which made them able 'to do' something that they could not otherwise do. In the moment of agency actors were able to act through the structuredness of resources (see Giddens 1979 p. 92). This structuredness is simultaneously a source of constraint. However, it is a constraint which is intrinsically important in the constitution of resources as resources. Constraint is the necessary prerequisite which prevents social action from degenerating into praxiological chaos. Without this constraint meaningful social agency would be impossible. In terms of Lukes' conceptualization of the relationship between agency and structure, this represented an important change in sociopolitical theory. Implicitly the 'could not have done otherwise' becomes linked, as a necessary prerequisite, to the concept of agency. Through this replacement of duality by dualism the image of separate realms of contingency versus realms of determinacy is abandoned. Instead, determinacy becomes necessary to the realization of contingent agency.

In the theorization of the duality of structure, Giddens had to maintain a link between structural constraint and determinacy, even if constraint and agency no longer constituted realms in opposition. If this link had not been maintained, structuration practices could not be theorized as realizable across varying spans of time and space. It is constraint which ensures that recursiveness is possible and it is recursiveness which reinforces constraint. The barrier between u.c. and d.c. forms the core internal drive necessary for the maintenance of constraint.

Inherent in the restructuration perspective is the total abandonment of Lukes' scalar analysis. In restructuration the concept of constraint is imposed by the restructuring practices of other. In some respects this can be described as a move away from the agent-centredness of Giddens and towards a more structuralist position. It is not only self who is responsible for constraint but it is also other. While this is less agent-centred, it is also a perspective which gives more autonomy to agents with regard to the recreation of structure. In Giddens it is 'the could not have done otherwise' aspect of structure which gives structural constraint meaning. However, with the differentiation of social reaction into restructuration, destructuration and non-restructuration, it is theoretically possible to remove determinacy from the concept of constraint without providing conceptual space for praxiological chaos or spontaneous social change. Structural contingency emerges both with respect to actors A and B. The central theoretical point which facilitates the break between structural constraint and determinism is the theorization of the creation of constraint as the mutual labour of both actors A and B. Unlike in structuration theory, in restructuration, constraint is not theorized as purely internal to A, it is derived from the need to verify a rule. While it would be untrue to argue that A does not experience constraint from his/her lack of knowledge of other rules (structuration), the actual imposition of constraint is realized in the choice between affirmation or falsification by another actor B. This collaborative aspect of structural reproduction gives actors control over structural reproduction. In this respect, actors have a level of autonomy with regard to structural constraint. This pertains in particular to the re/creation of institutions and the maintenance of organizational edges. In Giddens' perspective, actor A experiences constraint as internal determinacy which constitutes the sole theoretical barrier to social change. However, with the theorization of constraint as collaborative effort, actor A is freer to invent new rules. For an actor A who perceives a problem at the level of d.c., this allows him/her considerable structural possibilities for solving the problem through the creation of new d.c. rules. When an actor invents a new rule $a_n = n^4 - 22 + n^6$, instead of the more usual $a_n = n^2 + n - 1$, it is B who decides whether or not to allow the rule to be converted into a structure or if the imposition of structural constraint would be more appropriate. In other words, the fact that all interaction *does not* reproduce structure becomes the source for constraint. In short, figs 8.2, 8.3 and 8.4 can be interpreted as manifestations of the mutual labour necessary for the realization of structural constraint. With regard to actor B, it is analytically fundamental that constraint is not necessarily automatic. It is automatic when actor B does not understand the new rule used by A. In that case the only option open to B will be non-restructuration. However, if B understands the rule he/she has a *choice* whether or not to impose structural constraint upon A's structuration practices. B can choose between affirming or falsifying the new rule invented by A. If B engages in destructuration he/she will have prevented social change from taking place. *Inherent in the option of restructuration or destructuration there is both choice and contingency.* B can choose either restructuration or destructuration. In the realization of constraint upon A, B 'could have done otherwise'.

In the act of making a choice between restructuration or destructuration, B is producing a significant effect on two levels: 1) with regard to A, the imposition or non-imposition of constraint means a choice between allowing for the production of power or not, 2) with regard to a social system or organization, it means the active monitoring of structural/institutional social change. This dual effect significantly changes the theoretical status of agency. Agency is not only linked to structure in the sense that actors realize agency through the reproduction of structure but agents also manipulate the reproduction of the structural. In so doing, agents significantly affect others. By destructuration B has made use of a specific method of affecting A. This implies that agency can be realized through the manipulation of institutions. In other words, agents can affect each other *either* by the exercise of power or though strategic destructuration practices. In short, the theoretical severance of any link between structural constraint and determinacy also implies a change in the concept of agency. *Actor B can either be an agent through the production of power in restructuration or he/she can impose structural constraint upon A through destructuration.* Once an organization is set up and its institutions reproduced, the stabilisation of organizational edges involves the continual monitoring of institutional edges. The maintenance of organizational bias entails vigilant imposition of institutional constraints upon any actors A who wish to initiate institutional change. Since the machinery of organizational bias is produced through the activation of structural constraint *it would be analytically inconsistent to call this phenomenon power.* When exercised by B, institutional constraint is a method for realizing agency through a specific institutional control over A. This form of agency will be referred to as institutional control. Actor A experiences the exercise of institutional control by B as institutional constraint. In effect, institutional control is the agency/contingency side of structural constraint. *Actor B realizes his/her agency through the exercise of institutional control. Actor A experiences this exercise of control as a manifestation of constraint.*

As theorized so far, institutional control is exercised by limiting the scope of organisationally defined interaction to relatively safe issue areas. In this way potentially dangerous issues can be prevented from entering the process of organized social interaction. "For example, the demands of rent-strikers can be blunted or dulled by insisting that tenant-landlord relations are purely a private

216

matter." (Bachrach and Baratz 1970 p. 46). Once A's grievances are carefully placed outside organized decision-making, it is possible for actors B to be sympathetic to A while simultaneously keeping his/her grievances outside the decisional realm of an organization. B can engage in destructuration practices while continually emphasizing the non-existence of certain institutions. Institutionalized impotence is emphasized. In turn, this has the effect of recreating institutional impotence and powerlessness with respect to certain issues. On the personal level of interaction, destructuration can take many forms. There can be sympathy plus an explanation: "If I were to make an exception of you then everyone would want X". In other words, new institutions would be set up whereby it would always be possible to create power with respect to X. An example of such an interchange is given by Kathy Davis in her (1989) analysis of the reproduction of inequalities of power in doctor patient interaction. In one particular dialogue a patient requests a test for a liver ailment as part of a routine check-up for the contraceptive pill. In response, the doctor informs her "...that blood tests do not belong to routine pill check-ups." (Davis 1989 p. 211). The doctor's reply to the request is as follows: Doctor: "'We don't do that....(sarcastic) because then there's no end to it... come now.'" (Davis 1989 p. 210) In other words, yielding to the request for liver blood test would inherently imply the creation of new institutionalized practices; new practices whereby patients could request any number of tests as part of a pill check-up.

If it is very apparent that an organization 'should' contain the structures to deal with a specific grievance, then B can appeal his/her personal lack of access to certain institutions. This would mean a statement with respect to his/her institutionally defined authority. A is told that B is not in a position to restructure but possibly another actor B2 is. B2 can then refer A to B3 and this process can be repeated ad infinitum. Alternatively, it can take the form described in a transcript from an interview with an executive in Bigtown: "'We freeze out these New Dealers and other Reds. When we appoint people to important committee posts, we look at their record. If an individual has gone all out on some crazy idea, his goose is cooked. If I am chairman of a group that is making appointments, I go *stone deaf* whenever someone suggests the name of one of these radicals. My *hearing improves* when a good reliable person is mentioned as a possibility.'" (Pellegrin and Coats 1956 p. 417 emphasis not orig.). In other words, people who are likely to create new institutional practices are kept out by nondecision-making through feigned deafness.

Institutionalized social control is the manipulation of the social mechanisms by which power is produced. Consequently, institutionalized social control precludes overt conflict. It is a method by which the potential power resources of actor A are rendered useless because he/she cannot mobilize them in order to engage in conflict with B. This point is implicitly made by Crenson: "Gary's anti-pollution activists were long unable to get U.S. Steel to take a clear stand. One of them, looking back on the bleak days of the dirty air debate, cited the evasiveness of the town's largest industrial corporation as a decisive factor in frustrating early efforts to enact a pollution control ordinance. The company executives, he said, would just nod sympathetically and agree that air pollution was terrible, and pat you on the head. But they never *did* anything one way or the other. If only there had been a *fight* then something might have been accomplished!" (Crenson 1971 p. 76-7. Emphasis on fight not orig.). In other words, conflictual power was inherently preferable to powerlessness derived from an inability to engage in meaningful (pat on the head) interaction with respect to the issue of air pollution.

In institutionalized social control, what makes actor B more powerful than actor A is the ability to maintain A's powerlessness. With respect to air pollution, U.S. steel was powerful because they could avoid conflict and, in that manner, prevent clean air activists from using their power resources. In conflictual power actor A is more powerful than B because of his/her greater access to institutionally constituted social resources. Implicit in this is the alternative option whereby B can also increase his/her power by reducing the resources of A. This can be done through social control by placing A's resources outside organizational edges. Hence, A's resources are no longer power resources because they do not carry social structures/institutions.

In the long term, the preservation of organizational edges, through nondecision-making, is reinforced by A's knowledge of institutional practices. Like social structures, institutions exist in potential form, outside the moment of interaction, at the level of p.c. and d.c. knowledge. A will learn which acts of structuration are liable to meet with institutional restructuration or destructuration. Just as every competent actor knows what constitutes rule affirmation in every-day interaction, so he/she will gain knowledge of institutionalized destructuration practices. In this case, structural constraint is no longer a contingent, agent-specific, phenomenon.

Over time, through continual exposure to institutionalized social control, A will cease to structure in a particular manner because of his/her knowledge of institutional constraint. A knows that certain acts of structuration will meet with destructuration. In such a case of institutionalized social control, anticipated reactions in B signifies anticipated defeat for actor A. Consequently, A will cease to engage in interaction involving certain forms of structuration practices. A culture of apathy will prevail among actors A (see Gaventa 1980 p. 21). Over time, contingent exercises of structural control have created determinate levels of structural constraint. Routinized falsification of rules has contributed to a changing of paradigmatic knowledge of rules. As observed by Gaventa, it is at this point that Bachrach's and Baratz's 2-D power becomes inseparable from Lukes' 3-D: not only is A made less powerful by changed consciousness but nondecision-making has turned into a non-event (Gaventa 1980 p. 15, 20). This will form a theme in the next chapter.

13 Structural constraint and inequalities of power

The previous chapter concluded with the observation that institutional social control is inherently linked to the maintenance of certain paradigmatic perceptions of restructuration and destructuration practices. In this chapter, this theme will be combined with a conceptual broadening of analysis which covers the relationship between agency and structural constraint. It is an analysis of structural reproduction which will be prefaced with a short discussion of Lukes' perception of 3-D. This will include an assessment of the theoretical defensibility of the concept of 3-D. The concluding section of the chapter is a discussion of restructuring perspective reformulation and resolution of the relationship between agency, power and structure.

The need to retheorize and/or abandon Lukes' concept of 3-D is a recurrent theme in much contemporary political theory. For example, Giddens claims that there are two dimensions of power not three (see 1984 p. 15; 1979 p. 91). In developing the hypothesis of a modernist crisis in political theory, Clegg argues that the concept of 3-D inherently involved the theorist in an indefensible moral relativism vis a vis interests (1989 p. 127). Such criticisms of the concept of 3-D inevitably place a question mark over the existence of the phenomenon and/or its theoretical defensibility.

In dealing with any explanatory retheorization of 3-D, I would argue that large areas of the conceptual space occupied by the concept have to be abandoned. Many of the commonly made criticisms of 3-D necessitate serious qualifications and rethorizations of the phenomenon. It has to be accepted that the concept of true/false consciousness is premised upon an indefensible moral relativism vis a vis interests. Similarly, it is also a valid observation that 3-D does have certain tendencies towards a conspiracy theory (for an example of such criticisms see Clegg 1989 p. 86-128). Accepting that much of the conceptual space occupied by 3-D is theoretically questionable, I would wish to argue that the important contribution made by Lukes is not to be found in the particulars of his development of the concept of 3-D. What is of theoretical consequence is that Lukes managed to highlight the necessity to theorize a set of phenomena which exist beyond the conceptual terrain occupied by 2-D. This is not an esoteric defence of Lukes. What is at stake is neither Lukes nor *Power: A Radical View*. When Lukes observed that "...the bias of the system is not sustained simply by a series of individually chosen acts, but also, more importantly, by the socially structured and culturally patterned behaviour of groups and practices of institutions,.." (Lukes 1974 p. 21-2) he was formulating the need to theorize the relationship between the broader realm of praxis and the recreation of structured inequalities of power. In short, Lukes has perceived the importance of the relationship between the every-day reproduction of structure and the recreation of systemic bias.

At another level Lukes made a significant contribution to the understanding of the relationship between social consciousness and the praxiological manifestation of interests. He made this contribution in the context of attempting to formulate a theoretically acceptable concept of false consciousness. Wishing to preempt the accusation of occupying moral high ground with respect to the issue of 'true' and 'false' interests, Lukes tried to develop a new set of criteria for distinguishing 'true' from 'false' interests. To date, all theoretical attempts to define 'true' and 'false' consciousness have been unable to find acceptable criteria for assessing 'truth' and 'falsity'. The most commonly used technique for analysing false consciousness is for the political theorist to distinguish between what actors think and what they should be thinking. However, the prescriptive conditional inherent in such an analysis is implicitly premised upon an indefensible contempt for the competence of social actors. Wishing to distance himself from such a position, Lukes argues that 'true' interests must be expressed, at some level, by actors themselves. The idea of gauging an actor's false consciousness with respect to their own articulation of interests would appear to constitute an oxymoron - if an actor can make his/her interests known he/she is not suffering from false consciousness. In order to resolve this apparent contradiction, based on Gramsci, Lukes "...draws a contrast between 'thought and action, i.e. the co-existence of two conceptions of the world, one affirmed in words and the other displayed in effective action'" (Lukes 1974 p. 47). In a theoretically interesting manner, Lukes applies this novel concept of false consciousness to an analysis of the Indian caste system (1974 p. 48-9). Here he focuses on inconsistencies between discursively expressed interests and their manifestation in praxis. According to Srinivas' study of the Indian caste system, with uniform consistency, the lower caste profess a strict adherence to a set of values which explicitly forbid caste mobility. Yet, despite these professed beliefs, in practice it is a system which is characterised by high levels of upward mobility. "[O]pportunities of the lower caste to rise within the system are often, if not invariably, seized." (Lukes 1974 p. 49). Thus there is revealed "... *a gap between thought and action*, since the adoption of the Brahminic way of life by a low caste is theoretically forbidden and in general caste position is held to be ascriptive, hereditary and unchangeable." (Lukes 1974 p. 49, emphasis not orig.). The contradiction inherent in the idea of actors upholding the principles of the caste system, while praxiologically recreating a social system characterized by social mobility, reveals a dual articulation of interests. It is a dual expression of interests which displays the commensurability of contradictions between the promulgation of interests and their manifestation in practice. The perception of a possible disjuncture, between the articulation of interests and their manifestation in social practices, constitutes a significant addition to the number of conceptual tools available to the theorizer of power. However, it is doubtful if 'false consciousness' is the best term for this phenomenon. The use of 'true' and 'false' inherently implies an inside knowledge of motives and outcomes which is, by and large, unavailable to the political theorist. Who is to say whether social practices or promulgated preferences represent an actor's 'true' or 'false' interests? Consequently, I would suggest abandoning the use of the term 'false consciousness' in the analysis of this phenomenon. Removed from the prescriptive overtones of 'true' and 'false', the analysis of commensurable disjuncture can be retheorized using the vocabulary of d.c. and p.c.. With respect to d.c. and p.c., Lukes can be interpreted as arguing that it is possible for actors to have and/or express dissimilar interests at the level of p.c. and d.c.. Expanded to take account of beliefs and perceptions more generally, it can be argued that individual actors can engage in social practices which reveal contradictory d.c. and p.c. social paradigms. With respect to the Indian caste system, the lower orders held a set of d.c. convictions, concerning the inviolability of the caste system, which were clearly inconsistent with the p.c. knowledge used in the praxiological recreation of structure.

Taking an overview of the conceptual terrain salvaged from Lukes' concept of 3-D, it is essentially being argued that many of the more specific aspects of Lukes' formulation of the concept of 3-D have to be abandoned and others have to reinterpreted. However, this should not obscure the fact that Lukes' analysis is profound in its intuitive grasp of the importance of a set of phenomena which exist beyond the conceptual barriers of conflictual power and institutional control. In particular it is a position which throws two facets of systemic bias into bold relief: a) the relationship between praxiological structural reproduction and inequality and, b) the analytical separability of d.c. and p.c. articulation of interests. Both these themes will form central elements in the analysis which follows.

Within restructuration theory, social power is an ability produced in the moment of restructuration. Power has neither an 'out there' existence nor can it be stored. It is resources that have an objectified existence which lends itself to storage. What makes the traffic police more powerful than Dahl, the propertied actor more powerful than the propertyless one and the owner of 1000 coats more powerful than the owner of one coat, is their access to resources. As emphasized, things are constituted as social resources by the structures which they 'carry'. It is the social structures 'carried' by a material object or a d.c. concept (ideas/knowledge) which turns it into a social resource. The power of the traffic police, Dahl, the owner of 1000 coats and the proprietor of land is systemically defined. Solar powered cookers, clocks or the discourse of political science can be resources within one system and not within another.

If it were possible to imagine a structurally totally static system, then the relative power of actors could be analysed in terms of the straightforward pursuit of resources. However, in this work the image of structures as a set of static relations has been replaced with a dynamic concept of structures. Structures only exist in the moment of restructuration. Consequently, they are potentially continually subject to demise. Similarly, there is also a continual potential for the creation of new structures. It is the combination of both these factors which constitutes the essence of the dynamic of social change. Because resources are structurally constituted, their existence and distribution is inherently defined by a system in continual flux. Hence, the continual reproduction of social resources is inherently contingent.

The contingency of structural reproduction places the structural edges of social systems in a continual state of expansion and contraction. Due to the higher incidence of p.c. over d.c. knowledge of rules, the rate of flux in the time-space edges of systems is inherently higher than in organizations. It is a flux which involves the structuring of new resources and the destructuring of old resources. Edges expand through the introduction of new resources. The result of such expansion is a decrease in the zones of disorder and an increase in the structural power potential of a system. For example, the introduction of clock-time meant an increased systemic structuredness as higher levels of systemic certainty became created. It is an increased systemic rationalization which enables actors to produce new levels and forms of consensual and conflictual power. Similarly, the demise of certain structures will involve a contraction of certain systemic structural edges. This contraction results in a decrease in the potential for the production of certain forms of social power. For social actors, such a constant flux in the structural edges means a continual change in the distribution of systemic resources. It is a change that continually alters the relations of empowerment and disempowerment which characterize interactive relations between actors.

In a structuralist perspective social actors are the passive observers of this continual creation and demise of social structures. In Giddens' structuration theory actors are the initiators of flux and change without having any control over it. In restructuration theory the initiators of change also have the possibility of managing structural reproduction. Because rules have to be converted into structures, actors have substantially higher levels of control over structural reproduction than in previous sociopolitical theories. It is an increased control which does not pertain to actors as individuals. It is the property of actors A and B who are involved in the collaborative endeavour of reproducing social order by the conversion of rules into structures through affirmation.

As has been observed, one of the most commonly made criticisms of Lukes' position is that the concept of 3-D has an inherent tendency to degenerate into conspiracy theory. This tendency is derived from a misplaced intentionality with regard to the causal effects of agency. For example, it is true that a concerted disinformation campaign is a 3-D type phenomenon which can be attributed to specific agency. However, this should not be taken to imply that all 3-D phenomena must, in some respect, be attributable to this type of specific agency. The recreation of structurally and culturally constituted inequality involves many levels of agency. Not only is the agency inherent in institutional reproduction significantly different from structural reproduction but there are many facets to the relationship between agency and control over structural reproduction. Consequently, in the theorization of the praxiological maintenance of systemic edges, it is important to distinguish between different forms of agency. Otherwise, theoretical distortions are likely to take place. Since, within restructuration theory, the structural strategies of actors A and B are significantly different, I will begin by analysing the agency of each separately.

An actor A wishing to engage in interaction with other has two potentially systemically meaningful options open to him/her. He/she can engage in a structuration practice using 'old' rules with a high potential to contribute to structural reproduction within existing systemic edges. Alternatively, he/she can attempt to expand existing edges by structuring according to new rules. If A does the former and *if* B collaborates by verifying established rules, this will have three consequences: 1) power will be produced, 2) the structural constitution of existing inequalities of power will be recreated and 3) there will be an automatic feed-back reinforcing existing paradigmatic perceptions of rules and rule verification. If actor A decides to invent a new rule to structure his/her praxis, the collaboration of B will have a number of important consequences: 1) existing structural edges will be changed, 2) new resources created, 3) new forms of power will be produced, 4) systemic power potentials will be increased, 5) the creation of new structural resources will alter existing distributions of power, 6) there will be a decrease in the zones of disorder and 7) paradigmatic perceptions of social order will be changed. With regard to this multiplicity of potential implications inherent in novel structuration practices, it is important to note that any one could be instrumental in initiating A's invention of a new rule. It could be that A invents a new rule in order to change balances of power in his/her favour. It is equally likely that he/she invents a new rule in order to decrease zones of disorder. It is of course also possible that A engages in novel structuration practices by mistake - he/she is socially incompetent. Similarly, it must not be assumed that actor A structures according to well-established patterns because he/she has a vested interest in reinforcing existing structural inequality. It could be the case that existing structures are well-suited to produce a particular desired form of power. It is also possible that A may lack the structural imagination to invent new rules. Alternatively, A may have sufficient knowledge of B to know he/she will destructure or non-restructure to novel structuration practices.

Like actor A, actor B has several forms of social action open to him/her. Actor B can either restructure, destructure or non-restructure. Only the latter of the three does not actually involve a deliberate choice. Non-restructuration takes place when an actor does not know how to verify the rule used by A. In this case a lack of paradigmatic commensurability between actors prevents structure from being reproduced (see fig 8.4). If B does understand the nature of A's structuration practices, he/she does have a meaningful choice between restructuration and destructuration. This choice between restructuration and destructuration pertains both to the verification of new *and* old rules. The act of restructuration results in the production of power and the recreation of structure. If it is restructuration to new rules, new forms of power and types of resources will be created. In turn, this will change existing distributions of power. If B restructures to old rules the status quo will be recreated. The consequences of restructuration to new and old rules has already been theorized as a facet of the agency of A. Since, on its own, structuration has no systemic affects, restructuration was taken as a given in theorization of the agency of A. The above theorization of actor A took the form 'if A structures and *if* B collaborates then...'. Consequently, a methodological bracket will be placed on the phenomenon.

The choice between restructuration or destructuration is a choice between two forms of agency. Restructuration constitutes the power side of agency and destructuration is the structural control side of agency. Even if B does understand the rule used by A, he/she may not wish to confirm it. This act of destructuration constitutes the ability of B's to realize his/her agency through the imposition structural constraint upon A. The realization of agency through destructuration, as opposed to restructuration, represents the other side of agency. It is possible for B to be an agent either by collaborating with A in the production of power or by preventing the re/creation of structure and production of power though structural control over other.

The concept of structural control is the agency side of structural constraint. The traditional perception of constraint, as an autonomous facet of structure, is rather typically represented by

Lukes when he argues that structural consequences are analytically similar to C. Wright Mills' concept of fate in politics (Lukes 1974 p. 56). In contrast, in restructuration theory, the actual implementation of constraint belongs to the realm of agency and 'could have done otherwise'. Structural control is a facet of the agency of actors B attempting to influence or monitor reproduction of structure. Of course, this is not to deny that actors A often fail to engage in innovative structuration either out of a lack of structural imagination or an accurate knowledge of probable destructuration by B. In other words, it is only the actual implementation of constraint upon other, through structural control, which is attributable to the agency of B. It is not being denied that there are internalised structural constraints which shape the structuring practices of A. This internalised constraint represents A's p.c. and d.c. knowledge of relative probabilities of rule affirmation or falsification. However, the actual act of affirming or falsifying is the property of B.

In the theorization of control by B, the imputation of vested interests to B should not be taken for granted. Many forms of structural control are not specifically intended to influence relations of relative power and powerlessness. The regulation of systemic edges is not invariably intended to recreate the unequal distribution of power resources. Even though most acts of destructuration will influence relative relations of empowerment and disempowerment, most destructuration practices are not motivated by a desire to undermine the resources of others. While it is true that certain structural edges favour some actors over others, this does not necessarily imply that the maintenance of these edges is a conspiracy by the more powerful to keep out the relatively powerless.

When actor B exercises structural control over other he/she may have a number of reasons for doing so. Destructuration practices are often a manifestation either of ontological or epistemological insecurity with respect to A's structuration practices. This is particularly the case with novel structuration practices. In the Garfinkel experiments, the point was not that the violation of greeting behaviour inherently altered the power resources of A vis a vis B. The issue at stake was a lack of willingness to give consent to alternative perceptions of the structuredness of greeting behaviour. Actors were engaging in conflict over structural reproduction due to paradigmatically based disagreement on rules and their verification. In effect, when Garfinkel instructed his students to interpret "Hello, how are you? as a request about a person's well-being, he was asking his students disconfirm certain rules and introduce others. As such, the students were agents of potential social change. It was a change which was blocked by others who prevented the transformation of new rules into structures through destructuration. On a systemic level, the breaching experiments can be viewed as a struggle over the preservation of existing systemic edges which are not linked to vested interests. They are manifestations of an epistemologically based resistance to change.

In every-day social life, the assumption of structuredness is paradigmatically reinforced in routine every- day social interaction. In social life an anomalous experience constitutes a disruption of a particular paradigmatically assumed social order. As in science "Without waiting, passively, for impressions to impress or impose regularities upon us, *we actively try to impose regularities upon the world.*" (Popper 1963 p. 46 emphasis not orig.). However, with regard to the options open for imposition of ordered regularity, the social actor is in a very different position to the scientist. In social life the creator of an anomalous experience is another actor; it is other actors who introduced new rules. The attempt to impose order on the social world can take a more active form. The recreation of the order of a social system is not synonymous with the re/creation of certain rules. A social system is made of structures not just rules. *The distinction between rules and structures is fundamental here. Actor B has no control over the rules used by A. However, B can prevent the conversion of these new rules into structures.* Because structural reproduction is a collaborative endeavour, the creator of new rules can be prevented from introducing new structures through destructuration. It is a mechanism which allows actor B to falsify rules which are perceived as anomalous with respect to his/her paradigmatic understanding of the rule-governedness of social life. Destructuring is a vital mechanism for actors B to preserve systemic edges out of a desire for epistemological security.

One of the most important contributory factors to systemic stability is the imposition of structural constraint motivated by a desire for epistemological security. To the extent to which the systemic structuring of resources implies inequality, all imposition of structural constraint contributes to the recreation of relations of relative empowerment and disempowerment. Consequently, the desire to maintain epistemological security is an important factor in the constitution of power and powerlessness. In terms of previous theorizations of power, it is important to emphasize that this

228

reproduction of inequality neither involves the exercise of power nor the desire to influence power relations. In other words, Lukes' observation to the effect that there is an inherent relationship between structural reproduction and systemic bias, does not necessarily imply either that an exercise of power takes place or that deliberate structural inequality is being recreated. Similarly, when Clegg assumed that the creation of an uneven billiard table was a manifestation of power (Clegg 1989 p. 209, also see chapter 3), he made unwarranted theoretical assumptions. The recreation of the structural constitution of resources is a routinized phenomenon which is kept in check through destructuration and non-restructuration. Through the imposition of constraint, this control almost invariably means the reconstitution of structurally constituted relations of empowerment and disempowerment. With respect to such routinized recreation of structured inequality, not only is the reproduction of inequality of power resources not necessarily an exercise of power but the recreation of inequality is an unintentional effect of structural control motivated by the necessity for epistemological security. Of course, the reproduction of structurally constituted inequality is not always motivated by a desire to maintain epistemological security, structural control can also be a manifestation of conflict over distributions of power resources.

The attempt to influence distributions of resources through destructuration can either be a reaction to novelty or an attempt to initiate change. The former involves the monitored maintenance of existing systemic edges and the latter entails the contraction of edges.

When an actor A decides to replace the old rule $a_n = n^2 + n - 1$ with a new rule $a_n = n^4 - 22 + n^6$ a change of relations of empowerment and disempowerment will take place. In effect, if B refuses to verify rule $a_n = n^4 - 22 + n^6$ he/she is refusing to affirm the creation of new forms of structured inequality. In this case, the maintenance of existing systemic edges is linked to the continued reproduction of the unequal distribution of power resources. In short, through the implementation of structural constraint, social change is resisted and system stability can be maintained in the interest of the continued reproduction of structural inequality.

Destructuration to *novel* structuration practices is an effective form of agency for a more powerful actor B to maintain the relative powerlessness of actors A. On the other hand, destructuration to *established* patterns of structuration is an effective tool for a less powerful actor B to challenge a more powerful actor A. Here it is actor B who is engaging in novel practices of falsification in order to influence systemic edges. Destructuring to established rules has the immediate consequence of contracting systemic edges. It is a contraction of edges which leaves the 'normal' resources of the more powerful actor A outside the system. Consequently, A experiences a loss of resources.

Power motivated destructuring to established structures can take place in two alternative contexts. An actor B can destructure to established rules purely because he/she considers the *structures* recreated as contrary to his/her interests. Alternatively, B could be destructuring because he/she considers the *power* produced undesirable. Destructuration can take place either due to a lack of consensus on rule affirmation and/or consensus on the power produced. In the former case, B is destructuring in an interaction which has the potential to produce consensual power. In the latter B is destructuring in order to prevent the production of conflictual power. In destructuring to the production of consensual power, B is acting out of a lack of willingness to contribute to the reproduction of structured inequality. In the case of conflictual power, B does not necessarily perceive the structures reproduced as contrary to his/her interests. Instead, B considers the use made of the structures in question as undesirable. Some of these facets of destructuration practices can be illustrated by a further interpretative analysis of the Mrs. Anderson/Dr.Day medical example contained in chapter 10.

In the interaction between Mrs. Anderson and Dr. Day there is little reason to suspect that there is not consensus on the desired outcome of their interaction. As an expression of their interests, both would appear to desire power to help Mrs. Anderson's' cystic fibrosis. Yet, despite this consensus on outcomes, Mrs. Anderson deliberately engages in destructuring practices which are contrary to her interest in producing power 'to do'. Wright and Morgan give two reasons for Mrs. Anderson's lack of cooperation with Dr. Day: 1) "...she likes to be treated as an equal,..." (Wright and Morgan 1990 p. 954) and 2) [h]er beliefs,..., conflict with the medical model. Thus, argument over the correct view of reality occurs... in interaction with medical personnel." (Wright and Morgan 1990 p. 956). Each of these facets of Mrs. Anderson's destructuration practices will be dealt with in turn.

As observed by Wright and Morgan, "[i]t is a truism that physicians have substantial political, financial, and social power both as individuals and as a profession over patients....Such power is symbolized in the doctor-patient interaction by a set of asymmetrical rules regarding touching, initiation of conversation, expression of perceptions of the illness, and the determination of the content of the discussion." (Wright and Morgan 1990 p. 957). This situation of rule-governed inequality is one which many older physicians consider integral to their ability to treat patients (Wright and Morgan 1990 p. 957). In other words, it is a structural inequality which is perceived to be a necessary prerequisite to the production of consensual power 'to do'. It is a paradigmatically constituted perception of social order where there is a perceived relationship between the recreation of structured inequality and the production of power.

When Mrs. Anderson engages in interaction with Dr. Day she is interacting with an actor who subscribes to the 'older' medical paradigm. In the act of destructuring to Dr. Day, Mrs. Anderson is preventing the recreation of the particular structures which Dr. Day considers essential to the production of power. If it is assumed that Mrs. Anderson desires power to treat her condition, the direct effect of destructuration is the failure to produce power to do what she wants. In other words, the consequences of destructuration are contrary to her interests as they are articulated in the d.c. act of making a medical appointment. However, the other effect of destructuration is the non-reproduction of structured asymmetries of power resources. As such, the destructuring practices of Mrs. Anderson represent an effective method for challenging existing inequalities of power. In this sense, Mrs. Anderson's destructuration can be interpreted as an act of structural conflict directed at averting the reproduction of structurally constituted inequality. In terms of agency, this gives the less powerful actor an effective tool for engaging in conflict which does not involve the actual production of power. In other words, in a situation of structured inequality, where the production of conflictual power would invariably result in A prevailing over B, actor B can challenge the power of A through structural control. The less powerful actor can engage in conflict with a more powerful actor through the manipulation of existing systemic edges. Such an analysis is consistent with Wright and Morgan's observation: "while the physician has more power, it is far from complete. Patients use behaviour as a means of asserting control, commonly by violating the rules for 'good' behaviour. For example, Mrs. Anderson did not accept the medical model, and indicated her disagreement by interrupting, contradicting, and ultimately refusing the proposed therapy. Other patients used deviant behaviour to assert control over their care, including not showing up for surgery, noncompliance with medications, not 'hearing' the physician's educational messages, not giving the proper information or doing so at the wrong times, postponing hospitalization to their convenience, and requesting particular drugs." (Wright and Morgan 1990 p. 957).

Due to the theorization of destructuration as an act of falsification, it is easy to make the mistake of thinking that destructuration is a less skilled form of agency than restructuration. As a manifestation of a lack of p.c. or d.c. knowledge of rule verification, non-restructuration is obviously less skilled than restructuration. With regard to commonly reproduced social structures, non-restructuration can be regarded as a form of social incompetence. However, destructuration implies a p.c. understanding of the relationship between structure and the reproduction of systemic inequalities of power resources. The perception of a relationship between the reproduction of structure and the recreation of inequality implies a high level of p.c. knowledge and social competence. Not only does the destructuring actor know how to affirm rules but he/she understands that such affirmation implies a recreation of the relative powerlessness of self. It is interesting to observe that in University Hospital the type of strategies used by Mrs. Anderson against Dr. Day are "...particularly common among patients with chronic diseases, who develop a high level of knowledge about the system... which they may use to achieve their own goals and to participate more actively in decisions regarding their care." (Wright and Morgan 1990 p. 957).

In the Mrs. Anderson/Dr. Day interaction, Mrs. Anderson is willing to sacrifice the production of consensual power. Instead of contributing to the production of power, she engages in conflict in order to prevent the reproduction of structured inequality. There is consensus on desired outcomes but conflict over the consensus necessary for the production of power. In other words, Mrs. Anderson is in agreement with Dr. Day on the purpose of their interaction. However, she is unwilling to give consensus to the affirmation of certain rules which, if turned into structures, would contribute to the reproduction of structured inequality. This divergence of consensus highlights the levels of interest and perception at work in interaction. Because the production of power necessitates the recreation of structure the issue of primacy of interests can arise. In the case of the successful exercise of conflictual power, actor B accepts the production of power - which is contrary to his/her interests - out of an interest in structural

232

reproduction. The inverse of this is an actor B who sacrifices his/her interests in the production of power out of a lack of willingness to reproduce structures contrary to his/her interests. To take the example of Mrs. Anderson, she is an actor B whose interests would be served by the production of power. However, because the satisfaction of these interest can only take place through the affirmation of rules which are contrary to her other interests, she forgoes the production of power. In other words, the interests which are satisfied by the production of power would appear to be of less consequence than nonfulfilment of interest represented by the recreation of structure. The knowledge pertaining to the reproduction of structures is primarily p.c.. The expression of interests and knowledge represented by the production of power is, by and large, d.c.. Consequently, such a disjuncture between structural and power interests will tend, though not invariably, to manifest itself as a conflict between the p.c. and d.c. articulation of interests.

Mrs. Anderson's act of destructuration also represents the nonfulfilment of Dr. Day's d.c. interests. While Mrs. Anderson is willing to sacrifice her power based interests, Dr. Day is apparently not willing to do this. In this respect, Dr. Day is the opposite of Mrs. Anderson. He is willing to consent to the recreation of undesirable structures in order to satisfy his interests through the production of power. In the second interaction between Dr.Day and Mrs. Anderson, Dr. Day changes to the 'modern' medical paradigm in order to be able to produce power with respect to Mrs. Anderson's condition. Due to his interest in the production of power 'to do', Dr. Day engaged in a set of social practices which recreated a more egalitarian set of structures. In short, he contributed to a change in systemic edges because he considered the production of consensual power of greater significance than the recreation of a certain structured inequality (see Wright and Morgan 1990 p. 956-7).

In the short term, an actor A wishing to produce power of the type which could have been produced by his/her destructuralized 'resources' may tend to persist in attempting to get B to restructure. In the longer term, actor A may can try to find/invent new rules which B will affirm. If correctly constituted, these different structures can produce power for the same ends as the older destructuralized 'resources'. In analysing such a case it cannot be argued that there is a direct determined causal feedback from B's act of destructuration to A's act of innovative structuring. However, it can be argued that there has been an indirect feedback. Actor A experiences B's act of destructuration both as an act of falsification of a rule and a block on his/her ability to produce power. If the desire to produce power is sufficient, A will be motivated to look for other structures which can produce power of the desired kind. A's ability to do this will depend upon his/her ability to find/invent rules which B is likely to affirm.

As observed, destructuration is an effective method for a more powerful actor B to maintain an inequality of power resources vis a vis a relatively powerless actor A. Such destructuration pertains to *novel* structuration practices by A. On the other hand, for a less powerful actor B, destructuration to *established* structures can be an effective method of resisting a more powerful A. In particular it enables B to block the production of conflictual power. As theorized in chapter 11, the production of conflictual power is premised upon consensus on rule affirmation. It is a knowledge which is primarily carried at the level of p.c.. Here actor B is resisting the production of power by refusing to give consensus to the affirmation of certain rules. With regard to potential conflictual power, such a withdrawal of consent is not necessarily motivated by any objection to the rules used by A. Instead, actor B is refusing to verify rules because he/she considers the power produced contrary to his/her interests. The possibility of destructuration to the potential production of conflictual power is theoretically significant because it represents the conditionality inherent in the constitution of the inequality of power. However many power resources an actor may have at his/her disposal, he/she is still dependent upon the restructuration practices of other. Consequently, irrespective of the relative power of A and powerlessness of B, there are very real limits to the extent to which an actor A can prevail over an actor B. If an exercise of conflictual power is sufficiently contrary to B's interests, there always exists the option of contracting systemic edges through destructuration. However powerful an actor A, actor B does have a method of countervailing the power of A. In this respect, structural constraint represents an ultimate limit upon the potential misuse of conflictual power. Beyond these borders violence is the only means for A to prevail over B.

By way of conclusion, I would like to look at the manner in which this theorization of structural constraint necessitates a reinterpretation of Lukes' articulation of the power/structure problem. Possibly the best way of doing this is to re-evaluate some of the central analytical assumptions and premises used in the original formulation of the relationship between power and structure. In particular there are two analytical perceptions and premises that lie at the root of the problem: firstly, the relationship between power and structure has always been perceived as synonymous with the relationship between agent and structure; secondly, power is conceptualized as inherently contingent and structure as determinant; thirdly, it is usually an assumed premise that all forms of significant affecting between actors involves the exercise of power and; fourthly, the creation of inequalities of power must, in some respect, be attributable to the exercise of power.

For those who perceive of the power/structure problem as synonymous with the agent/structure problem, the relationship between power and structure manifests itself in the form of contradictions with respect to agency. An agent is an actor who affects others through the realization of his/her agency in the production of power. In this act of agency the actor in question could have done otherwise. In short, the realization of agency is a contingent act involving choice. On the structural side of the equation, structures implied determinism: the 'could not have done otherwise' side of social action. However, if the existence of 2-D and 3-D is accepted, this implies a series of unresolvable dilemmas. In 2-D and 3-D actors affect each other through the creation of systemic bias. Sometimes they 'could do otherwise' and sometimes they couldn't. In 2-D and 3-D there is sometimes contingency, this implies power and agency. However, the routinized reproduction of systemic bias is often not attributable to specific agents and does not involve choice. The latter implies determinacy, the absence of agency and consequently structure. In turn, such a theorization of routinized structural bias is incommensurable with the premise that the ability to affect others, or their relative power resources, must in itself constitute an exercise of power.

In the restructuration explanatory theorization of the production of power and re/creation of structure, the relationship between power and structure is not perceived to be synonymous with the relationship between agency and structure. Agency is not realized solely through the production of power. It is possible for an actor to actualize his/her potential agency through structural control. Actors can be agents who affect others either through the production of power or the imposition of constraint upon other. It is possible for powerful actors to realize their agency by maintaining the reproduction of systemic bias. Similarly, it is possible for relatively powerless actors to be agents by preventing the production of conflictual or consensual power. To be an agent affecting other means either to contribute to the production of power or to impose structural constraint upon other.

This conceptualization of agency is part of a fundamental break with previous theorizations of the re/creation of structure. In particular it is an integral part of the perception that the re/creation of rules is not the same as the reproduction of structure. Rules are only converted into structures when they are verified by others. Structures are re/created in the act of affirmation through restructuration. Restructuration is not inevitable, it involves choice and contingency. For actor B, it is a choice between affirming a rule (collaborating in the production of power and the re/creation of structure) or, alternatively, imposing structural constraint upon other through destructuration and falsification of a rule. In other words, constraint is not inherently linked to determinism. Neither is it purely an internalised lack of structural imagination or a desire for epistemological/ontological security. In these circumstance, structural constraint is a form of destructuring agency which involves contingency - 'could have done otherwise'. This introduction of contingency into the structural side of agency does not represent a denial of the significance of determinacy as an aspect of social action. The restructuration perspective is not radical agent-centred phenomenological voluntarism. Rather it is being denied that the division between contingency and determinism is in any respect identical to the analytical separation of power and structure. Lack of structural imagination, non-restructuration, ontological and epistemological insecurity are all representative levels of determinacy which pertain to the purely structural. In short, both contingency and determinacy are an integral part of social life. However, this division is not the same as the division between power and structure. Both determinacy and contingency pertain to the constraining side of structure.

In the theory of restructuration things or ideas are constituted as resources within systemic edges in continual flux. Within these edges objects become resources by virtue of becoming 'carriers' of structure. Outside these edges 'resources' become emptied of their structural content through destructuration. In other words, the conceptualization of resources as 'carriers' of structure creates a potential for the controlled demise of certain resources and the constitution of others. This creation or demise can be a momentary act, pertaining to a specific interaction, or it can form part of an accumulative contribution to major systemic change. The implication of such a theorization of resources undercuts any assumption to the effect that the recreation of structured inequality is invariably linked to the exercise of power. Both the routinized and the highly strategically controlled reproduction of structure, to a greater or lesser extent, involve the reproduction of a systemic bias which is not a direct product of the exercise of power. Both routinized structural reproduction and strategic destructuration practices are commensurable elements which form an integral part of the constitution of structured inequality. The theorization of recreation of systemic bias, as a direct consequence of structural reproduction, neither denies the possibility of the deliberate creation of structured inequality nor does it inherently link inequality and intentionality. Consequently, on a theoretically explanatory level, it is possible to provide conceptual space both for deliberate re/constitution of bias and for the routinized reproduction of structured asymmetries of power resources.

Appendix 1

The choice of how to handle Bachrach's and Baratz's two uses of the concept of power was not an easy one. The general development of the second dimension of power takes place in "Two Faces of Power" published in 1962 and their typology of power and related phenomena is developed in "Decisions and Nondecisions" of 1963. Consequently, it would be tempting to conclude that the observed inconsistency between the concept of 2-D power and its typological development represents a development in Bachrach's and Baratz's ideas on the subject between the years 62 and 63. However, this is not plausible because both articles are included as chapters one and two of their book *Power and Poverty* of 1970.

Lukes' solution, of substituting 'coercion' for 'power' in its restricted form, is unsatisfactory for my purposes. It obscures the contribution, to the conflictual power debate, of the thesis that power (unlike force) is an inherently relational concept referring to meaningful social interaction between actors A and B. The alternative solution, of restricting the general term 'power' to include only the ability of A to affect B through threatened sanctions, is inherently inadequate because it places most forms of nondecision-making outside the conceptual ambit of power. The process of nondecision-making, which interests Bachrach and Baratz most, centers around the ability of actors A to create and maintain an organizationally defined decision-making process which precluded B's interests or grievance from reaching the decision-making stage. The effectiveness of such an organization depends on the subtle manner in which certain issues are organized out of the decision-making procedures. Consequently, an organization's efficiency, as a tool of 2-D power, has nothing to do with the ability to impose sanctions. Speaking in general terms, it would probably be true to say that the threat of sanctions is much more central to 1-D power than to 2-D power.

The solution of using the twin concepts of Power and Power* is in many respects deficient in the sense that it sidesteps the whole problem of Bachrach's and Baratz's dual usage of the term. However, I chose this option because it is, in many respects, a more faithful rendering of their position.

While procrastinating on how to resolve this theoretical dilemma, I developed an alternative more theoretically satisfactory solution than the one I actually used. However, as it involves taking great liberty with Bachrach's and Baratz's work I have relegated it to this appendix.

Theoretically more satisfactory would be the hypothesis that power is a general term which embraces 1-D and 2-D control of B by A through socially meaningful interaction between the two actors. As such this concept would include coercion, authority and some forms of influence. However, it would not include force which is not a from of social interaction but rather an active A acting *upon* a passive B.

Within this framework coercion would be a form of power where A prevails over B through the threat of sanctions. In this case B's action should be the result of a reasoned assessment of the advantages to be gained by compliance or noncompliance taking account of, among other factors, the severity and nature of the threat posed by A (see Bachrach and Baratz 1970 p. 22-4). Authority would be where B was prevailed upon due to his/her perception of an inherent connection between A's demand for compliance and his/her socially or institutionally defined legitimate position. Influence would be where A controlled the behaviour of B through persuasion. If A succeeds (through skill or otherwise) in making B act in a manner beneficial to A, but disadvantageous to B, then A's act of influencing B constitutes an exercise of power. However, if A influences B to act in a manner which is consistent with B's own interests then the causal relationship between A's 'advice' and B's action is not based upon power. In short, coercion and authority are always categories of power, whereas the classification of influence as power is inherently linked to the interests of A and B.

Appendix 2

Note on *Who Governs?*

This appendix is an aside which is intended to indicate how a restructuration perspective throws familiar empirical political analysis into a different theoretical relief. For this purpose I have taken one aspect of *Who Governs?* and held it up for examination within the framework of restructuration theory. As has been observed before (e.g. Lukes 1974 p. 23), the narrowness inherent in Dahl's 1-D focus made him unable to theorize many aspects of his study of New Haven. However, the quality of his empirical research make his descriptions of political life theorizable from a different angle than the one used by him. The actual material which I have chosen to reinterpret is the story of Mayor Lee and the redevelopment programme. For the sake of clarity I have divided this examination into two parts. The first is a descriptive synopsis of Dahl's account of the story. The second is an analysis of this chronicle through the application of restructuration theory as a methodological tool for making sense of 'what is going on'.

Urban redevelopment had a very low profile in New Haven until it "... became attached to the political fortune of an ambitious politician." (Dahl 1961a p. 115). The ambitious politician was Richard Lee. In 1949 and 1951 Lee was narrowly defeated for the position of Mayor. These defeats made him a skillful politician who

"...was unusually sensitive to the important consequences of minute shifts in the opinions, habits, or vagaries of voters." (Dahl 1961a p. 118). During his 1951 campaign he had visited some of the worst slums of New Haven. These visits convinced him of the necessity of slum clearance and redevelopment. During his successful 1953 campaign "... he emphasized the importance of doing something about the condition of New Haven." (Dahl 1961a p. 120). However, at this stage he still had not made urban redevelopment a major issue nor was it possible "...to foresee the extent to which the emphasis on redevelopment would turn out to be politically profitable." (Dahl 1961a p. 120). It was after his narrow victory (2 %) that Lee pushed redevelopment to the centre stage and held it there year after year (Dahl 1961a p. 126).

Having won the 1953 election by the narrowest of margins "...the election of 1955 gave him solid grounds for concluding that the political appeal of redevelopment far exceeded any other conceivable issue within his grasp. " As a result he made redevelopment even more central to his policy. In the 1955 election he received 65% of the vote - a larger majority than any previously incumbent mayor including Roosevelt. When he repeated this phenomenal majority in 1957 the result definitively proved the spectacular appeal of redevelopment (Dahl 1961a p. 121). On the basis of his success Lee began to attract attention throughout the United States as a person of potentially national political stature. With respect to the programme itself, having been started on a relatively modest scale in 1953, the redevelopment project became the largest and most ambitious in the whole country. In short, the whole phenomenon could be encapsulated in the title of an article which appeared in Harpers: "Lee of New Haven and His Political Jackpot".

The burden of the technicalities of redevelopment fell to the Development Administrator and the Director of the Redevelopment Agency. It was Mayor Lee's task to whip up support for the scheme (Dahl 1961a p. 129). Central to his scheme for creating support for redevelopment was the establishment of the Citizens Action Committee. The CAC was a crucial part of an elaborate structure of citizenship participation *created* by Mayor Lee (Dahl 1961a 133). In the words of Mayor Lee the CAC was composed of "...the biggest set of muscles in New Haven..." (Dahl 1961a p. 130). The muscle of this personnel derived from their leadership of all the main interest groups of New Haven. In this sense "...the CAC was public opinion..." (Dahl 1961a p. 137) The purpose of the CAC was not to initiate or change proposals rather it served the function of legitimating,

242

through democratic ritual, decisions already made. (Dahl 1961a p. 131, 135). As an organ of ritualized democracy the CAC performed a dual function.

When decisions were first to be made by the Mayor and his team "[i]t acted as a sounding board for proposals which the city administration wished to try out before announcing them to the general public." (Polsby 1980 p. 72). The existence of this ritual forced Lee and his associates to shape their policies so that they would receive the support of the CAC (Dahl 1961a p. 137). "If none of the administration's proposals on redevelopment and renewal were ever opposed by the CAC, the explanation probably lies less in the Mayor's art of persuasion than in his capacity for judging with considerable skill what the existing beliefs and commitments of the men on the CAC would compel them to agree to if a proposal were presented in the proper way time and place." (Dahl 1961a p. 137). In this sense it became a tool for sniffing "...out the faint smell of distant political success, generate demands, and activate the latent consensus." (Dahl 1961a p. 139). It was here that the secret of Lee's success lay: in his "...capacity for anticipating what the organized interests, the political stratum, and the voters in general would tolerate." (Dahl 1961a p. 140).

Once a decision was ratified the CAC served a second function. This centered on the hypothesis "...that whatever received the full assent of the CAC would not be strongly opposed by other elements in the community." (Dahl 1961a p. 136). The representative nature, and consequent democraticness of the CAC, "...presented to the public an appearance of power and responsibility diffused among a representative group of community notables, and inhibiting criticisms of even the most daring and ambitious parts of the programme as 'unrealistic' or 'unbusinesslike'. Indeed, by creating the CAC the mayor virtually decapitated the opposition" (Dahl 1961a p. 133).

The most obvious general comment which can be made about the above account is that it is reasonable to conclude that this chronicle of success made Mayor Lee a powerful individual. However, it is a much wider form of power than that which can be detected within the narrow parameters defined by prevailing in conflictual decision-making (see Dahl 1961a p. 129). It is cumulative power which can be measured or assessed through indicators such as: Mayor Lee's ability to get things done, the 'decapitation' of opposition, his dual majority of 65% and his emergence as a political figure of national importance. However, while he was a powerful individual the key to his political jackpot did not derive from the exercise of power. Instead his success and that of the redevelopment project originated from Lee's ability at structural and institutional control.

On an institutional level the setting up of the CAC provided Lee with an organization of massive political potential. On a structural level, the key to Lee's jackpot was his ability to create/discover issues which the populous of New Haven had not as yet articulated as demands. He understood their anticipated reactions and used the CAC as a tool for reinforcing that knowledge. In a sense he used the ordered reactions of others to build his power base. Prior to his interest in the issue there was no manifest ordered reaction to urban renewal. Within a short period everyone reacted positively to it (Dahl 1961a p. 134-7). It became synonymous with the 'democratic will' variously described as a 'dream' or 'prosperity' or the formula for a better 'economic atmosphere' (Dahl 1961a p. 136). In other words, development became loaded with meaning which conveyed inherent legitimacy. All the social actors of New Haven saw redevelopment in the same fashion and consequently could be predicted to react in the same manner to it. In other words, it became the carrier of new social structures.

Redevelopment became a carrier of social structures in a manner analogous to the way in which a clock carries the structure of time. As a carrier of new structures, redevelopment had a new meaning which is part of the ordered existence of the system of social interaction in New Haven. When it was mentioned people reacted in exactly the same ordered fashion as actors react to the question 'Hello, how are you?'. This new ordered reaction to to redevelopment, through restructuration, was a contribution to the total structural practices in New Haven. In some respects this example is both analogous to the way in which clock-time increased the number of structures within society from the sixteenth century onwards and the Christmas card introduced new structures in 1843. In short, the introduction of new structuration practices, pertaining to redevelopment, constituted a decrease in the zones of disorder. A decrease in disorder which enabled new systemically constituted levels of power to be created. As observed by Mayor Lee, prior to his political intervention the citizens of New Haven "'...*were all working at cross purposes. There was no unity of approach.*'" (Dahl 1961a p. 120).

While Lee was successful, it should be noted that his redevelopment plan was accompanied with a certain 'risk'. Lee's structuration practices vis-a-vis redevelopment could have been perceived as 'odd' and consequently undermine his authority and ability to get things done. The capacity of peculiar behaviour to undermine a power base is, to a certain extent, summed up by a corporate executive from Bigtown when commenting upon the process whereby deviants or 'cranks' are weeded out: "'If an individual has gone all out on some crazy idea, his goose is cooked'" (Pellegrin and Coats 1956 p. 417). Analytically speaking, the person who's 'goose is cooked' is in a similar position to Dahl when he insisted that he could direct traffic. In other words, rather than introducing new structures an actor can make it obvious to other social actors that he/she has a 'deviant' social paradigm. Consequently, most of that actor's more unusual structuration practices will fail to meet with restructuration. Hence, he/she will be powerless to do anything 'new'.

With respect to the process by which Lee created the structural practices pertaining to redevelopment, Lee's use of the CAC can be interpreted as a theoretically interesting attempt to resolve the problem of risk. On a general level it should be reiterated that the source of Lee's and his colleagues' success was not derived from being "...pressed into action by public demand. On the contrary, they had to sniff out the faint smell of distant political success, generate demands, and activate the latent consensus." (Dahl 1961a p. 139). In other words, they had to search for new structuration practices - do something 'new'. It is here that the first function of the CAC was central. It enabled them anticipate and test for rule affirmation in the creation of new meaning. In essence the CAC was a sounding-board for restructuration. As such, it became a forum within which the risks associated with new structuration practices could be assessed. Simultaneously, it also forced Lee and his team to formulate even the most radical proposal in a manner which would decrease the risk of destructuration.

Once the proposal had been 'tested' in the CAC, using the democratic process, the ritualistic elements of this decision- making procedure constituted a legitimating device (see Kertzer 1988 p. 50). The ritual conferred upon decisions a structure whereby such resolutions would be perceived as consistent with the 'natural order' of things. Even if such a decision were highly ambitious it would be not be labelled as, in the words of Dahl, 'unrealistic' or 'unbusinesslike', or, in the words of the executive from Bigtown, 'some crazy idea'. The use of democratic procedure meant that any decision reached would be an expression of the will of the people. Hence, any other reaction than a positive reaction would appear as a contradiction of self. In short, the creation and use of democratic institutional procedures played into other's paradigmatic social perceptions so that any decisions reached, through the use of these institutions, became carriers of social structure which 'demanded' restructuration. Non-restructuration or destructuration would be as inherently unthinkable as a rejection of the question 'Hello, how are you?' as a form of phatic communion.

In chapter 10 I showed the total quantity of power in a system is non-zerosum and that the systemic meaning of a material object is constituted through the structures which it 'carries'. Similarly, the authoritatively defined power and/or systemic significance of an individual actor can be altered through structural change. When an actor whose authority is structurally defined decides to create or reinforce certain structuration practices he/she has the possibility of making his/her position more powerful. This increase in power is dependent upon the restructuration practices of others. In much the same way as a material social object has systemically constituted significance, through the structures which it 'carries', so individual actors also have meaning conferred upon them through other actors' paradigmatically constituted perception of them as manifest in restructuration. Consequently, an individual actor can also change his/her relationship to others by becoming a 'carrier' of different social structures.

In the case of Mayor Lee, the creation of new structuration practices, pertaining to redevelopment, not only constituted an enlargement of the total amount of power in the system, by managing to identify himself with redevelopment (see Dahl 1961a p. 126), his person became a 'material carrier' or 'container' of the structures belonging to the new social praxis surrounding the redevelopment issue. To an actor in New Haven it became paradigmatically impossible to separate Mayor Lee from redevelopment (see Dahl 1961a p. 134). In other words, the structurally conferred legitimacy of redevelopment became associated with him. In effect, Lee managed to create restructuration practices which became associated with him in just the same manner as directing traffic is inherently the 'property' of the traffic police. However, unlike in the case of the institutionally constituted authority of the traffic police, they were structures which pertained to Lee as an individual actor. Hence, through redevelopment, Lee simultaneously enlarged the power in the social system of New Haven and changed people's paradigmatically constituted perception of his person. It was a change of perception which systemically fed back to making him a highly successful and powerful political leader.

Notes

Chapter 1:

1. Among the more well known reputational elite theorists are the following: Abu-Laban B. (1963 and 1965), Barth E. (1961), D'Antonio W. V. et al (1961, 1962a and 1962b), Erlich H.J. (1961), Erickson E. C. (1967), Hunter F. (1953), Miller D. C. (1958, 1961 and 1963), O'Schulze R. (1958), Pellegrin R. J. and Coats C. (1956).

2. For example, with the exception of the mayor, in the five years 1953 to 58 the decision-making elite of New Haven changed completely (See Dahl 1961a p. 114-40).

3. For some examples of the many variations of this procedure see: Abu-Laban and Barth 1970 p. 383; Hunter 1953 p. 11-2; O'Schulze and Blumberg 1957 p. 291.

4. The accusation levelled by the Pluralists against the Reputational elite theorists, that they fail to distinguish between actual and potential power, is in many respects exaggerated. It has a certain validity as a critique of the methodology used by F. Hunter in *Community Power Structure* (1953) but less so with respect to the work of D'Antonio and his followers from the early sixties onwards. For details of the debate surrounding this issue, for example, see: Polsby 1960 p. 483; 1962 p. 845; Wolfinger 1960 p. 644; D'Antonio et al 1962b. p. 848; Ehrlich 1961 p. 91-2.

5. Emphasis is always original unless stated otherwise.

6. Among the many resources which actors have at their disposal Polsby lists the following:
1) Money and credit
2) Control over jobs
3) Control over the information of others
4) Knowledge and expertness
5) Popularity, esteem, charisma
6) Legality, constitutionality, officiality, legitimacy
8) Ethnic solidarity
9) The right to vote
10) Time
11) Personal (human) energy
(Polsby 1980 p. 120)

It is this great range of resources which enables Pluralists to claim that all actors have power resources at their disposal(Dahl 1961b p. 89) - an important element of their normative defence of the democratic workings of Polyarchy.

7. I have taken the liberty of reversing the type of example used by Dahl to illustrate the distinction between having and exercising power. I did this for two reasons: 1) primarily because it fitted the context and, 2) because his own 1968 example (of A having power and B exercising it), when extended to its logical conclusion, appears to imply a critique of the hypothesis he maintained with regard to the workings of pluralist democracy. Using that example it could be argued that the key decision makers exercise power whereas the business elite have it. Hence, the study of key decision-makers and decisions made only tells you who exercises power but not how it is distributed.

8. Bachrach and Baratz did not conceive of themselves as 'radical' power theorists. My classification of them as such is purely a convenient labelling device which enables me to bracket them together with Lukes as part of a common tradition of power theory.

9. In *Power and Poverty* pages 44 to 46, Bachrach and Baratz make a list of what they consider the four most important forms of non-decision-making. For analytical purposes, I have changed their order and enlarged on the number of listings.

Chapter 8:

1. In this chapter, I have changed student and experimenter to A and B. A is female and B is male.

Chapter 10:

1. This is consistent with the point made at the end of chapter two (on Parsons) where it was argued that consensus and legitimacy are not necessarily mutually theoretically exclusive. It is conceptually possible for a given intentional actor to contribute unintentionally to the re-creation of a systemic product which he/she perceives as illegitimate. Put another way, a given act could be consistent with the p.c. consciousness of an actor and yet be considered illegitimate on the level of d.c.. However, this point will be methodologically bracketed as an aside for the moment.

2. Even if there were an abstract concept of weight, within a large complex system, the usefulness of the idea depends upon constant and consistent weights. Without such there could not be the order necessary for a sophisticated economy. As such, the introduction of weights and measures was a key element in the transition from the medieval locally based organization to the more ordered mercantilist economies of the seventeenth centuries(Heckscher 1934 p. 111). Prior to seventeenth century attempts to standardize weights and measures, the most unusual practices took place. For example, in Sweden a distinction was made between the unit of weight for copper and iron in cities along the coast and the unit employed in cities farther inland in the mining districts. In the latter the same unit of weight was ten percent less due to transport cost. "It was thus considered preferable to alter the unit of weight itself, rather than have a common unit and add the price for transport cost from the pit or the works to the coast." (Heckscher 1934 p. 112)

3. However, this was not always the case. In 1661, when Johan Palmastruck introduced paper money in Sweden, he was the first one in Europe to attempt this experiment. At first it was a great success. This success ultimately proved a temptation to print too much money and, consequently, there was a run on the bank. The impression this failure made was so strong that it took nearly one

hundred years for paper money to be introduced into Sweden again (see Heckscher, 1934 and 1963).

Chapter 11:

1. A point which is interestingly illustrated by recent territorial conflicts between the Canadian Government and the Innuit hunters and trappers. The former perceive of land as defined and measured in square miles while the latter consider land and air as an inseparable nonquantifiable unit (see *The Independent*, 30/6/90 p. 27).

Bibliography

Abercrombie N., Hill S. and Turner B. (1980) *The Dominant Ideology Thesis*, Allen and Unwin, London.

Abu-Laban B. (1963) "Social Origins and Occupational Career Patterns of Community Leaders", *Sociological Inquiry*, vol. 33.

Abu-Laban B. (1965) "The Reputational Approach in the Study of Community Power", *Pacific Sociological Review*, vol. 8.

Abu-Laban B. and Barth E.A. (1970) "Power-Structure and the Negro Sub-Community", in Aiken M. and Mott P.E. (ed.) *The Structure of Community Power*, Random House, New York.

Agger R. (1956) "Power Attributions in the Local Community", *Social Forces*, vol. 34.

Agger R. and Goldrich D. (1958) "Community Power Structure and Partisanship", *American Sociological Review*, vol. 23.

Agger R., Goldrich D. and Swanson B. (1964) *The Rulers and the*

Ruled, Wiley, New York.

Aiken M. and Mott P. (1970) (eds.) *The Structure of Community Power*, Wiley, New York.

Alexander J.C. (1984) *The Modern Reconstruction of Classical Thought: Talcott Parsons*, Routledge and Kegan Paul, London.

Althusser L. (1982) *For Marx*, Verso, London.

Althusser L. (1984) *Essays on Ideology*, Verso, London.

Althusser L. and Balibar E. (1970) *Reading Capital*, Verso, London.

Archer M. (1982) "Morphongenesis versus Structuration", *British Journal of Sociology*, vol. 33.

Arendt H. (1970) *On Violence*, Allen Lane, London.

Aristotle (1947) *The Basic Works*, (ed.) McKeon R., Random House, New York.

Aron R. (1950) "Social Structures and the Ruling Class", *British Journal of Sociology*, vol. 1.

Aron R. (1986) "Macht, Power, Puissance: Democratic Prose or Demoniacal Poetry", in Lukes S. (ed.), *Power*, Basil Blackwell, Oxford.

Ashley D. (1982) "Historical Materialism and Social Evolution", *Theory, Culture and Society*, vol. 1.

Atkinson J.M. Heritage J.C. (1984) *Structures of Social Action: Studies in Conversation Analysis*, Cambridge University Press, Cambridge.

Avineri S. (1971) *The Social and Political Thought of Karl Marx*, Cambridge University Press, Cambridge.

Bachrach P. (1962) "Elite Consensus and Democracy", *Journal of Politics*, vol. 24.

Bachrach P. (1967) *The Theory of Democratic Elitism*, Little Brown, Boston.

252

Bachrach P. and Baratz M.S. (1962) "The Two Faces of Power", *American Political Science Quarterly*, vol. 30.

Bachrach P. and Baratz M.S. (1963) "Decisions and Nondecisions: An Analytical Framework", *American Political Science Review*, vol. 57.

Bachrach P. and Baratz M.S. (1970) *Power and Poverty: Theory and Practice*, Oxford University Press, Oxford.

Baker G.P. and Hacker P.M.S. (1980) *Wittgenstein: Understanding Meaning*, Basil Blackwell, Oxford.

Baldwin D.A. (1989) *Paradoxes of Power*, Basil Blackwell, Oxford.

Ball T. (1978) "Power Revised", *The Journal of Politics*, vol. 40.

Ball T. (1988) *Transforming Political Discourse*, Oxford.

Ball T. and Farr J. (1984) *After Marx*, Cambridge University Press, Cambridge.

Barbalet J.M. (1985) "Power and Resistance", *British Journal of Sociology*, vol. 36.

Barbalet J.M. (1987) "Power, Structural Resources and Agency", *Current Perspectives in Social Theory*, vol. 8.

Barnes B. (1988) *The Nature of Power*, Polity, Cambridge.

Barry B. (1976) (ed.) *Power and Political Theory*, Wiley, London.

Barth E. (1961) "Community Influence Systems", *Social Forces*, vol. 40.

Barth E. and Abu-Laban (1959) "Power Structure and the Negro Sub-Community", *American Sociological Review*, vol. 24.

Bauman Z. (1988) "Sociology and Post Modernity", *The Sociological Review*, vol. 36.

Belknap G.E. and Smuckler R. (1956) "Political Power: Realities in a Mid-Western City", *Public Opinion,* vol. 20.

Bell D. (1958) "The Power Elite Reconsidered", *American Journal of Sociology*, vol. 64.

Bendix R. (1952) "Social Stratification and Political Power", *American Political Science Review*, vol. 46.

Bendix R. (1977) Max Weber, Berkeley. Bendix R. and Lipset M.S. (1953) *Class, Status and Power*, Glencoe Free Press, Glencoe.

Berger P and Luckmann (1967) *The Social Construction of Reality*, Penguin, Harmondsworth.

Berlin I. (1978) *Karl Marx*, Oxford University Press, Oxford.

Bernstein R. (1976) *The Restructuring of Social and Political Theory*, Blackwell, Oxford.

Bernstein R. (1989) "Social Theory as Critique", in Held D. and Thompson J.B. (ed.) *Social Theory of Modern Societies*, Cambridge University Press, Cambridge.

Bershady H.J. (1973) *Ideology and Social Knowledge*, Oxford University Press, Oxford.

Bierstedt R. (1950) "An Analysis of Social Power" *American Sociological Review*, vol. 15.

Bierstedt R. (1981) *American Sociological Theory*, McGraw-Hill, New York.

Birnbaum P. (1976) "Power Divorced from its Sources", In Barry B. (ed.) *Power and Political Theory*, Wiley, London.

Black M. (1961) *The Social Theories of Talcott Parsons*, Prentice Hall, Englewood.

Blankenship V.L. (1964) "Community Power and Decision-Making", *Social Forces*, vol. 43.

Blau P.M. (1964) *Exchange and Power in Social Life*, Wiley, New York.

Blauner R. (1964) *Alienation and Freedom*, Chicago University Press, Chicago.

Bleicher J. and Featherstone M. (1982) "Historical Materialism Today: An Interview With Anthony Giddens", *Theory, Culture and Society*, vol. 1.

Block I. (1981) *Perspectives on the Philosophy of Wittgenstein*, Basil Blackwell, Oxford.

Bolton Derek (1979) *An Approach to Wittgenstein's Philosophy*, Macmillan, London.

Bonjean C.M. (1963) "Community Leadership", *American Journal of Sociology,* vol. 68.

Bottomore T. (1964) *Elites and Society*, Watts, London.

Bottomore T. and Nisbet R. (1979) *A History of Sociological Analysis*, Heineman Educational, London.

Bourdieu P. (1979) *Algeria 1960*, Cambridge University Press, Cambridge.

Bourricaud F. (1981) *The Sociology of Talcott Parsons*, University of Chicago Press, Chicago.

Bradshaw A. (1976) "A Critique of Steven Lukes 'Power: A Radical Analysis'" *Sociology,* vol. 10.

Bunday G. (1964) *A History of the Christmas Card*, Spring Books, London.

Burke T.E. (1983) *The Philosophy of Popper*, Manchester University Press, Manchester.

Burnham J. (1942) *The Managerial Revolution*, Putnam, London.

Buzan B. (1983) *People, States and Fear*, Wheatsheaf, Brighton, Sussex.

Callinicos A. (1985) "Anthony Giddens: A Contemporary Critique", *Theory and Society,* vol. 14.

Carr E.H. (1966) *The Twenty Year Crisis*, Macmillan, London.

Carr M. (1988) "Technologies for Rural Women: Impact and Dissemination" in Ahmed I. (ed.) *Technology and Rural Women*, Allen and Unwin, London.

Cartwright B.C. and Warner R.S. (1976) "The Medium is Not the Message" in Loubser J.J. (ed.) *Explorations in General Theory in Social Science*, Collier Hamilton, London.

Cartwright D. (1959) (ed.) *Studies in Social Power*, University of Michigan Press, Ann Arbour.

Cartwright D. (1965) "Influence, Leadership, Control", in March J. G.. (ed.) *Handbook of Organizations*, Rand McNally, Chicago.

Cassinelli C.W. (1953) "The Iron Law of Oligarchy", *The American Political Science Review,* vol. 47.

Clarke T.N. (1967a) "The Concept of Power", *South Western Social Science,* vol. 48.

Clarke T.N. (1967b) "Power and Community Power Structure", *The Sociological Quarterly,* vol. 8.

Clarke T.N. (1972) "Community Power and Decision-Making", *Current Sociology,* vol. 20.

Clegg S. (1975) *Power, Rule and Domination: A Critical and Empirical Understanding of Power in Sociological Theory and Organizational Life*, Routledge and Kegan Paul, London.

Clegg S. (1979) *The Theory of Power and Organization*, Routledge and Kegan Paul, London.

Clegg S. (1989) *Frameworks of Power*, Sage, London.

Clelland D.A. and Form W. (1964) "Economic Dominants and the Concept of Power", *The American Journal of Sociology*, vol. 69.

Cohen G.A. (1982) *Karl Marx's Theory of History*, Clarendon Press, Oxford.

Cohen I. (1987) "Structuration Theory and Social Praxis", in Giddens A. and Turner J. (eds.) *Social Theory Today*, Polity, Cambridge.

Cohen I. (1989) *Structuration Theory*, Macmillan, Basingstoke.

Cohen P.S. (1968) *Modern Social Theory*, Heineman Educational, London.

Collett P. (1975) *Social Rules and Social Behaviour*, Blackwell, Oxford.

Cook T. (1939) "Gaentano Mosca's 'The Ruling Class'", *Political Science Review*, vol. 33.

Cousins M. and Hussain A. (1984) *Michel Foucault*, Macmillan, London.

Craib I. (1984) *Modern Social Theory*, Wheatsheaf, Brighton.

Crenson M.A. (1971) *The Un-politics of Air Pollution*, The John Hopkins Press, Baltimore.

Dahl R.A. (1957) "The Concept of Power" *Behavioural Science*, vol. 2.

Dahl R.A. (1958) "Critique of the Ruling Elite Model", *American Political Science Review,* vol. 52.

Dahl R.A. (1961a) *Who Governs? Democracy and Power in an American City*, Yale University Press, New Haven.

Dahl R.A. (1961b) "Equality and Power in America", in (ed.) D'Antonio W. and Erlich H., *Power and Democracy*, University of Notre Dame Press, Notre Dame.

Dahl R.A. (1968) "Power" in *International Encyclopaedia of the Social Sciences*, New York.

Dahl R.A. (1971) *Polyarchy*, Yale University Press, New Haven

Dahl R.A. (1984) *Modern Political Analysis*, Prentice Hall, Englewood Cliffs.

Dallmayr F. (1982) "The Theory of Structuration", in Giddens A. (ed.)

Profiles and Critiques in Social Theory, Macmillan, London.

Dankelman I. and Davidson J (1988) *Women and the Environment in the Third World*, Earthscan in association with I.U.N.C., London.

D'Antonio W. and Erlich H. (ed.) (1961) *Power and Democracy in America*, University of Notre Dame Press, Notre Dame.

D' Antonio W., Form W., Loomis C.P. and Erickson E. (1961) "Institutional and Occupational Representations in Eleven Community Influence Systems", *American Sociological Review*, vol. 26.

D' Antonio W. and Erickson E. (1962a) "The Reputational Technique as a Measure of Community Power" *American Sociological Review*, vol. 27.

D'Antonio W., Ehrlich H. and Erickson E. (1962b) "Further Notes on the Study of Community Power", *American Sociological Review*, vol. 27.

Davis K. (1988) *Power Under the Microscope*, Foris Publications, Dordrecht.

Debnam G. (1984) *The Analysis of Power: A Realist Approach*, Macmillan, London.

Deleuze G. (1988) *Foucault*, Minnesota University Press, Minneapolis.

Drew P. "Analysing the Use of Language in Courtroom Interaction" in van Dijk T. *A Handbook of Discourse Analysis: Genres of Discourse*, vol. 3, Academic Press, London.

Durkheim E. (1982) *The Rules of Sociological Method*, Macmillan, London.

Easton D. (1953) *The Political System: An Inquiry into the State of Political Science*, Knopf, New York.

Easton D. (1966) *Varieties of Political Theory*, Prentice Hall, Englewood Cliffs.

Ehrlich H.J. (1961) "The Reputational Approach to the Study of Community Power", *American Sociological Review,* vol. 26.

Eldrige J.E.T. (1983) *C.Wright Mills*, Horwood, Chichester.

Elster J. (1976) "Some Conceptual Problems in Political Theory", in Barry B. (ed.) *Power and Political Theory*, London.

Elster J. (1978) *Logic and Society*, Wiley, Chichester.

Elster J. (1985) *Making Sense of Marx*, Cambridge University Press, Cambridge.

Emerson R.M. (1962) "Power and Dependence Relations", *American Sociological Review,* vol. 27.

Erickson E. C. (1964) "Review of The Rulers and the Ruled", *Social Forces,* vol. 43.

Evans M. (1975) *Karl Marx*, Allen and Unwin, London.

Fararo T.J. (1987) "Concrescence and Social Order", *Current Perspectives in Social Theory*, vol. 8.

Fell J.P. (1979) *Heidegger and Sartre*, Columbia University Press, New York.

Findlay J.N. (1984) *Wittgenstein: A Critique*, Routledge and Kegan Paul, London.

Fogelin R.J. (1976) *Wittgenstein*, Routledge and Kegan Paul, London.

Form W.H. and D'Antonio (1959) "Integration and Cleavage among Community Influentials in Two Border Cities", *American Sociological Review,* vol. 24.

Foucault M. (1971) *Madness and Civilization*, Travistock, London.

Foucault M. (1979) *Discipline and Punish*, Penguin, Harmondsworth.

Foucault M. (1980) *Power/Knowledge*, The Harvester Press, Brighton.

Foucault M. (1982) "The Subject and Power", in Dreyfus H. and Rabinow P. *Michel Foucault*, The Harvester Press, Brighton.

French J.R. and Raven B. (1959) "The Bases of Social Power" In Cartwright D. (ed.) *Studies in Social Power*, University of Michigan Press, Ann Arbour.

Freund J. (1968) *The Sociology of Max Weber*, Allen Lane, London.

Frey F.W. (1959) "Comment: 'On Issues and Non-Issues in the Study of Power", *American Political Science Review,* vol.65.

Gane M. (1983) "Anthony Giddens and the Crisis of Social Theory", *Economy and Society*, vol. 12.

Garfinkel H. (1984) *Studies in Ethnomethodology*, Polity, Cambridge.

Gaventa J. (1980) *Power and Powerlessness*, Clarendon Press, Oxford.

Gerth H. and Mills C.W (1948) (ed.) *From Max Weber: Essays in Social Theory*, Routledge Kegan Paul, London.

Giblan R. (1981) "White Collar from Start to Finish", *Theory and Society,* vol. 10.

Giddens A. (1968) "'Power' in the Recent Writings of Talcott Parsons", *Sociology,* vol. 2.

Giddens A. (1976) *New Rules of Sociological Method*, Hutchinson, London.

Giddens A. (1977) *Studies in Social and Political Theory*, Hutchinson, London.

Giddens A. (1979) *Central Problems in Social Theory*, Macmillan, London.

Giddens A. (1981) *A Contemporary Critique of Historical Materialism*, Macmillan, London.

Giddens A. (1982a) *Profiles and Critiques in Social Theory*, Macmillan, London.

Giddens A. (1982b) "A Reply to My Critics", *Theory Culture and Society,* vol. 1.

Giddens A. (1984) *The Constitution of Society*, Polity, Cambridge.

Giddens A. (1985) *The Nation State and Violence*, Polity, Cambridge.

Giddens A. (1989) "A Reply to My Critics", in Held D. and Thompson J. (ed.) *Social Theory of Modern Societies*, Polity in Association with Basil Blackwell, Cambridge.

Giddens A. (1990) *The Consequences of Modernity*, Macmillan, Cambridge.

Giddens A. and Held D. (1982) (eds.) *Classes, Power and Conflict*, Macmillan, London.

Giddens A. and Turner J. (1987) (eds.) *Social Theory Today*, Polity, Cambridge.

Gilbert C.W. (1972) *Community Power Structure*, University of Florida Press, Gainesville.

Gitlin T. (1965) "Local Pluralism as Theory and Ideology", *Studies on the Left*, vol. 5.

Glucksmann T. (1974) *Structuralist Analysis in Contemporary Social Thought*, Routledge and Kegan Paul, London.

Goffman E. (1979) *The Presentation of Self in Everyday Life*, Penguin, Harmondsworth.

Goldhamer H. and Shils E. (1939) "Types of Power and Status", *American Journal of Sociology*, vol. 45.

Goldman A.I. (1986) "Toward a Theory of Social Power", in Lukes S. (ed.) *Power*, Basil Blackwell, Oxford.

Gramsci A. (1971) *Selections from the Prison Notebooks*, Lawrence and Wisehart, London.

Grathoff R. (1978) (ed) *The Theory of Social Action: The*

Correspondence of Alfred Schutz and Talcott Parsons, Indiana University Press, London.

Gregory D. (1989) "Presence and Absence", in Held D. and Thompson J.B. (ed.) *Social Theory of Modern Societies*, Cambridge University Press, Cambridge.

Gross D. (1982) "Time-Space Relations in Giddens Social Theory" *Theory, Culture and Society*, vol. 1.

Habermas J. (1986) "Hannah Arendt's Communicative Concept of Power", in Lukes S. (ed.) *Power*, Basil Blackwell, Oxford.

Hamilton P. (1983) *Talcott Parsons*, Horwood, Chichester.

Heckscher E.F. (1934) *Mercantilism*, Allen and Unwin, London.

Heckscher E.F. (1963) *An Economic History of Sweden*, Harvard University Press, Cambridge (Mass.).

Heidegger M. (1973) *Being and Time*, (Trans. Macquarrie J. and Robinson E.), Blackwell, Oxford.

Held D. (1982) "Review of A Contemporary Critique of Historical Materialism", *Theory, Culture and Society*, vol. 1.

Heritage J. (1984) *Garfinkel and Ethnomethodology*, Polity, Cambridge.

Herson L.J. R. (1961) "In the Footsteps of Community Power", *American Political Science Review*, vol. 55.

Hindness B. (1972) "The Phenomenological Sociology of Alfred Schutz", *Economy and Society*, vol. 14.

Hindness B. (1982) "Power, Interests and the Outcome of Struggles", *Sociology*, vol. 16.

Hirst P.Q. (1982) "The Social Theory of Anthony Giddens: A New Syncretism", *Theory, Culture and Society*, vol. 1.

Hobbes T. (1651) *Leviathan*, London.

Hobbes T. (1839) *De Cive*, London.

Homans G.C. (1961) *Social Behaviour: Its Elementary Forms*, Routledge and Kegan Paul, New York.

Hughes D. (1982) "Control in Medical Consultation", *Sociology*, vol. 16.

Hunter F. (1953) *Community Power Structure*, University of North Carolina Press, Chapel Hill.

Janowitz M. (1962) "Community Power and 'Policy Science' Research", *Public Opinion*, vol. 26.

Jessop B. (1976) "On the Commensurability of Power and Structural Constraint", Revised version of a paper presented to the E.G.O.S. symposium on 'Power', (Photocopy) Colchester.

Jessop B. (1982) *The Capitalist State*, Robertson, Oxford.

Jessop B. (1985) *Nicos Poulantzas*, Basingstoke, Macmillan.

Jessop B. (1989) "Capitalism, Nation-States and Surveillance" in Held D. and Thompson J.B. *Social Theory of Modern Societies*, Cambridge University Press, Cambridge.

Kant I. (1963) *Critique of Pure Reason*, Trans. Smith N.K., Macmillan, London.

Keckskemeti P. (1973) "Propaganda", in de Sola Pool (ed.) *Handbook of Communications*, Rand McNally, Chicago.

Kertzer D.I. (1988) *Ritual, Politics and Power*, Yale University Press, New Haven.

King M. (1964) *Heidegger's Philosophy*, Blackwell, Oxford.

Klapp O. and Padgett V. (1960) "Power Structure and Decision-making", *American Journal of Sociology,* vol. 65.

Kolakowski L. (1975) *Husserl and the Search for Certitude*, Yale University Press, London.

Kolakowski L. (1978) *Main Currents of Marxism*, Trans. P.S. Falla, vol.s 1-3, Oxford University Press, Oxford.

Kolakowski L. (1988) *Metaphysical Horror*, Basil Blackwell, Oxford.

Kornhauser W. (1960) *The Politics of Mass Society*, Routledge and Kegan Paul, London.

Kuhn T.S. (1970) *The Structure of Scientific Revolutions*, Chicago University Press, Chicago.

Lakatos I. (1978) *The Philosophical Papers of Imre Lakatos*, (ed.) Worrall J. and Currie G., Cambridge University Press, Cambridge.

Lash S. (1982) "Critical Theory and Postmodernist Culture", *Current Perspectives in Social Theory*, vol. 8.

Lash S. (1985) "Postmodernity and Desire", *Theory and Society*, vol. 14.

Lasswell H.D. (1952) *The Comparative Study of Elites*, Stanford University Press, Stanford.

Lasswell H.D. and Kaplan A. (1950) *Power and Society*, New Haven.

Layder D. (1985) "Power, Structure and Agency", *Journal for the Theory of Social Behaviour*, vol. 15.

Layder D. (1987) "Key issues in Structuration Theory: Some Critical Remarks", *Current Perspectives in Social Theory*, vol. 8.

Lenski G. (1986) *Power and Privilege: A Theory of Social Stratification*", Mc Graw-Hill, New York.

Lively J. (1976) "The Limits of Exchange Theory", In Barry B. (ed.) *Power and Political Theory*, Wiley, London.

Long N.E. (1958) "The Local Community as an Ecology of Games", *The American Journal of Sociology*, vol. 64.

Lukacs L. (1971) *Political Writings*, NLB, London.

Lukacs L. (1972) *History and Class Consciousness*, Merlin Press, London.

Lukes S. (1973) *Emile Durkheim, His Life and Work*, Allen Lane, London.

Lukes S. (1974) *Power: A Radical View*, Macmillan, London.

Lukes S. (1976) "Reply to Bradshaw", *Sociology,* vol. 10.

Lukes S. (1977) *Essays in Social Theory*, Macmillan, London.

Lukes S. (1986) (ed.) *Power*, Basil Blackwell, Oxford.

Lynd R.S. and Lynd H.M. (1929) *Middeltown*, Harcourt, Brace and World, New York.

Lynd R.S. and Lynd H.M. (1937) *Middeltown in Transition*, Harcourt, Brace and World, New York.

Mann M. (1986) *The Sources of Social Power*, vol. 1, Cambridge University Press, Cambridge.

Margolis J. (1973) "Meanings, Speaker's Intentions, and Speech Acts", *The Review of Metaphysics*, vol. 26.

Marx K. (1973) *Grundrisse*, Penguin, Harmondsworth.

Marx K. (1975) *Early Writings*, Penguin, Harmondsworth.

Marx K. (1976) *Capital*, Vol. 1, Penguin, Harmondsworth.

Marx K. (1981) *Capital*, Vol. 3, Penguin, Harmondsworth.

May J.D. (1965) "Democracy, Organization, Michels", *American Political Science Review*, vol. 59.

McHugh P., Raffel S., Foss D.C. and Blum A.F. (1974) *On the Beginning of Social Enquiry*, Routledge and Kegan Paul, London.

McIntosh D. (1963) "Power and Social Control", *American Political Science Review*, vol. 57.

Meszaros I. (1970) *Marx's Theory of Alienation*, Merlin, London.

Michels R. (1915) *Political Parties*, Jarrold, London.

Miesel J.H. (1962) *The Myth of the Ruling Class*, University of Michigan, Ann Arbour.

Miller D.C. (1958) "Industry and Community Power Structure", *American Sociological Review*, vol. 23

Miller D.C. (1961) "Democracy and Decision-Making in the Community Power Structure", In D'Antonio W.V. and Erlich J. (ed) *Power and Democracy in America*, University of Notre Dame Press, Notre Dame.

Miller D.C. (1963) "Town and Gown: The Power Structure of a University Town", *American Journal of Sociology*, vol. 68.

Miller D.C. and Dirksen J.L. (1965) "The Identification of Visible, Concealed and Symbolic leaders in a Small Indiana City", *Social Forces*, vol. 43.

Milliband R. (1969) *The State in Capitalist Society*, Weidenfeld and Nicholson, London.

Milliband R. (1973) "The Capitalist State: A reply to Nicos Poulantzas" in Urry J. and Wakeford J. (ed) *Power in Britain*, Heinneman Educational, London.

Mills C.W. (1956) *The Power Elite*, Oxford University Press, London.

Mills C.W. (1958) "The Structure of Power in American Society", *British Journal of Sociology*, vol. 9.

Mills C.W. (1959) *The Sociological Imagination*, Oxford University Press, Oxford.

Mills C.W. (1963) *Power, Politics and People*, Oxford University Press, New York.

Mitchell W.C. (1967) *Sociological Analysis and Politics: The Theories of Talcott Parsons*, Prentice Hall, Engelwood Cliffs.

Molotch H.L. and Boden D. (1985) "Talking Social Structure", *American Sociological Review*, vol. 50.

Mommsen W. (1974) *The Age of Bureaucracy*, Blackwell, Oxford.

Morriss P. (1987) *Power: A Philosophical Analysis*, Manchester University Press, Manchester.

Mosca G. (1939) *The Ruling Class*, McGraw-Hill, New York.

Mumford L. (1966) *The City in History*, Penguin, London.

Nagel J. (1975) *The Descriptive Analysis of Power*, Yale University Press, New Haven.

Nicholls D. (1980) *Three Varieties of Pluralism*, Macmillan, London.

O'Hear A. (1980) *Karl Popper*, Routledge and Kegan Paul, London.

Olafson F.A. (1987) *Heidegger and Philosophy of Mind*, Yale University Press, New Haven.

Oppenheim F.E. (1961) *Dimensions of Freedom*, St. Martin's Press, New York.

Oppenheim F.E. (1976) "Power and Causation", in Barry B. (ed.) *Power and Political Theory*, Wiley, London.

O' Shulze R. (1958) "The Role of Economic Dominants in Community Power Structure", American Sociological Review, *American Sociological Review*, vol. 23.

O'Shulze R. and Blumberg U. (1957) "The Determination of Local Power Elites", *American Journal of Sociology*, vol. 63.

Parry G. (1969) *Political Elites*, Allen Unwin, London.

Parsons T. (1949) *The Structure of Social Action*, Free Press, New York.

Parsons T. (1951) *The Social System*, Routledge and Kegan Paul, London.

Parsons T. (1960) *Structure and Process in Modern Societies*, (Collection of essays including: "Authority, Legitimation and Political Action and "The Distribution of Power in America"), Frank Cass. New York.

Parsons T. (1967a) *Sociological Theory and Modern Society*, (Essays including: "On The Concept of Political Power", "Some Reflections on the Place of Force in Social Process" and "On the Concept of Influence"), Free Press, New York.

Parsons T. (1967b) "The Political Aspects of Social Structure and Process", in Easton D. (ed.) *Varieties of Political Theory*, Prentice Hall, Englewood Cliffs.

Parsons T. (1969) *Politics and Social Structure*, Free Press, New York.

Parsons T. and Smelser N.J. (1956) *Economy and Society*, Routledge and Kegan Paul, London.

Parsons T. and Shils E. (1967) *Towards a General Theory of Action*, Harvard University Press, Cambridge (Mass.).

Partridge P.H. (1963) "Some Notes on the Concept of Power", *Political Studies*, vol. 11.

Pellegrin R. and Coats C. (1956) "Absentee-Owned Corporations and Community Power Structure" *American Journal of Sociology*, vol. 61.

Pitkin H.F. (1972) *Wittgenstein and Justice*, University of California Press, Berkeley.

Polsby N.W. (1959) "Three Problems in the Analysis of Community Power", *American Sociological Review*, vol. 24.

Polsby N.W. (1960) "How to Study Community Power: The Pluralist Alternative", *Journal of Politics*, vol. 22.

Polsby N.W. (1962) "Community Power: Some Reflections on the Recent Literature", *American Sociological Review*, vol. 27.

Polsby N.W. (1980) *Community Power and Political Theory*, Yale University Press, New Haven.

Popper K. (1959) *The Logic of Scientific Discovery*, Hutchinson, London.

Popper K. (1963) *Conjectures and Refutations*, Routledge and Kegan Paul, London.

Popper K. (1972) *Objective Knowledge: An Evolutionary Approach*, Clarendon Press, Oxford.

Popper K. (1986) *Unended Quest: An Intellectual Autobiography*, Flamingo, London.

Poulantzas N. (1973) *Political Power and Social Classes*, NLB, London.

Poulantzas N. (1973b) "The Problem of the Capitalist State", in Urry J. and Wakeford J. (ed.) *Power in Britain*, Heineman Educational, London.

Poulantzas N. (1978a) *State, Power, Socialism*, NLB, London.

Poulantzas N. (1978b) *Class in Contemporary Capitalism*, Verso, London.

Raceuskis K. (1983) *Michel Foucault and the Subversion of the Intellect*, Ithaca.

Ricci D. (1976) *Community Power and Democratic Theory*, Random House, New York.

Rocher G. (1974) *Talcott Parsons and American Sociology*, Nelson, London.

Rorty R. (1989) *Contingency, Irony, and Solidarity*, Cambridge University Press, Cambridge.

Rossi P. (1960) "Power and Community Structure", *Midwest Journal of Political Science*, vol. 4.

Rueschemeyer D. (1986) *Power and the Division of Labour*, Polity, Cambridge.

Russell B. (1938) *Power: A New Social Analysis*, Allen and Unwin, London.

Saunders P. (1989) "Space, Urbanism and the created Environment", in Held D. and Thompson J. (ed.) *Social Theory of Modern Societies*, Cambridge University Press, Cambridge.

de Saussure F. (1974) *Course in General Linguistics*, Fontanna, London.

Savage S.P. (1983) *The Theories of Talcott Parsons*, Macmillan, London.

Schattschneider E.E. (1960) *The Semi-Sovereign People*, Holt, Rinehart and Winston, New York.

Schram S. F. (1991) Review of *Frameworks of Power*, American Political Science Review, vol. 85.

Schumpeter J.A. (1976) *Capitalism, Socialism and Democracy*, Allen and Unwin, London.

Schutz A. (1971) *Collected Papers*, Vol. 1, Dryden Press, The Hague.

Schutz A. (1972) *The Phenomenology of the Social World*, Heinemann Educational, London.

Schutz A and Luckmann T. (1974) *The Structures of the Life-World*, Heinemann, London.

Sereno R. (1937) "The Anti-Aristotelianism of Gaetano Mosca and its Fate", *Ethics,* vol. 48.

Shaw W.H. (1978) *Marx's Theory of History*, Hutchinson, London.

Smart B. (1985) *Michel Foucault*, Ellis Horwood, Chichester.

Steiner G. (1978) *Heidegger*, Harvester Press, Brighton.

Sudnow D. (1972) *Studies in Social Interaction*, Free Press, New York.

Swingewood A. (1975) *Marx and Modern Social Theory*, Macmillan, London.

Therborn G. (1980) *The Ideology of Power and Power of Ideology*, Verso, London.

Thiele L. P. (1990) "The Agony of Politics: The Nietzschean Roots of Foucault's Thought", *American Political Science Review*, vol. 84.

Thompson J.B. (1989) "The Theory of Structuration", In Held D. and Thompson J.B. (ed.) *Social Theory of Modern Societies*, Cambridge University Press, Cambridge.

Tilley N. (1980) "Popper, Positivism and Ethnomethodology", British Journal of Sociology, vol. 31 Turner J.H. (1986) "The Theory of Structuration", *American Journal of Sociology*, vol. 91.

Urry J. (1982) "The Duality of Structure: Some Critical Issues", *Theory, Culture and Society*, vol. 1.

Vail L.M. (1972) *Heidegger and Ontological Difference*, Pennsylvania State University Press, Pennsylvania.

de Vree K.J. (1976) "On Some Problems of Political Theory", in Barry B. *Power and Political Theory*, Wiley, London.

Walker J.L. (1966) "A Critique of the Elitist Theory of Democracy", *American Political Science Review*, vol. 60.

Waltz K.N. (1979) *The Theory of International Politics*, Reading Mass.

Weber M. (1947) *The Theory of Social and Economic Organization*, Free Press, Glencoe.

Weber M. (1948) *Max Weber: Essays in Social Theory*, (ed.) Gerth H.H. and Mills C.W., Routledge and Kegan Paul, London.

Weber M. (1968) *Economy and Society*, 3 vol.s., Bedminster Press, New York.

White D.M. (1971) "Power and Intentions", *American Political Science Review*, vol. 65.

White D.M. (1972) "The Problem of Power", *British Journal of Political Science*, vol. 2.

Wickham G. (1983) "Power and Power Analysis", *Economy and Society,* vol. 12.

Wickham G. (1990) "The Political Possibilities of Postmodernism", *Economy and Society,* vol. 19.

Wittgenstein L. (1967) *Zettel*, Blackwell, Oxford.

Wittgenstein L. (1968) *Philosophical Investigations*, Blackwell, Oxford.

Wittgenstein L. (1969) *Blue and Brown Books*, Blackwell, Oxford.

Wood A. W. (1981) *Karl Marx*, Routledge and Kegan Paul, London.

Wolfinger R. (1960) "Reputation and Reality in the Study of Community Power" *American Sociological Review,* vol. 25.

Wolfinger R. (1962) "A Plea for Decent Burial" *American Sociological Review*, vol. 27.

Wolfinger R. (1972) "Why Political Machines Have Not Withered Away and Other Revisionist Thoughts", *The Journal of Politics*, vol. 34.

Wright A.L. and Morgan W.J. (1990) "The 'Problem Patient' in Medical Interaction" *Social Science and Medicine*, vol. 30.

Wright L. (1968) *Clockwork Man*, Elek, London.

Wrong D. (1968) "Some Problems in Defining Social Power", *American Journal of Sociology*, vol. 73.

Wrong D. (1979) *Power: Its Forms, Bases and Uses*, Blackwell, Oxford.